## BEHIND THE SCENES WITH THE
## TOP LEADERSHIP EXPERTS IN SPORTS

*CREATED BY*

# MATT MORSE & BRETT BASHAM

Leadership VIP:

Behind the Scenes with the Top Leadership Experts in Sports

Printed in the United States of America

Published by Compete Publishing

Co-Creators: Matt Morse & Brett Basham

Audio Editor: Brandon Barrett

ISBN: 978-0-9969367-3-6

# ABOUT THE CREATORS

**Matt Morse** is an entrepreneur, coach, consultant, author, and speaker. He is a former NCAA Division I student-athlete who was a leader on and off the field during his playing career. After having the opportunity to learn from and work alongside some of the best mental performance coaches in baseball, Matt had a vision of bringing them all together in an active research type project. As the process evolved, *Mental Game VIP* was built during Matt's senior season at the University of Alabama at Birmingham.

After the release of *Mental Game VIP*, Matt teamed up with leadership expert Brett Basham to create the second VIP compilation, *Leadership VIP: Behind the Scenes with the Top Leadership Experts in Sports*.

In addition to coaching, Matt also consults with and speaks to teams, organizations, coaches, athletes and leaders around the world. For more information on Matt, to have him come speak to you and your team, or if you want to create your own VIP collection, visit **Matt-Morse.com** and follow @MattMorse_17 on Twitter!

# ABOUT THE CREATORS

**Brett Basham** is a leadership development coach, author, and speaker. As a former NCAA Division I baseball player at Ole Miss, professional baseball player, and national champion collegiate baseball coach, Brett has had the opportunity to play with and learn from some of the best leaders in collegiate and professional sports.

Sports leadership and team building have always been a passion of Brett's. So much so, he co-authored a leadership development manual titled *The Leadership Clock* with noted mental conditioning coach Brian Cain. Within this book, Brett speaks to his experiences in sports, both as player and coach, and what he feels are the 12 most important character traits a leader can possess.

In addition to being an author, Brett also consults with and speaks to teams, organizations, coaches, and athletes of all ages. For more information on Brett or to have him come speak to you and your team, visit **BrettBasham.com** and follow @BashLeadership on Twitter!

# CONTENTS

## GAME TIME Q&A

# MILLION DOLLAR QUESTION

# HOT SEAT

# CONCLUSION

# LEADERSHIP VIP DEFINED

The *Leadership VIP* program is a compilation of interviews with some of the top leadership experts, authors, speakers, and coaches in sports. These audio interviews have been transcribed and sorted into chapters by topic for you to read, or simply reference while listening to the corresponding audio program.

This program can be read and listened to in any order by selecting specific chapters or audio sections that you wish to learn about.

**Meet the Experts** contains a set of specific questions for each featured coach. **GameTime Q&A** is a series of questions asked to all of the coaches and includes their various responses to these frequently asked questions among leaders around the world. All of the coaches were then put on the **Hot Seat**, where they were asked to provide their initial thoughts on several popular topics. **The Conclusion** contains recommended reading, insights on the future of leadership and closing comments from each expert.

The material covered in this program covers a wide variety of topics that are crucial to maximize your potential and experience as an athlete, coach, parent, fan, business owner, entrepreneur, or leader in any field! Go behind the scenes with each of these experts with the *Leadership VIP* program!

*Interviews have been modified and condensed by the Leadership VIP team.

# MEET THE EXPERTS

## Introductions + Exclusive Q&A

# JON GORDON

**Wall Street Journal Best-Selling Author, Speaker, Coach, and Consultant**

**You graduated from Cornell, hold a Master's in Teaching from Emory, and you are passionate about developing positive leaders, teams, and organizations. You have many best-selling books and talks to inspire readers and audiences around the world. Tell us a little bit about your journey and what has led to such a successful career.**

**Gordon:** My journey is one of being a student first and a teacher second. I learn from so many great leaders and then I share best practices of what I learn about. I've been fortunate. In writing *The Energy Bus* I've been able to work with all these different coaches, sports leaders, business leaders, and non-profit leaders. So, I get to see what great leaders do, what great organizations do. I'm continually learning, growing, and acquiring new and best practices. Then, in that process I get to share

what I've learned, share what I know works in organizations based on my work with teams, organizations, and what I see other leaders do. It really makes for a great journey, to be always learning and then always be sharing.

**We mentioned *The Energy Bus* (a *Wall Street Journal* bestseller), *The No Complaining Rule*, *Training Camp*, etc... – all of which have their own great leadership theme. Which was your favorite to write and which has been the most**

# well received with organizations you've worked with?

**Gordon:** I enjoyed writing them all. I think *The Energy Bus* is by far the most popular. It actually is more popular than all the other books combined. I think the idea of staying positive and really building a positive team and eliminating those energy vampires that sabotage your team, that's something that really has resonated with people. But *Soup*, I think, is the best book for a leader in terms of building a great culture. If you want to build a great culture, you'd use *Soup*.

Carl Liebert, who's the president of USAA – he was the former CEO and president of 24 Hour Fitness and was with The Home Depot before that – he played basketball at Navy with David Robinson, an incredible leader. He says he gives *Soup* to leaders to help them build their culture, then he gives *The Energy Bus* to help them lead their teams, and then he gives them *Training Camp* to be their best for themselves. I think that's a pretty cool framework on how he does that.

# With all the success that you've accumulated over the years, what's been the most rewarding aspect of it all?

**Gordon:** The most rewarding thing is hearing from people and organizations that have read the books, been touched by them, benefited from them, and have utilized them. Then, I love hearing when people say, "Oh, yeah, we use this at work. I brought it home to work with my kids, and my kids are doing great. We have a stronger family." So, knowing that these principles apply to your home team as well as your work team; that is really rewarding. I wrote a children's book, *The Energy Bus for Kids*, so it's fun when they do *Energy Bus* at work, then the next thing you know, their kids are reading *The Energy Bus for Kids* at home. It's just great to hear those kind of stories. I get a lot of e-mails, and that's the best part of it. It keeps me going, keeps me energized knowing that you're touching people's lives and making it different. That's what it's all about. At the end of the day, I'm very aware that 50 years from now, 100 years from now, no one will ever remember my name most likely, or my books. It's part of a generation. Your job now is to touch people's lives, so a life touches a life that touches a life. That's what it's all about.

### For more from Jon Gordon, visit LeadershipVIP.com/JonGordon

# JEFF JANSSEN

**Sports Leadership Consultant and Author of *Team Captain's Leadership Manual***

## Tell us a little bit about your journey. How did the Janssen Sports Leadership Center come about?

**Janssen:** I was fortunate. About 20 years ago, I started as a sport psychology consultant at The University of Arizona. I got to work with all of their teams there. Over that time, I got to see how important and impactful leaders were to success on the field, on the court, in the locker room, and off the field. But, I also saw that, a lot of times, it was just by chance. They weren't really trained. They weren't really developed. I thought, "Wow, if we could invest some time and resources into developing these people into strong, impactful leaders, then we can really make a difference." So, I started about fifteen years ago putting together the *Team Captain's Leadership Manual*. It was just a tool that was really practical and made a lot of sense. It showed leaders not only how to lead themselves but to lead other people. That went really well.

We moved over to North Carolina and, fortunately, started doing some work with NC State and The University of Carolina (UNC). In 2004, UNC athletic director, Dick Baddour, really saw how important their leaders were. He kept hearing about that from his coaches like Anson Dorrance of the women's soccer program. He said, "We need to develop leaders not only for on-the-field success but what's happening off the field as well." So, back in 2004, North Carolina created the first and most comprehensive leadership academy for college athletics.

We were at the forefront in starting all of that. We'll be starting our 12<sup>th</sup> year coming with that program. Since then, we've been fortunate to work with about 25 different colleges all across the United States from NCAA Division I to Division III. We even have some schools in Canada getting involved where we provide comprehensive leadership development for their student athletes and coaches. It's been a really great journey. I've gotten to learn from a lot of amazing coaches and student-athletes. We're just trying to keep getting better and keep developing great leaders.

## How do you go about setting up the leadership academies when you go in to those schools?

**Janssen:** We work with the administrators. We work with the coaches. Usually, there is a main point person that we have, and we work with them. The main thing that we do is set up a tiered approach with the student-athletes because, obviously, some of them are at different levels and different stages of their leadership development. So, we have an Emerging Leaders program for, usually, the younger kids. Our main focus there is teaching them how to effectively lead themselves. Assuming they can do that well, then move up, level up, and graduate to the next level, which we call Veteran Leaders. That's often the juniors. There, we focus a lot on being a vocal leader and really starting to gain your voice and have an impact on the team that way. Then, last but not least, with the student-athletes, we have a Leadership 360 level, which is where the kids really apply what they learn as an Emerging Leader and as a Veteran Leader to impact their teams both on and off the field.

A part of it, too, is the coaches are huge in terms of not only developing their student-athlete leaders but professional development for them is critical. So, we also do a leadership component for the coaches. In a few instances with our academies, we also work with the administrators and, sometimes, even have specialized programming for assistant coaches who want to be head coaches. We try to really hit all the different layers of leadership that are available at a team and then try to really take a developmentally based approach to walk them along that leadership journey.

## You've got the highest endorsements from Hall of Fame coaches and athletic directors such as Pat Summitt, Roy Williams, Jeff Long, and Anson Dorrance. What has it been like working with the best coaches and athletic directors in all of college athletics? How have your leadership messages been received?

**Janssen:** It's a dream come true. I pinch myself when I get a chance to go to some of the universities or interact with some of the coaches who are the best of the best in their sports and in their field. It's a real joy to learn from these people while getting to pick their brains, pick up their strategies, and pass that along to other aspiring coaches. Fortunately, it's been very well received. I think what we do really well is our approach is extremely practical. It makes sense to people and things that they've experienced.

What we do is put it into a framework – terminology and evaluations that really make sense and can be implemented in today's practice. I think that's why we've been really successful. The other thing is our approach has been proven. We don't want just "smile sheets" at the end of the program. We say, "Hey, did you like this?" We want to know that our programming has real impact. One of the things that we do is a pre and post test. We also do what's called a retrospective pre and post test at the Center for Creative Leadership where we have student-athletes look at their change. We also have the coaches look at the change.

Fortunately, we've seen in our programming that 95, 96, 97, or, sometimes, 99% of kids feel like they improve from the start to the finish. It's usually 15 or so percent – or 15 points – in terms of their improvement, which is a really nice gauge for us to see, over a year's time, that multiple leaders are improving.

The other thing we do is called the net promoter score, which is what a lot of businesses use to see how well they are doing. In using that score, we're fortunate to see that our programming is right along with some of the best companies like Apple, Google, and Nordstrom's, usually the ones that lead the field. That's the same kind of response we're getting from our coaches and athletes. We do a tremendous amount of feedback. We get that from them, and we make tweaks and adjustments. Having done that now with 25 schools over the last 11 years and thousands of student-athletes and coaches, you really get to see what works and what may not work and then make adjustments accordingly.

## You've authored several very popular books. *The Team Captain's Leadership Manual, The Commitment Continuum System,* and *How to Build and Sustain a Championship Culture.* Are there any other projects or resources we should be on the lookout for coming in the future?

**Janssen:** There are. I'm very, very excited about a new book called *The Team Captain's Culture Manual.* Obviously, *The Team Captain's Leadership Manual* is one that's been around for a while. We've had tens of thousands of people go through that. We've gotten such great feedback on it that, as I've kind of evolved over time, I've seen how important culture is.

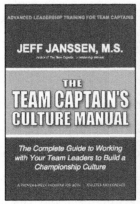 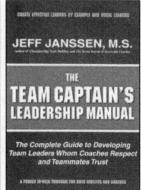 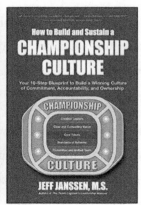

I did write a book for coaches, *How to Build and Sustain a Championship Culture*. But, you've got to have your captains involved in the creation of the culture as well. So, what I'm doing is putting together an advanced level of training for team captains on the whole culture aspect because it's your captains, along with the coaches, that really help you create that championship culture. They've got to champion, or drive, that culture throughout the rest of the team. They've got to connect people to what that culture is all about and what that means. Last, but not least, and one that a lot of student-athletes struggle with: They've got to be the caretakers of that culture. They've got to be the people that, when teammates are starting to drift outside of that championship culture and they see or hear that in the locker room or on the weekends, step up and serve as the guardians or caretakers of that culture and say, "Hey, we don't do that here. You need to step things up. This is the expectation. This is the standard. This is what we need from you."

So, I'm really excited about this resource because I think it is going to take the leadership training to a whole new level by involving your captains in creating that championship culture that so many coaches want.

## If a coach, a team, or organization listening along wanted to utilize the Janssen Sport Leadership Center, what would be the best way to go about doing that?

**Janssen:** We put a lot of resources on the website, *JanssenSportsLeadership.com*. We've got a lot of information about who we are and what we're all about. We've got a lot of resources and articles that coaches can use. It has information on the programs that we offer for teams, colleges, and high schools, as well as some information on our products and resources. That's probably the best one, *JanssenSportsLeadership.com*. People can always e-mail me at *Jeff@JeffJanssen.com*. That's the best way to get a hold of us.

### For more from Jeff Janssen, visit LeadershipVIP.com/JeffJanssen

# ROD OLSON

## Author & 21st Century Coaching and Leadership Consultant

# Talk briefly about what led you to where you are today and how you got to do what you are doing on a daily basis.

**Olson:** I think, first of all, I don't believe that anyone plans to grow up, leave college, and is going to be a leader or trainer of leaders and a coach of coaches. There's no major for that! I've coached for a long time. My life was changed basically around fifteen years ago when a guy came to me and showed me a different way to coach. It changed my life, and it also resonated with the twenty-first century athlete. That led to me doing some things in regards to very special things with our teams, in regards to capturing the heart of the today's athlete, and in finding the greatest ways to motivate them from the inside out. Started having a lot of guys calling me – "Hey. What are you doing? Is it team building? What is it? How do you do it?"

Next thing you know, I seemed to have more opportunities to share and that led to me getting into a position where we started coaching coaches and training trainers. That evolved into the secular world of leading leaders. What I mean *secular* is just the government, the military, and these kinds of places, along with CEOs, top companies, and their leadership. Basically, how to coach their people. Not supervise them, not manage them, but coach them and get the most out of them. We just talk a lot about that a coach's job is to help an individual or team get to a level they can't get to by themselves. Executives, parents, teachers, and coaches are all in that boat. So, we just started doing that and I've been doing it ever since.

# You have written one of the best books I have ever read, and I know a lot of people who have really enjoyed *The Legacy Builder*. Can you talk a little bit about where you were inspired to write that book and where the listeners can pick

# it up?

**Olson:** I appreciate that. You know it's funny; I'm not a guy that wrote books and started speaking and training people. I'm not an author that turned speaker. I'm actually a guy that's a coach then was speaking. People would come up pretty consistently after a talk and would say, "Hey, do you have a book?" I would say, "No, I'm not that guy. I'm a PE major, and I'll probably never have a book." Then, they would say "No, no, we really wish you had a book because we could take the principles away with us and just resonate."

So, a good friend of mine, Clint Hurdle, the current manager of the [Pittsburgh] Pirates, he and I exchanged books an awful lot. We have three rules on any book that we exchange:

1) It has to be short enough that you can read it on an airplane from Denver to Pittsburgh.

2) It had to be in story form so that you couldn't put it down. Had to have nice, short chapters so that you felt like you were getting something done.

3) It had to have principles in it that were not only applicable to sport, business, and leadership, but also to life. And the book had to make it come alive.

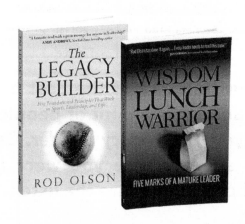

So, that was my goal when we put *The Legacy Builder* together: to take the principles from the trainings that I was doing and put it in story form. I just weaved in people that were important in my life. As they always say in the beginning of a book, none of these characters are actually real people, but some of them are, in a way – or they're a mixture. So, it seems to have resonated with people. We have the sequel coming out in the fall [2015] called *The Wisdom Lunch*. We are looking forward to that. Right now, they can get the book at *LegacyBuilderBook.com* or at *Amazon.com* too. *LegacyBuilderBook.com* is the best place to grab it.

## You are also involved with Coaches of Excellence. Can you expand on what Coaches of Excellence is and what you do with that? How can someone take the next step to work with you or have you speak to them?

**Olson:** Coaches of Excellence is a 501(c)(3) non-profit that we developed. I founded that roughly seven years ago. What we really wanted to do is have an opportunity for schools, youth programs, Boys and Girls Clubs organizations, YMCAs – all of those types of things – along with college and pro levels, whether they need a keynote speech at a banquet or a convention.

We wanted to have an organization that would focus specifically on coach's development and that of developing the coach and athletic director. Helping them navigate the twenty-first century and all the pitfalls of it. We wanted to help them save time, save money, and really make sure that their coaches are

coaching the way they need to in the twenty-first century. It's funny –
sometimes people go, "So, you are just trying to eradicate the world of bad
coaches." I say, "Yes, pretty much." But, we are actually just trying to help
coaches maximize their potential as a coach and get the most out of their
players. Again, teach those players and those families life lessons and use
sports to do it. It's more than just character; it's how to coach in this day and
age. We are finding that it is resonating with people at every level, in every
sport, and even at the Olympic level and in individual sports. Even in martial
arts and all those kinds of things. Again, coaching is coaching. You need to
be able to connect with people and get the most out of them. Coaches of
Excellence is a great organization that allows you to bring in someone to help
you do that and empower you to do the things you need to do as a leader in
your organization, high school, or college.

## For more great content from Rod Olson, visit LeadershipVIP.com/RodOlson

# MO ISOM

## Speaker, Author, and Former All-American Soccer Player at LSU

# You had quite the accomplished career as a soccer player at LSU earning All-SEC and All-American honors. You also became a pioneer of sorts, becoming the first female athlete to train with a major NCAA Division I football team. Tell us a little bit about your journey and how it has led you to this point of your life.

**Isom:** It has been quite a journey. Athletics have always been a part of my story. I grew up playing all types of sports and really found my niche with soccer and especially back between the pipes as a goalkeeper. The fact that I was able to work hard enough and things fell into place for me to get an education alongside of playing sports was just amazing. Deciding on LSU was one of those things you didn't expect that that would be your choice, but I stepped on campus and just knew it was where I was meant to be. I looked at a lot of different universities, but I really saw a chance with LSU of stepping into a program that was growing, being a key element in leading that, helping to support it, and seeing it really develop. The coaches sold me pretty hard on that, and that's always been something that I've been drawn to.

So, I made the LSU decision. I had just an unbelievable athletic career and time there. The program grew tremendously. We were three-time SEC West Champions. We came so close to winning the SEC just by a few points shy at the end of the season, but we just had a great run into the NCAA Tournament multiple times and really grew the program and grew as a people, honestly. Then I realized, right before my senior soccer season that I, and actually every NCAA athlete, had five years of eligibility. I thought, "I'm about to finish up soccer in four years, but I have a fifth year here that I could really do something with. This is a 'once in a lifetime' type deal." I started thinking what that would be. Soccer always trained in the same facility as the football team, so we had great friendships and just long-standing relationships there. We'd always mess around, kick footballs, and just play around inside football ops. It struck me one day that, "Wait a second. I've got thunder thighs for a reason here. I could kick a football. That could work." I just started asking the guys, "Is this possible? What do you guys think?" They just welcomed it, really, with open arms and made it very clear that if I wanted to take on that task it was going to be two years of work before I ever got a Yes or No answer. One full year, while I was still playing my soccer season, I was in and out with the football team, training every day, lifting, and kicking with them. Then, an additional eight or nine months once soccer was done and until that August tryout time. It was a massive question mark, and it was a huge leap of faith.

Ultimately, the guys made it clear that if it was something I wanted to go for, then to go for it. But, understand that it was going to take a tremendous amount of work. There was no male-female dynamic – it was "best athlete" dynamic. So, I was welcomed to give it a go, and I just had a really incredible time with them. I enjoyed that journey a lot. It's tough to say but probably just that short time with the football team really taught me so much more about myself, about true leadership, and about real commitment than, maybe, most of my youth. I can dive into that but there's a big difference when it comes to learning leadership when you're a big fish in a small pond and leading comes easy, than when you're the smallest fish in a big pond and leadership is still required of you.

It was an interesting journey. It was amazing, and I miss LSU every single day. I left there – going about that football journey really gave me the courage to go about whatever my heart really desired work-wise. And what that was for me was getting up on stage and speaking to people – to Millennials, to young women, to young men – about what it looks like to live boldly despite your circumstances. There was a lot of personal adversity that had gone on during that time in college. I just think it's an untapped oil bank in this society. Especially with Millennials, we're just so defined by our circumstances, and we forget that we have the opportunity to live, to lead, and to love really boldly.

So, that's what I do now! I travel the country speaking, internationally speaking. I'm working on my first book actually; just signed a book deal as well. It's all growing and it's all great, but I had to hang up the cleats after a while. My body is sore and thanking me for it.

# You've also had to experience some tremendous adversity for a person who's had such a short time on this earth so far. What has that taught you about yourself? How has that affected you as a leader on your team and personally throughout your life?

**Isom:** It's been a roller coaster. You know, it's interesting because so much in my life on the surface looks like unbelievable success. I think sometimes we can look at success stories or these people in these really established positions, leadership positions, or whatever it may be and think that they don't know the hardships, they don't know the brokenness, or they've been just given something on a silver platter. The fact of the matter is a lot of skills and talent commanded leadership in my life, but there was, really, a lot going on behind closed doors. At the same time that some of these unbelievable successes were happening on the soccer field and with the football team, I struggled growing up understanding my identity, fully. I was pretty desperate for control in a lot of ways and wanted so badly – sort of grew up in a home where my dad just loved me so much. My parents loved me so much that they really did want the best in me. They pushed me very hard, but it equated in my mind of like, "If I do well and if I'm successful and I lead well then I'm praised. But, if I don't do well, then I'm punished, and I'm actually given the silent treatment." It just really drove me to a place of beyond perfectionism, kind of an obsession. The way that really started to manifest itself in a dangerous way was a pretty vicious eating disorder as a young teen. For many girls, and even for many guys, it's something you could control. It's a lot more than just a body image issue. It is, really, a control issue at the core, and I struggled with it a lot and moved through that eating disorder for about four years.

When I decided to commit to LSU, I surrendered that. That was a long

27

process, but I began to sort of crawl out of the valley of struggling with that. I saw this opportunity for transition and change in going off to college. I surrendered a bit of that and had an amazing freshman year. It was just incredible, athletically. I received blessings left and right. I scored a 90-yard goal that year; ridiculous stuff that started to catapult our team into the national limelight. People started actually listening and looking at our stories more so than just the scores of the final games. I thought I was just on top of the world. I had overcome this eating disorder. Things were good.

Winter break of my freshman year, my dad very unexpectedly, without warning, didn't come home one night. To make the long portion of the story short, he ended up in a hotel in Alabama with a gun to his heart and pulled the trigger. He committed suicide, and it just rocked our world. It just destroyed us. Well, it *tried* to destroy us. I don't think that grief ever fully won out, but it took its toll on our family, on myself – I had to go back to school just a few weeks later and played the Dr. Jekyll and Mr. Hyde. On the outside, everything's good. I'm fine, and I'm still required to be leading this team. I'm this face on campus now because of such a great freshman year. But, inside I'm just depressed and anxious, turning to all these things I really never should have. I tried to fill up a very big hole in my heart and just really struggled for little over a year with that. I really lost myself, but I was pretty good at faking that everything was fine.

Almost one year after that, I headed home for Thanksgiving break; this was after my sophomore season now. After my freshman season, I lost my dad. Fought through it, played through my sophomore season, and really struggled with a lot. After that sophomore season, I was headed home to Atlanta for Thanksgiving

break and was in a horrific car accident. I broke my neck, ribs, lungs, liver, face, and had brain damage. It was brutal, but it was amazing because that car accident was a turning point for me. I can dive into that a little later, but it was just a unique journey. Like I said, there was so much on the outside that looked so well held together, yet there was so much adversity just ripping my family and myself at the seams on the inside. The eating disorder, the suicide, the car accident, just all the grief and all the healing that has to happen in conjunction with those things. I think they served a beautiful purpose in the end. I don't think we can discount the power in our adversity. I think we can grieve it, and I think we can, obviously, mourn, struggle, and work hard to overcome it. But, at the end of the day, that adversity shapes us just as much as the victory in our life.

It was a crazy ride that ultimately worked to use all of that to make me grow into a more whole woman. Someone who understands the perspective of the broken, as well as the perspective of the brave. I forced it to serve a purpose because I just couldn't keep crying myself to sleep every night. Learned a lot of leadership from that as well.

## If a team or organization wished to have you speak, what is the best way to get in touch with you?

**Isom:** Absolutely. The best way to get in touch with me – I'm really just an e-mail away – is through my website, which is *www.moisom.com*. On there, you can find a lot of resources. We're in the midst of revamping it, but you can find a lot of resources, a lot of videos, lot of fun videos, lot of challenging videos, as well as a lot of writing. It primarily serves as written blog and in addition, all of the contact information, the e-mail that I can be reached at, the speaking request forms that you can fill out to bring me to their organization. Soon, when we revamp the blog, we will have an additional section for consulting. All of that can play out for you in your organization, with your team, or whatever it may be. It's my heart, and it's my passion to really just plug in and power people up in those ways. It's a blessing that I get to do it, and it can all be found at *MoIsom.com.*

## *For more great content from Mo Isom, visit LeadershipVIP.com/MoIsom*

# MARSHALL GOLDSMITH

*New York Times & Wall Street Journal*
**Best-Selling Author, Speaker, and
Executive Coach**

**The Marshall Goldsmith Group includes associates who you have hand-picked to deliver on his mission – to help successful leaders get even better. From executive coaching, keynote speaking, leadership education and more, group members are highly skilled and experienced consultants who effectively impact individual, team, and organizational challenges. What has made your group so successful?**

**Goldsmith:** It's one thing we do that's a little different. In my coaching, I don't get paid if my clients don't get better. Better is not judged by me or my client. It's judged by everyone around my client. It's a great way to test if someone actually believes what they're saying. You can ask them one question and instantly determine their level of belief. A very simple question, "Do you want to bet on it?" If they say, "I believe it, but I wouldn't bet on it," they don't really believe it that much. If they say, "Here's your money," they believe it. So, we bet on this every time.

**When working with a group, it seems as if you hit three major parts: the leader, the team and how they come to respect leaders, and on the higher organization level. How did that philosophy come to be?**

**Goldsmith:** I went to work originally giving 360° feedback. I've learned after we started giving confidential 360° feedback, to start measuring who gets better, why they get better, and why they don't get better. And then, from there, we went onto, how can you use the same process to build the team? How can you create a larger cultural change in the whole organization? We started with the micro level, at the individual level, and expanded out from there.

## You have written best-selling books such as *What Got You Here Won't Get You There* and *MOJO*. What was the inspiration for those books and what impact have you seen them have on organizations you have worked with?

**Goldsmith:** The book *What Got You Here Won't Get You There* – Peter Drucker-- I was on his advisory board for 10 years. He's the world's authority on management and the founder of modern management. He basically taught me and said, "We spend a lot of time helping leaders learn what to do. We don't spend enough time helping leaders learn when to stop." He said, "Half the leaders I meet, they don't need to learn what to do, they need to learn when to stop." That one comment led to *What Got You Here Won't Get You There*. In that book I talk about interpersonal behavior – how to change an individual at the interpersonal level.

Then, my book *MOJO* is more intrapersonal; that's looking at yourself from the inside. My new book, *Triggers,* is going to be focused more on the environment; how does the world outside us change us? So, look at it as three perspectives. One, interpersonal behavior – that's *What Got You Here Won't Get You There*. Two, looking inside ourselves and that is the book *MOJO*. And then, three, my new book *Triggers* focuses on our relationship with the outside world around us.

# If our readers are interested, where can they pick up those books?

**Goldsmith:** Yeah, you can go to the website or go to Amazon.com. You can get all the books there, or you can go to my website.

# If a team or an organization wanted to utilize the Marshall Goldsmith Group, what would be the best way to go about doing that?

**Goldsmith:** Just give me an e-mail *Marshall@MarshallGoldsmith.com*. Very simple.

*For more great content from Marshall Goldsmith, visit*
*LeadershipVIP.com/MarshallGoldsmith*

# STEPHANIE WHITE

## Head Basketball Coach of WNBA's Indiana Fever

**You had quite a decorated career as an athlete. You were the National Player of the Year and part of the first NCAA National Championship team in school history at Purdue University. You also had a pretty successful WNBA career, setting Indiana Fever records in several categories. Tell us about your journey as both a collegiate and professional athlete.**

**White:** I grew up in Indiana. That's all we do; play basketball. It is funny because I often get asked, "When did you start playing?" I have a picture – my dad was holding me when he first brought me home from the hospital. He had me in one hand and a basketball in the other. It is all I've ever known. I played other sports growing up, but basketball was the one that I loved. Basketball was the one that I always went back to after practices for the others. It has been a passion of mine for as long as I can remember. I've always had an inner drive to be successful. I've always had a competitive spirit about me that knew if I wasn't out there working, somebody else was.

I came from a small town. I will never forget – when I was in fourth grade I told my parents that I wanted to go to college to play basketball, and I wanted to get a scholarship. I think they were supportive like parents are, but the same time, it was, "Okay, well, good luck. We will support you any way that we can." I came from a small town, and that just didn't happen. If you didn't go to a big school, at that time, you weren't well known. So, my parents did whatever they could to put me in a position to be successful. Letting me play AAU, which was completely different than AAU is now. Taking me to camps and wherever I could go to be visible. I just worked all the time. That's all I ever wanted to do was to play. I was competitive by nature in all areas of my life. I was a competitive student. I have two younger sisters; we'd be walking across the street to our grandparents' house, and it would turn into a dead-out sprint. We all wanted to win, all the time.

I really was a community project. My school only had four hundred kids in our whole high school. Our entire county went to one high school. We didn't have any stoplights in our county. It was just a typical "Hoosier-esque" story. I ended up going to Purdue so I could stay close to home. Those people continued to be a part of my journey. I played for three coaches in four years, so certainly went through some trials while in college. I played on a team as a freshman that was probably one of the most talented teams in the country and drastically underachieved. Our coach didn't get her contract renewed. We graduated five seniors, lost five others to transfer, returned three scholarship players, and the next year, win the Big Ten. It taught me a lot about what it takes to be successful in the kind of culture that you want to be a part of. Then, two years later, won a national championship at Purdue and had just an incredible experience, an incredible career with wonderful teammates, and really enjoyed my time playing at Purdue. I had a pretty good, pretty decent WNBA career. We were, at that time, playing for an expansion team with the Indiana Fever. Injuries kind of derailed me a little bit, and I got into coaching.

## You've also been successful in the coaching ranks. You were an associate head coach with the Indiana Fever. Now, you're in your first season as the head coach of the Fever, the most successful organization in the history of the WNBA. Tell us a little bit about your coaching journey and what that experience has been like.

**White:** In the last couple of years of my playing days, I really wasn't sure what I wanted to do after that. I had a little bit of personal struggle; I was going through a divorce and trying to come back from injuries. I had a couple of ankle surgeries and a knee surgery. I was approached by a woman named Tracy Roller who is the head coach at Ball State University. She asked me if I would be interested in coaching, and I said, "Yeah, I think I would like to give that a try." She was willing to work with me in becoming an assistant coach, at that time, while I was still playing. That was while I was in the middle of my Indiana Fever season. Towards the end of that season I ended up tearing my ACL. So, while I was at Ball State, I was rehabbing an ACL and was attempting to come back again to play.

I'll never forget the first time I stepped foot on the floor at Ball State. I knew that coaching was the direction I wanted to go. I knew that was where I was meant to be. I coached that year, rehabbed my knee, and played the next year for the Fever. Then, went to Kansas State, decided to retire from playing, and get into coaching full-time. I spent a year at Kansas State; a couple years at Toledo working for a guy named Mark Ehlen that I knew from my Purdue basketball camp days. A wonderful guy who really helped teach me about perspective and about balance.

I got the call to come to the WNBA level by a guy that was getting the job in Chicago with the Chicago Sky. He called me; I said no twice. I didn't want to do it, really had a comfort zone at the collegiate level, and wasn't quite sure I wanted to jump into WNBA coaching. The league was still fairly new, fairly young. I knew it was solid to coach in college. There was a solid career opportunity there. I was really struck by a woman named Margaret Stender who was the COO of the Chicago Sky and Michael Alter who was the owner. They wanted it to be more than just basketball. They wanted former players to get involved, to really teach the young players – the new players – what life before the WNBA was like so that they can realize the opportunity that was there and embrace a transition period but still have the perspective of, "Look, this league is only going to survive if we do things the right way." I think being more than just a basketball piece drew me back to the pro level. So, I spent four seasons in Chicago and then came back home to Indiana. I'm just really excited about the opportunity that I have to be the head coach of the Fever – the franchise that I played with, the franchise that I was with in the inaugural season, and won the first championship with. I now have the opportunity to be the head coach, and I'm really looking forward to it.

# What is your leadership philosophy and/or the core values of your organization? How do you communicate that philosophy to the members of your organization?

**White:** There are certainly core values of our team that were in place before I got there. I played for Lin Dunn in college and then worked with her [with the Indiana Fever]. The core values that were established through her in terms of our toughness, our warrior-like mentality, and our defensive and rebounding prowess - the things that you do on the court - are certainly going maintain. To me, it's also about your work ethic, your ability to communicate in a positive way, and about trusting one another. If you don't want to work your tail off, if you don't want to sacrifice for the greater good of our organization, then you don't need to be here. It's not about individual ego and individual accomplishment. It's about team success. Ultimately, team success leads to more individual success. Work ethic, sacrifice, and trust, to me, are non-negotiable.

The other thing is communication. I am a very open person. I was a player who openly communicated with her coaches on the floor with what I was seeing. So, I am open to two-way communication. It's not a one-directional thing with me. I want it to be honest, open communication. Having that builds trust. It builds togetherness, and it allows players to be coachable because they also feel like they have a voice. I certainly believe that leadership starts with work ethic. If you don't do the work, you can't expect your players to do the work. I really believe that, and I think that is part of the benefit of being a player and now being the head coach; you've been there, you know what they're going through, and you trust in what you see. You trust in your gut because you know what that sacrifice on a daily basis is like. You know if your team is giving you everything that they have, and you know when they're holding back. Because I've been a former player it allows me to call them out on that. But, it also allows me to applaud them when I know, regardless of the outcome, that they're still giving their best effort.

### *For more great content from Stephanie White, visit LeadershipVIP.com/StephanieWhite*

# JIM KOUZES

**Leadership Coach, Speaker, and Best-Selling Author of *The Leadership Challenge***

**You are a best-selling author, an award-winning speaker, and according to the *Wall Street Journal*, one of the twelve best executive educators in the United States. However, your start in leadership began when you were one of only a dozen Eagle Scouts to be selected to serve in John F. Kennedy's honor guard when he was inaugurated President of the United States. What was that experience like?**

**Kouzes:** Yes, that was probably one of the most unique things that ever happened to me in my life. I grew up in the northern Virginia suburbs of Washington, D.C. I don't know if you know the area, but there is Arlington, Alexandria, and Fairfax, and I grew up in those three cities. My dad worked for the Federal Government downtown so we spent a lot of time in the nation's capital. That gave me a great appreciation for the history of our country and the leaders who helped shape it.

I was an Eagle Scout at the time JFK was elected. He wanted to have a group of Eagle Scouts as part of his honor guard. I was 15 at the time, and to this day, I still don't know how or why I was selected. But I was. It was just a thrilling experience at that time - probably, at that age, the most important thing that happened to me in my life. I was so inspired by that experience, and the words he spoke, "Ask not what your country can do for you. Ask what you can do for your country" - those words are as meaningful today as they were when I heard them.

**You are a co-author of the best-selling book, *The Leadership Challenge*. It has sold more than two million copies worldwide and has been called "one of the top ten best leadership books**

## of all time." Tell us a little about how this book came to be and the inspiration behind it.

**Kouzes:** I think like the previous story about my experience with John F. Kennedy's honor guard, a lot of things happened to me quite serendipitously. When you're really passionate and dedicated to what you're doing, whether it's playing an athletic sport, coaching, or in my case, leadership, things happen because you are on that path.

I was hired as the director of the Executive Development Center in the business school at Santa Clara University. On my very first day at work in my new office, I met Barry Posner, who was, at the time, an assistant professor of Management. Barry knocked on my door, invited me to join him for lunch, and said if I needed any help, he'd be happy to help me get acquainted with people on campus. Show me around, where things were, and also talk to me about the work he did with the Executive Development Center. We became friends. Over time, within the first few days of meeting each other, found that we had a common interest in leadership and in corporate culture. There was an opportunity for us to work with Tom Peters, who wrote the book *In Search of Excellence.* Through the Executive Development Center, I asked Tom if he would come and conduct a seminar with us. So, he did day one of the seminar on excellent companies. Barry and I signed up to do day two on excellent managers. While Tom had a book and all this experience behind him at McKinsey for his presentation, Barry and I had not yet done our research, but we had an idea. The idea was to investigate personal-best leadership experiences. We asked the people in the seminar if they would prepare those as pre-work and then share them in the seminar. They did. We used the personal-best methodology, by the way, from sports. We actually thought, "Well, if they're personal bests in athletics, they are personal bests in leadership." From those stories, we noticed that there was a common pattern to those experiences. That discovery of the commonalities between personal-best leadership experiences led us to start doing the original research for the book. Eventually, about three years later, that led to the publication of *The Leadership Challenge*.

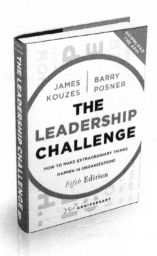

# You also developed the highly acclaimed Leadership Practices Inventory (LPI), a 360-degree questionnaire for assessing leadership behavior, which is one of the most widely used leadership assessment instruments in the world. What are the components of the LPI that has made it so effective?

**Kouzes:** The LPI grew out of our research for *The Leadership Challenge*. We saw patterns; we eventually ended up with *The Five Practices of Exemplary Leadership®*: Model the Way, Inspire a Shared Vision, Challenge the Process, Enable Others to Act, and Encourage the Heart. That became the framework, but one of our clients at the time, Apple Computer, said to us, "Well, do you guys have something to measure these behaviors? Here is the model and the framework and we understand the research from the case studies, but do you have some way we can assess our leaders on these dimensions?"

So, they invited us to work with them to develop that, and we did. That became, eventually – after several iterations – the Leadership Practices Inventory. What it is is a questionnaire that consists of 30 items; there are five practices, so there are six items per practice. Each of those items is measured on a frequency scale from one (not at all) to 10 (all the time). We asked both leaders themselves and their constituents, whether they're managers, direct reports, or peers, to indicate the extent of which they observe these behaviors occurring in what degree of frequency.

So, the LPI is an assessment of leader behavior. One of the reasons it has been as successful as it has is we have nearly 30 years of data. We just analyzed 2.5 million responses. We have a data-rich environment. We have lots of information about leaders from 70 different countries; male and female; all kinds of industries and functions; age groups. Over 600 studies have been done using this tool – other than our own research – so it has a lot of validity and reliability. It is predictive of performance so people use it both to provide feedback for development but also to help people understand the impact that they're having. I think that's one of the reasons.

Another reason: It's short. It is 30 items. It takes less than 15 minutes to complete, and that makes it easier for people. We don't get any pushback because it is too long.

The third thing: It is about behavior. It's not about personality. It is about behavior, so it is something that other people can observe making the information you get not about what your attitudes are but what your behavior demonstrates to other people.

## *For more great content from Jim Kouzes, visit LeadershipVIP.com/JimKouzes*

# TIM ELMORE

**Best-Selling Author, International Speaker, and President of Growing Leaders**

# You're a leading authority on how to understand the next generation and preparing tomorrow's leaders today as well as being a best-selling author, international speaker, and president of Growing Leaders. Tell us about your journey, and how you've gotten to this point in your career.

**Elmore:** I get asked about my journey a lot, as you probably do as well. It's a little bit of a combination of a number of elements that I didn't see how or why they came together and but they did. Looking back, I can see how they came together. I began working with students, high school and college students, way back in 1979. I was still finishing up my degree and began to see that I wanted to invest my life in the next generation, the emerging student.

In 1983, I joined the staff with John Maxwell in San Diego, California, and immediately, I got bit by the leadership bug. So, I had a love of students that had already been cultivated, and I wanted to invest my life in the young, moldable, and shapeable. I began to see immediately how leadership played a critical role. Growing Leaders, the organization I lead now, has put those two loves together. My love of students, or the emerging generation, and my love of leader development, where I do more than just teach them or do more than try to help them survive school. We're really equipping them to thrive in the future.

So, my journey does include John Maxwell, no doubt about it. Other great leadership mentors - long distance and up close, executives at Chick-Fil-A,

Jim Collins, and others. I feel very fortunate. I always tell people, "If I don't do a good job, it's my own fault." That's where I am today, and I love what I get to do. I know I owe a lot to the people that have invested in me over the last 30 years.

## Your work with Millennials is groundbreaking, especially with the book *Generation iY*. You've also created the *Habitudes* series, which are images that form leadership habits and attitudes. How did you come up with the idea to write *Habitudes*, the goal of that series of books, and the response that you receive from those teams and organizations that have used *Habitudes*?

**Elmore:** *Habitudes* is far and away our bestseller. Now, there are actually eight books, eight videos, eight podcasts - the whole deal. But, as you mentioned, *Habitudes* are images that form leadership habits and attitudes. As I worked with students over the years, I began to see that #1, the life skills that they naturally needed to become adults, or leaders as an adult, weren't necessarily being built into them by what was happening in their first 18 years. At the same time, I was noticing that the way teachers were connecting with students wasn't always working. That lecture the professor gives for 50 minutes, this one-way download, wasn't what they were wanting.

I was a double major in college. One of my majors was art, and I had been into graphic design and so forth. My love of leadership and my love of art really came together with *Habitudes*, where we were able to cease a word picture or a picture itself. Rivers and Floods, Iceberg, or Chess and Checkers - that image represents a timeless, universal principle that we believe everybody ought to know if they are going to lead effectively. Whether they are 15 or 35, it makes sense at that level. You understand it at a 15-year-old level if that's how old you are. We have folks in the White House, the Pentagon, and the Commerce Department who are going through *Habitudes*. The cool thing is that this idea of teaching with images seems to be universal in nature; they've been translated into 14 different languages.

The whole idea of teaching with the image, that whole right-brain thing, seems to be connecting with others. We believe we are living in a world that is full of icons and images. Doctor Leonard Sweet said images are the language of the twenty-first century. So, long answer to a short question, I began to see that, as I was teaching leadership, the students were remembering the metaphor or picture that I was giving them, not the 17 points that I was making. I thought, "Why not anchor the big idea with an image?" It's really been fun.

One more quick thought before we go on. Our culture is marvelous. I love America; I love the country we live in. It's full of speed, technology, and convenience. But, because it's so full of technology, our country doesn't automatically build into us the interpersonal skills, the life skills, or the emotional intelligence that we need. Staring at a screen doesn't build people skills in me, all the time. We felt like we've got to be way more intentional at building these principles into the students because they may not automatically get them going through school in this current state.

# What are the core values of your organization at Growing Leaders? How do you communicate those to your team members?

**Elmore:** That's a great question. We have based our entire mission off of a set of values and propositions, even a brand personality that we've developed. A couple of things might be relevant. One is that we believe that leadership capacity is within every person in the world. So, are there natural-born leaders? Absolutely, no doubt about it. But, I love what Peter Drucker once said years ago: "There is such a thing as a natural-born leader, but there are so few of them that it doesn't make any difference." The rest of us need to grow; we need to develop.

We find that when we stand in front of a group of athletes - or just students in general - I can say with all honesty that I am looking at a group of leaders. Here's something else I say, and this is our philosophy: We believe we are in front of a group of leaders in every audience because we believe the world is full of two kinds of leaders and everybody fits into one of these two kinds. They are either a habitual leader or a situational leader; habitual or situational.

The habitual leader is the one that leads out of habits; they're the natural-born leader. They are the ones that, whatever group they're in or whatever team they're on, they tend to take over. That's John Maxwell. That's Jim Collins. That's Steven Covey. They're just natural leaders. I think that's only 10 to 15 percent of the population. I think the other 85 to 95 percent of us are what I call a situational leader. We are the ones that would say, "You know what? I am not really a great leader, but you put me in the right situation - one that matches who I am, my strengths, my passions, and my gifts - in that one sweet spot, I'm pretty good. Naturally. I have intuition in that area and I've never taken a class on it. I'm comfortable in that area, I'm confident in that area, and I'm influential in that area."

So, we think one of the primary factors that a coach, teacher, or even a parent needs to take is, "I need to help this student find their situation where they will become the best version of themselves just by being placed in the right context, where their gifts will begin to flourish, and they're energized by them rather than being de-energized." So, that would be one big deal; there's leadership capacity in everyone. That doesn't mean that they're all going to be positioned as a CEO. We just believe leadership has less to do with the position and more to do with the disposition. It's a way of looking at life. That's what we are trying to do, is help every student we come into contact with look at life through the big picture lens and have a vision for solving problems and serving people.

## If a team or organization wished to utilize you and the Growing Leaders team, what would be the best way to go about getting into contact with you?

**Elmore:** Our website is the best. In fact, obviously, going to our website you can scan and see what our organization is about. So, *growingleaders.com*; it's very simple. *Growingleaders.com* is our site, and there is a set of tabs at the top on getting involved. There's a lot of free stuff; there's e-books and free downloads. I do a blog every day. We love to stay in touch with anybody that is interested in the same topic; we believe there's leadership potential in students and we want to pull it out now rather than wait till they're 40.

When I meet with a dean of a college or a principal of a high school and I tell them what we are really trying to do, they usually don't have any problem with it. In other words, they may disagree that there is a leader inside of every single person; but when we say leadership is about solving problems and serving people, there is not one educator that says, "I don't want to do that, we don't want to do that. That's what we need to graduate." So, that's really what we're after, and you find that all through the website that we are really about helping students learn to solve problems and serve people.

## For more great content from Tim Elmore, visit LeadershipVIP.com/TimElmore

# DAVE ANDERSON

## Author, Consultant, and President of LearnToLead

# You're the president of LearnToLead, an international sales, leadership training, and consulting company. Tell us about what has gotten you to this point in your career and how you've become as successful as you've become.

**Anderson:** I started in the automotive retail business selling cars and worked my way up to where I was running a large dealership group. We had about 300 million dollars a year in sales. That was bought out by a public company about 16 years ago. I use now a lot of the same leadership principles that we used in building that company to teach all around the world. The principles evolve from real-world experience running the dealership group.

**You've given over 1,000 workshops and speeches over the past decade on leadership development in 15 different countries. What has that experience been like and how has your message been received internationally?**

**Anderson:** I speak about 120 times a year. What I have found, it doesn't matter if I'm in Moscow or Bangkok or Okoboji, Iowa, most folks in leadership face the same challenges – finding the right people, getting them in the right places, and getting them to do the right things consistently. Those are challenges everybody faces. When I teach leadership, I teach leadership principles so they're widely applicable. They stand the test of time, and they transcend borders. So, the reception is very good.

**You've authored 12 books, including *If You Don't Make Waves, You'll Drown; How to Lead by The Book;* and *TKO Business Series*. You've had interviews and articles appear in a number of publications including the *Wall Street Journal, Investor's Business Daily,* and *US News & World Report*. You're also a frequent panelist on MSNBC's *Your Business* show. To what do you owe your continued success?**

**Anderson:** Our organization focuses solely on developing the leadership of an organization. Every once in a while, after we've trained the leadership, we will work with the frontline employees and get them into sales training and such. But, by focusing on the leadership, on the core of the organization, I believe that's where you get results. Until the leaders get better, nothing else really changes. So, as we're able to do that and help our companies get results, they keep doing business with us and fueling our success.

# If an organization, company, or team wished to utilize your speaking, coaching, or consulting, what would be the best way to go about getting in touch with you?

**Anderson:** Two quick ways: Our website, *LearnToLead.com*. It has a lot of our information. They can contact us through there. My sample speaking clips and topics are all there as well. Then, through Twitter. I communicate a lot to potential clients through Twitter. My Twitter address is *@DaveAnderson100*. Either of those ways would be great ways to get in touch with us.

### *For more great content from Dave Andersn, visit LeadershipVIP.com/DaveAnderson*

# JOSHUA MEDCALF

**Founder of Train 2B Clutch, Author,
Leadership & Mental Training Speaker**

# You're the co-founder of Train 2B Clutch, a heart's first approach to leadership, life skills, and mental training. Tell us a little bit about your journey and how you came to start this group.

**Medcalf:** About eight years ago, I was at Duke University. I was working on my master's program and finishing up my last year of eligibility playing soccer. I was supposed to be writing my master's thesis. At that time, I asked myself a question that I'd never asked before, which was: What would I do if money didn't matter? I realized that I wouldn't go to law school. I ended up not writing my master's thesis, skipping scholarships to law school, and moved across the country into a homeless shelter to serve people. I thought if money didn't matter then that's what I would do. That's what I needed to do if money didn't matter.

I really started focusing on that. I was there for six months, serving, and moved into the closet of a gym to start my organization. From there, a couple of years later, I ended up starting Train 2B Clutch. I was really grateful when my best friend, Jamie Gilbert, was able to come on board. Since then, a lot of really cool stuff has been happening.

# Your book, *Burn Your Goals*, is a great read. For those that haven't had a chance to read it yet, what's the message that you're trying to get across by saying burn your goals?

**Medcalf:** It's a really provocative title, but the real reason we wrote it was because we were really sick and tired of hearing people talk about their wish list, sit in rooms, and think that writing something down this big, audacious, sexy goal - basically all it does is give you an endorphin high. But, then, it puts you on this emotional roller coaster because most of the time the goals that people set are outside of their control. You get this huge high from setting the goal, then you get this huge crash whenever you don't actually achieve the goal. What we ask people to do is to focus, 100%, on controllables; things like true mental toughness - which we define as having a great attitude, giving your very best, treating people really well, and having unconditional gratitude, regardless of your circumstances. We believe that's a much higher standard. It actually forces people to focus on the stuff that's inside of their control. When you focus on stuff that's outside of your control, like these arbitrary outcome-based goals, all you do is end up increasing pressure, decreasing confidence, and making people miserable in the process. Making them feel like failures. That's why we've got kids jumping off of buildings and killing themselves in different ways - because they felt like they were a failure because they didn't reach some goal. Maybe that goal was outside of their potential.

Maybe we're setting goals too low. I think that if we're focused on controllable things – that's why we ask people, "What are you willing to do with your 86,400 seconds every single day to close the gap between who you are and who you want to become? What are you willing to sacrifice inside of your twenty-four hours a day to become that type of person that you want to become to close the gap between where you are and where you want to be?" That's actually controllable. Rather than focusing on things that are outside of our control, if we just focused on the stuff that's inside of our control, truthfully, we'd get a lot better results. Ultimately, when it comes to sports, I believe that we could actually start using sports to become the type of people we want to become instead of being used by our sports. Then, it becomes a transformational experience where we actually use the "worst circumstances" to develop the characteristics of true mental toughness. Last time I checked, everybody wants people on their team that have a great attitude, give their very best, treat people really well, and have unconditional gratitude, regardless of their circumstances.

## In your newest book, *An Impractical Guide to Becoming a Transformational Leader,* you talk about what it takes to become a transformational leader. Tell us a little bit about that and where the readers can pick that up.

**Medcalf:** Most of the stuff we write - it is not like we're sitting around in a room and we come up with cool ideas. We're actually in the trenches working with people. I was having a conversation with a person who coaches at a very high level in this country. We'd been hanging out, playing golf, and at the end he said, "That's the stuff that I want, the super practical stuff." I

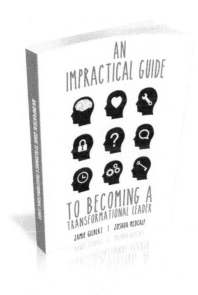

wanted to just yell at this guy like, "It's not practical! It is impractical! It's really freaking hard. If you want to become a transformational leader, it is ridiculously hard work. It's going to take serious sacrifice. It's going to take serious intentionality." We talk about having linguistic intentionality that every word that comes out of your mouth needs to be intentional. It's not just saying stuff. Stop calling people "talented" because you really mean they're skilled; you're using words that confuse people, that push people towards a fixed mindset instead of a growth mindset.

We want people to read every single day and make a commitment to reading. When they do find thirty minutes, an hour, or an hour and a half every day to read, stop going, "Oh, I'm just not a reader. That's just not what I do." No, that's crap; that's an excuse. What's more important, your excuses or your dreams? You want your kids to be coachable, so you need to be coachable. You need to get your butt in the training room. You need to start training yourself to become a transformational leader. It does not happen, especially coming out of the day and age that we've come out of with transactional leadership that came from the military where people are yelling and screaming.

One of the things I was just talking to my good friend, Jon Gordon, about this morning: What would happen if people had physical bruises the way that you do whenever you physically abuse something, the way that you get whenever people emotionally and mentally abuse you? That's the type of leadership that a lot of people were accustomed to. Hurt people end up hurting people. If we never go back, roll up our sleeves, and go, "You know what? This is going to be hard." You don't lose 150 pounds just by going, "Oh, you know, I'm just going to diet a little bit." No, it's going to be really hard work. For most of us, we're 150 pounds mentally overweight. For us to become transformational leaders, it's going to be impractical, it's going to be hard, but it's incredibly worth it.

We all have had people in our life, hopefully, that have been transformational leaders, put our heart first, and focused on using our sport to help us become the type of people that we want to become instead of using sports and manipulating people to get results over something that really doesn't matter - like hitting a ball around a field or shooting a ball around a court. Those things, at the end of your life, really aren't going to matter. But, that's what we put so much attention on. We actually end up ruining people and relationships over stuff that, at the end of the day, is not going to give us true satisfaction. It's not going to give us fulfillment. Go look at all the people that have won a ton, and they'll tell you, "It's not going to fill that hole in your sole."

We believe in doing that hard work and working to become a transformational leader. When you do that – when you put first things first and when you focus on the process. John Wooden, who won more national championships than anybody in March Madness, never talked about winning. Ever. He talked about the process, the process, the process. He talked about how you could never  find a player that he coached that ever heard him mention the word "winning." That's incredible because we've gotten so far away from that. Yet, like C.S. Lewis said, "If we'll put first things first, those second things will not be suppressed; they'll increase." But, we live in a society that is constantly pushing and pulling us towards putting second things first - put winning first, put money first, put your job title first, and put beauty, power, and fame first. All of these things are secondary things. There's not anything inherently wrong with any of those things, but, if we put first things to the second, then we're going to mess up everything. Those first things are who we become, the relationships that we develop, and the impact that we have on people's lives. If we're not putting those first things first, then, most likely, we're not even coming close to tapping into people's fullest potential. We're making things a lot worse for people and who they become in the process, and we pass on some really challenging characteristics and leadership qualities that tend to have a generational impact.

## If someone wants to get in touch with you and work with Train 2B Clutch, what's the best way to go about doing that?

**Medcalf:** There's a lot of different ways. It's not super hard to get a hold of us. Our website is *t2bc.com*. If you just Google *"Joshua Medcalf"* or *"Jamie*

*Gilbert*" we tend to pop up. We're pretty active on Twitter. My Twitter handle is *@joshuamedcalf* and Jamie's is *@jdgilbert19*. Those are pretty easy ways. If you e-mail us through our website, it comes straight to us, and that is the easiest way to get hold of us.

## *For more great content from Joshua Medcalf, visit LeadershipVIP.com/JoshuaMedcalf*

# BEN PETRICK

**Former MLB Player and Author of *Forty Thousand to One***

# Your journey has been loaded with inspiration, love, faith, and much adversity. Please share with us as much as you would like to share about how you got to where you are today.

**Petrick:** Wow. I was just a kid growing up in a small town and happened to have enough skill and talent to get drafted by the Rockies in the second round of the 1995 Amateur Draft. I got into pro ball and was over my head; I didn't know what I got into. I was a very naïve kid. I had great parents – still have great parents – and they raised me well. It was an eye-opening experience for me to see the real world and get into the world of minor league baseball. I went through all kinds of ups and downs and had to persevere to get through the minor leagues to get to the big leagues. I had a very successful start to my career and then Parkinson's hit. Both my dad and myself came down with Parkinson's within seven months of each other. It was a shock to my whole family. I tried to finish my career playing four years with the disease in the Big Leagues - which is crazy. At the time, I didn't realize I was as bad as I was. I retired in 2004, like you said, and I have lived the last eleven years trying to cope with the disease and be as normal as possible for my kids. I have three kids now and wrote a book, *Forty Thousand to One*. It's been a crazy last eleven years: from pro baseball to being a stay-at-home dad with a disease to trying to be a leader in the community with my disability and being as open and honest with it.

# Your battle with Parkinson's disease has been filled with ups and downs: Disappointment, hope, faith, and, obviously, an unstoppable love for the game of baseball. What are one or two things that helped you through it all?

**Petrick:** My faith is one, no doubt. It has given me strength, inner peace, and something to fall back on whenever I have troubles. Sports has been something I have done all my life. I played football, basketball, and baseball growing up, and my dad was an athletic director. Out of all the adversities you face in sports, he had to overcome a few, improve and get better, and never give up. I think those go in my everyday life now. Without them, I don't know if I would be the same person, be married, or have three kids, so I'm thankful for that.

## *Forty Thousand to One* is a tremendous story. Can you talk about what the title stands for, and where can the listeners purchase that?

**Petrick:** It stands for two reasons. First, I had a 1 in 40,000 chance of getting Parkinson's disease. The other, the main topic/title, is because when I was playing ball, my audience was 30,000-50,000 fans every day. Then, I suddenly retired and was sitting at my house feeding my daughter her lunch. It was just me and her; she was my audience. So I went from an audience of 40,000 fans to an audience of one, my daughter McKenna, who was seven years old and in first grade.

To purchase the book, they can either go to my website, *BenPetrick.com*, or they can also go to Amazon.com.

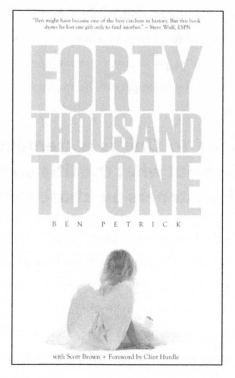

## You are now doing some consulting with Minor League Baseball players as they get acclimated to life in professional. What are some of the key points you try to focus on as they make this transition?

**Petrick:** One of the key points is the fact that everybody is different. So, when they get into pro ball, they react differently to the intensity of it. The skill level - even at the lowest levels - you are taking guys who are the best college and high school players, and you are putting them all onto one field. When you do that and have a lot of talent, the "self-weeding" begins; guys pulling themselves out of baseball because it is too hard to deal with the failure. It is a whole, new world for them. I try to tell them, "It's not that big of a deal," but when you get into it, it's pretty intense.

My first year was a mess. I was away from home. My last year of high school, I hit .520 which is four or five hits every 10 at-bats. In pro ball, my first month I hit .175. I was a mess; I couldn't handle it, like, "What is going on?" I thought I would be a lot better than that. It takes a while to adjust. I am trying to take young men that are struggling or need someone to talk to about life and try to be there for them. It has been fulfilling for me; I am grateful to the Diamondbacks organization for giving me a chance.

## *For more great content from Ben Petrick, visit LeadershipVIP.com/BenPetrick*

# KEVIN EIKENBERRY

Speaker, Author, and Chief Potential
Officer of the Kevin Eikenberry Group

**You're a world-renowned leadership expert, two-time best-selling author, speaker, consultant, and trainer. You recently were named to *Top 100 Leadership and Management Experts in the World, Top 100 Leadership Speakers for Your Next Conference,* and American Management Association's *Leaders to Watch in 2015.* Tell us a little bit more about you as a person and how you got to this point in your career.**

**Eikenberry:** What makes me different is that I'm a Midwestern farm boy. I grew up on a farm, and that has two big implications to the work that I do today:

1) I grew up with a very clear understanding that everything is about growth. We plant a seed in the ground, and it produces this amazing harvest. When I look at people, I see tremendous potential in them. For us to be successful leaders we fundamentally have to believe that the people we're leading have tremendous potential. That's a part of who I am that comes through in my work.

2) In growing up on a family farm, in a family business, with very young parents, I was very involved in a lot of things and was with my dad all the time. I grew up with a real sense of learning how to communicate with people of all ages and socio-economic strata and different types of work, if you will. That really helped me in my career and informed my work in making me able to communicate with people, whether they're frontline employees, in the c-suite, or any place in between.

Those are two things. I'm a farm kid. I would like to think that comes through in my writing in terms of values and also in terms of trying to take things that are complex and communicate them in a way that's accessible for people.

## You have an interesting title as the Chief Potential Officer of the Kevin Eikenberry Group. You include leadership, teams and teamwork, organizational culture, organizational learning, and more. I'd like to know a little bit more about your unique position and a little more about what the Kevin Eikenberry Group does.

**Eikenberry:** We've been at this for north of 20 years now. When you own a company, you can call yourself whatever you want. You know, I could say "janitor," and there have been days when that would be accurate. But I picked Chief Potential Officer because I wanted a title that no one else had. That was the number one thing. If there wasn't such a thing in the world as Chief Learning Officers, that's what I would've picked. I wanted to be unique and different, and I've already mentioned a little bit about my belief around the word "potential."

I think it informs a lot of our work, this idea of unleashing your potential. We talk about people's remarkable potential, and it seemed like the natural thing to call it Chief Potential Officer. We're a training and consulting company that's all about helping leaders, organizations, and teams get where they want to go.

Leadership is a great lever to help organizational results get achieved. It's how teams achieve greater things. Nothing great happens in the world without someone leading it. Our business is all about helping leaders, whether they have title and position or they're leading as an independent contributor. Our focus is on helping leaders grow so that they can grow their organizations.

## If a company, team, or organization wished to utilize your speaking or consulting, what would be the best way to go about getting in touch with you?

**Eikenberry:** The easiest way would be to go *kevineikenberry.com*, and you can learn everything you want to know there. Lots of free things available there. You can go directly to what you think you're interested in and be able to leave a message for us, send an e-mail to us, or get directly to what you would want. It's *kevineikenberry.com*, and you can always send an e-mail to *info@kevineikenberry.com*, or to me directly at *kevin@kevineikenberry.com*. Probably safer to send it to info; it will less likely get lost.

### *For more great content from Kevin Eikenberry, visit LeadershipVIP.com/KevinEikenberry*

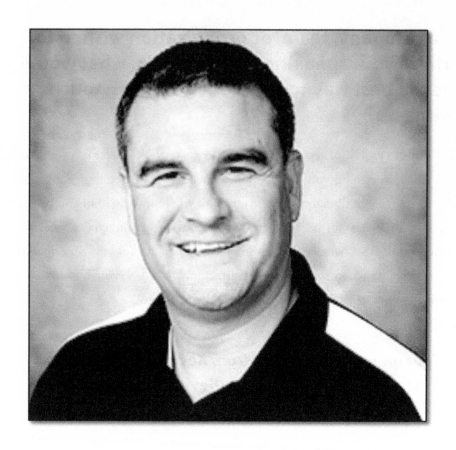

# DARRIN GRAY

**Speaker for All Pro Dad and Author of *The Jersey Effect***

## You work with All Pro Dad, a group of people passionately committed to bringing additional focus to fathers around the world. You have worked with many NFL coaches, such as Tony Dungy and Mike Tomlin. Tell us a little bit more about yourself and All Pro Dad.

**Gray:** We call it All Pro Dad, but I'm not an all pro dad. Tony Dungy's not an all pro dad. What defines us is that we want to get better. We've got that similar DNA about us whereby we want to constantly improve that particular quality in our lives so we can be the best husband, father, coach, and/or mentor that we can possibly be. We feel like that's important enough for us to invest time in, and All Pro Dad gives us the tools we need to help do that. For the last nine years, I've been able to walk alongside some very special men that have a great calling on their life in the NFL. As a result, they have a great ability to have a positive effect on those around them.

I get to work with them to help advance what it means to be an All Pro Dad. We teach millions of people every day at *AllProDad.com* and with the Play of the Day e-mail, the world's most widely read fatherhood e-mail. And then, certainly, through all our social media channels - Facebook pages, Twitter accounts, and Instagram - all those new ways to reach men and teach them what they most need to learn about being the best possible husband, father, and man. So, that's what I do, and I'm honored to do it each day.

## You co-authored a book titled *The Jersey Effect* with Super Bowl Champion punter, Hunter Smith. Tell us a little bit about that book. How did it come to be? What's the premise behind it? What is it really talking about?

**Gray:** That's a fun story. If I take you back, right after the Indianapolis Colts won Super Bowl XLI, which was on February 4, 2007. It was actually the 2006 Super Bowl. Tony Dungy and his team kneeled down in the locker room after that game and they gave credit, collectively, to God. And I thought that was pretty interesting. Usually, after championship games, people are popping champagne bottles and celebrating. They enjoyed themselves. But, they also wanted to stop and say, "You know what? This isn't just about us. It's about all those that came before and all those that'll come after us that really helped us along the journey to be champions." When they knelt down in the locker room and said that prayer, there was a photo that was taken by one particular guy at Getty Images. Tony asked everybody to turn off their cameras. Turn off the video cameras, turn off the individual cameras - they want to do it privately. One guy didn't. Thank goodness that he didn't because that photograph then went viral around the world. It was seen by tens of millions of people saying, "Hey, it's possible to win, to win the right way, and then give credit to God."

That for me is the proper lens. That's the proper perspective on sports. It's not about if you win or if you lose. Everybody's going to win some, and everybody's going to lose some. It's about what you do when you win, and what you do when you lose. And, in this case, it was about what the Colts did when they won. I thought that was remarkable. I

remember sitting in Tony Dungy's hotel room in New York City after that Super Bowl. This is about a year and a half later – "Tony, I want to tell that story. I want to write a book called *The Jersey Effect*. I want to go back, meet with some of your players, and talk with them about what that journey was like. What that experience taught them. What perhaps they learned along the way." And he said, "Well, I got just the guy for you. You need to talk to Hunter Smith." I knew Hunter, but I didn't know him well. Hunter and I connected over lunch, and I began to tell him the vision and about how Tony was excited about it. And wouldn't you know; Hunter caught the vision. I'm so blessed that he did.

From there, he introduced me to these champions, Jeff Saturday and Tarik

Glenn – these men that have these ginormous personalities and ginormous NFL contracts but were as humble as can be. They were willing to tell their story and allow me to capture that with the help of some of my other friends, Hunter and others. And that became *The Jersey Effect*. It's still having incredible ripple effects across America as teams and individuals are reading this book and learning how to keep sports in proper perspective.

Win the right way, and lose the right way. It's a lot of fun and been something that really blessed me, my family, and the community in so many ways.

## If a team or organization wanted to utilize you at All Pro Dad, or just have you come and speak or consult, what's the best way to go about getting in touch with you?

**Gray:** I'm pretty accessible. The quickest way to find me is on Twitter, *@AllProDadLeader*. If you want to see the work that I do - I was down at the Indiana State House yesterday doing some programs and talking with some key community leaders in Indiana, which is where I make my home, for your listeners to get some perspective on me and my life – they're also welcome to track me down at *allprodad.com*. There's a page where I'm listed as one of the key employees; I'm one of four directors of the organization. They can find my contact information there, or they're welcome to track me down by e-mail at *darrin@familyfirst.net*. However they want to seek me out will be fine. I'd be delighted to talk with them and coach them up on how they can use the All Pro Dad strategies to help improve their communities, schools, and, ultimately, make a difference in lives of kids.

### For more great content from Darrin Gray, visit LeadershipVIP.com/DarrinGray

# DON BEEBE

## Former NFL Wide Receiver and Super Bowl Champion

# Would you mind telling us about your road to the NFL and how you got to where you are today?

**Beebe:** Sure. I'm just a common guy. People look at me and they say, "Wow, that guy played in the NFL for nine years?" I'm living what every little kid's dream was and is. I only played two years of college football, one at Western Illinois in 1987 and one at a really small NAIA school called Chadron State in the northwest corner of Nebraska. It is an amazing story that I got invited to the NFL Combine out of that small school because they only take the top 300 players in all of college football. I went to the college combine a complete unknown. I didn't have an agent; didn't know I needed an agent. I ended up breaking two all-time records at the combine, and my whole world turned upside down.

I came back home to Chadron, Nebraska, to finish out my college degree. I had 21 personal workouts over the course of the next month and a half before the NFL Draft, then became the Buffalo Bills' first pick in the third round of the 1989 draft, which in itself is an amazing story. Obviously, it's one of faith. I'm a man of faith. My whole story is centered on my faith in the Lord, and I went through doors that were opened by Him. Now, I'm in the realm of coaching and owning a business called House of Speed which trains, encourages, and leads athletes of today's world.

# What led you to begin the House of Speed and how is it doing today?

**Beebe:** I was known for speed and running a 4.21 in the 40 yard dash is certainly going to open some eyes. I was gifted with that; it was my gift. When I retired, I knew that I still wanted to be involved in sports somehow, and I definitely knew I wanted to impact kids.

So, Dr. Jeff Schutt – who was a friend of mine and was training me at the end of my career in Green Bay – we were training and we went out to lunch one day and we were just talking, and I said, "Jeff, this is my vision." This was his vision too; he just loved working with athletes, and he did it out of the kindness of his heart. That's the kind of guy he is. We said, "Let's form a business." Back then, 17 or 18 years ago, nobody was training kids for speed. It was a complete unknown. So, we decided that we were going to start this business. My wife came up with the name on a napkin at dinner that night, House of Speed.

Here we are, 18 years later, with franchises and licensing agreements. We're training thousands of athletes every year. I'm just amazed at how far God has taken this because, initially, I just wanted to train some local kids and have fun with it. I never thought it would turn into the business that it's become.

## In 9 years in the NFL, you played in 6 Super Bowls. I'm sure you had to be around some great teams and leaders in the locker room. What stands out the most from your career in the NFL and the leadership that went into the success that you and your teams had on the field?

**Beebe:** I've learned a lot from some of the great leaders of our time. I played for Hall of Fame coach, Marv Levy; two Hall of Fame general managers, Bill

Polian and Ron Wolf, who are going into the Hall of Fame this year; two Hall of Fame defensive ends, Reggie White and Bruce Smith, arguably the two best ever; and two of the greatest quarterbacks to ever play, Jim Kelly, who's already in, and Brett Favre, who we know will go in.

I've been fortunate to be around some great people, great leaders, who understand and know what it takes to have high character that develops into some of the things that we are going to talk about in this interview. That's leadership. I have been blessed in that area, I never will forget it.

# Rumor has it that your book, *Six Rings from Nowhere,* is headed to the big screen. Is that true?

**Beebe:** It is. Well, we are hoping that it does. It needs to be funded, as everything does. Without money you don't have anything. The book is already done - *Six Rings from Nowhere.* I never thought, as a player, that I was a book guy. Certainly not a movie guy. I was just playing and having fun just going through the doors that were opened in front of me. When you have the story that I have - I should have never played in the NFL - it was an amazing thing that I was able to achieve that. Just to get in. Then, to go to six Super Bowls and winning one in a Packer uniform, that's just iconic.

I started listening to people. "Man, you need to write a book. This is crazy. What an unbelievable story that kids and people need to learn and read." So, I said, "Ok." We did the *Six Rings from Nowhere* because my whole life is that; I came from nowhere to go to six Super Bowls. It was more than that, though. It was about faith and putting my faith into something that was bigger than me. Way bigger than me. That's when the movie started coming about. Desert Wind Films, a faith-based film company out of Hollywood, approached me about a year and a half ago. I told them during our very first call, "Listen, if this has anything to do with me, you, how much money we can get, and fame, then I'll be honest with you: I have no interest in that. I really don't. But, if it does everything to give me a stage and a platform, more than I already have as an athlete, to travel the globe and speak to kids and people to never give up, be able to achieve things in life, and put their faith in something other than themselves, I'm all ears. I'm all in." That just blew them away.

In their world of Hollywood, they don't hear those kind of comments very often. So, we hit it off right away, and here we are, a year and a half later, trying to raise the funds to do it. If we do, it's going to come to fruition.

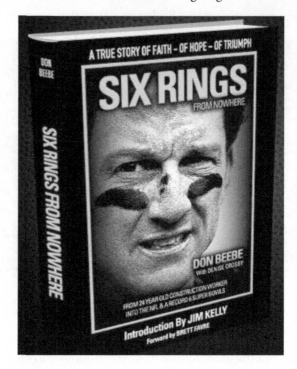

*For more great content from Don Beebe, visit LeadershipVIP.com/DonBeebe*

# JOHN BRUBAKER

## Award-Winning Author, Speaker, and Executive Coach

**Let's say one of your clients was the head coach of an NCAA Division I sport and felt like he was not being the leader he needed to be for his players. Where would you begin to assess his situation? How would you move him forward?**

**Brubaker:** This is what I tell him. You have a team, you have a title, and you have a mirror. If you're not being the leader you need to be, it's nobody's fault but your own. If your team's not getting the results they need to get, you need to look no further than in the mirror. I think it all starts with that self-assessment. Whether it's Narcotics Anonymous, Alcoholics Anonymous, Workaholics Anonymous, whatever it is, they say the first step is admitting it. So, a leader has got to admit that he's got a problem or at least got a real challenge on his hands or her hands. In order to move forward, you've got to be honest with yourself and realize, "Here's what I'm not doing. Here's what I need to do. Also, get a measurement of 'here's what I'm doing well and I ought to keep doing.'" Because everyone has different leadership strengths, and I don't think anyone is a complete failure as a leader. Usually we go astray in a couple of critical areas, but we have that foundation in place in others. So, what's working, what's not, and what do I need to start doing?

**Chapter 19 of *The Coach Approach* is titled "Little Things Win Big Games." What are a few of the little things when it comes to leadership?**

**Brubaker:** The founder of the Marriott Corporation I think said it best: "It's the little things that make the big things possible." Attention to detail, fine details in any operation, is what really makes for a first-class experience. If you ever stayed in a Marriott Hotel, you know they are the master of all those tiny details. So, I would say that the little things, when it comes to leadership, are the big things, but it's being consistent. Your players, your administration, and your staff - they want to know that every day they're getting that same guy or girl who's leading them.

I call coaches who are up one day then down the next; everything's good after a win and then the whole world's crumbling after a loss – there's a certain species in the animal kingdom that I call them. "Bipolar bears." Not a polar bear, a *bi*polar bear. You never know what you're going to get with that person. You look at it like a coaches' play book. What do successful teams do? They tend to have a steady diet and are consistent with the same scheme. They drill it and they drill and drill it until it's automatic, until it's flawless execution. They are successful because they know what to expect, they know what to do, and they've gotten the reps. I think successful leaders are consistent in their leadership style in the same way that they're consistent with their game strategy. People know what to expect; they know what they're getting every day.

But, it's really being a master of the little things, and I know coaches are masters of the little things. They leave no stone unturned in the recruiting process, on the recruiting trail, everywhere. They leave no stone unturned when it comes to film study and scouting reports. The teams that do the little things right are the ones that win. I think the leaders that really do the little

things - and the little things are keeping your finger on the pulse of your team, your staff, your boosters, or whatever it is - keeping your finger on the pulse every day. Maybe it's just the first five minutes going up and down the line in stretch and checking in one to one with each of those guys or girls, giving them a high five, asking them how they're doing, and not just, "Hey, how are you doing?" but "How are you really doing?" Just a quick check-in that lets them know you really do care and it's not a formality. "Hey, how are you really doing? I know you had a rough outing last game. What's going on?" Or, giving them a little praise, but it's all those little things that make the biggest difference.

## You've had a lot of experience working with business executives around the country and several competitive athletes. What do you think is one hidden aspect of leadership that almost all people miss entirely?

**Brubaker:** There is one staggering statistic I'm going to throw at you, and that's that 75% of a person's waking hours are spent on work. Not at work, on work. What I mean by that is getting to and from work - that morning commute; thinking about work while you're in the shower or brushing your teeth, combing your hair, or whatever you're doing; thinking about work after you get home or after you sit down for dinner. It's in those areas. Also, that 75% encompasses actually working on their job. So, hearing that ought to make you realize what an incredible, and enormous, responsibility we have as leaders. It's not just people thinking about work while they're at work; they're taking it home with home. They're going to bed with work at night. This is the hidden implication that a lot people miss completely as leaders. You're not just impacting your team members' lives, their life at work, or their life on the game field, but your leadership impacts their home life and their personal life in a huge way.

Think about the average roster size in your sport as you're listening to this. Those student-athletes probably have a boyfriend or girlfriend. Some of them have a wife and kids or a wife and a kid. Maybe they're living at home, and they have a family - their parents. Whatever it is, you're not just affecting that student-athlete. You're affecting the lives of the people they go home to: their roommates or the people they share an apartment with. Your average roster - you multiply that by four or five, easily. The people that your players surround themselves with when they're not on the playing field. Your leadership impacts more than just the results on the field or just the people on your team. Your influence extends so far beyond that locker room and that playing field. It extends to all the people around the people you lead. That's a big implication. That means we need to grow ourselves. We need to become better at leading. If we're not bringing our best, setting that example, realizing that your leadership footprint – let's say it's a football team - it isn't just your 85-man roster. It's all the people around. It's irresponsible of you as a leader if you don't recognize the fact that what you're doing doesn't just rub off on your players; it rubs off on everyone around them, sort of by osmosis, through your players.

## If our readers wanted to get more from you, where can they do that? Are there any social media accounts that they should be following?

**Brubaker:** Absolutely. They can go to my website, that's *coachbru.com*. When you go to the homepage you could sign up for my weekly newsletter. That is the single best entry point into all my resources. You're going to get a weekly newsletter that is all about and geared towards your leadership performance. It will be one article, one quote, and one actionable strategy. I'm not big on being thought-provoking. I want to be change-provoking and action-provoking. So it's all actionable strategy; stuff that you can take straight out of theory and right into practice immediately. I enjoy Twitter a lot and my Twitter handle is *@CoachBru* so we can continue the conversation there too.

### For more great content from John Brubaker, visit LeadershipVIP.com/JohnBrubaker

# ZAC WOODFIN

## Collegiate Strength & Conditioning Coach and Former Professional Football Player

# You've moved pretty quickly up the ladder into the professional and collegiate ranks of the strength & conditioning world. What characteristics do you possess that have allowed you to do that?

**Woodfin:** My faith drives everything I do, in regards to character or my characteristics. I've always tried my hardest to make every opportunity I've had the most important one. I've always believed that I was called to each opportunity for a specific reason.

With that being said - whether it be starting off interning at The University of Alabama at Birmingham (UAB) or volunteering at The University of Alabama as a strength and conditioning coach - anywhere I've been, I've really tried to be my best there and try not to think about the next stop. That's one thing I really focused on early in my career.

I've also tried to really focus on how I treat people, whether that being the athletes that I've coached, the coaches, the colleagues, the janitors, or anybody that I've come across. I've really tried to treat them with respect, serve them, and let them know that I really do care about them and care about their needs before mine.

Hopefully, that has come across to people I have worked with and been around. Relationships are key. Making people feel like they're important and backing that up daily. Again, my faith, how I treat people, and how I go about each opportunity I have has led me to where I am today.

## What did you learn as an NCAA Division I student-athlete that translates into your leadership today?

**Woodfin:** I had some good leaders and some good coaches when I was playing football at UAB. I also had some not-so-good leaders and some not-so-good coaches. So, I've seen every end of the spectrum.

As I really look back and think about that question, the most important thing that I've learned from playing football at UAB is that practicing what you preach is vital if you want people to follow what you're trying to get them to do. Being transparent in your life, not having secrets, and not having walls. If you're a coach and athletes and other people can see that you are genuine and you are trying to do yourself what you are coaching and teaching them to do - knowing that you're going to make mistakes, practicing what you preach, and being consistent in that - people will listen to you and people will follow a lot quicker than if they know, "Hey, he's trying to tell me this, but he doesn't do it." That's a hard pill to swallow with me.

## Besides enhancing your physical capabilities, how can a team become more unified through a strength and conditioning program?

**Woodfin:** Our biggest deal is not even strength, power, or speed. Mindset is our number one pillar which we talk about. We have four within our philosophy. Under that umbrella of mindset you have culture, mental toughness, and character. I really believe culture - the kind of environment that you create, the connection that you have with your players, the connection that they have with themselves - will always trump a team's ability or athleticism. When it comes to winning or losing, I truly believe the culture you create is what's going to lead to championships or not. So, a lot of things fall under culture, but I think culture is the number one thing for any team or organization.

# In your first year as the head strength and conditioning coach at UAB, you carried a paralyzed member of the team to the top of Legion Field. What inspired you to do this? Was it predetermined, or was it a spur-of-the-moment thing?

**Woodfin:** That was Tim Alexander, who was paralyzed from the waist down. It was definitely not predetermined. I would never want to do something like that for me to get recognition. It ended up going viral. Everybody that was there knows that wasn't meant to be; it just happened. I'm glad it happened because it raised some awareness for Tim, some of the goals he has, and his dream to walk again. If it can inspire people, then I'm all for it. It was definitely a spur-of-the-moment decision.

We were at Legion Field - our team was - running stadiums and doing a lot of on-field agility and different things. I was at the bottom of the stadium while our whole team was running them. I just looked over, and I saw Tim in his chair looking up. He was almost in a daze. Again, I try to live as much of my day trying to be open-eared to my faith, my conscience, and listening to anything God puts on my heart to do. In that moment, it was very heavy in my heart and in my mind to take him to the top, if that's what he wanted.

I look over and think to myself that he's basically dreaming of himself running those stadiums. That's what he's doing right there. He's in a daze - in a trance - and I say, "Tim," and he kind of snapped out of it. I said, "Do you want to go?" And he said, "Yeah!" All this happened within a matter of about five seconds. I didn't really think it through. I'm glad I didn't because then I wouldn't have carried him because Tim is 6'4", 250. I put him on my shoulders and started to walk up the steps. I started to stumble halfway up, and that's when the whole team came to my side. We carried him up together, but it was definitely not planned. It was something that just hit my heart and didn't really think about it; just did it.

**For more great content from Zac Woodfin, visit LeadershipVIP.com/ZacWoodfin**

# BILL CLARK

## NCAA Division I Head Football Coach

**You went from being an extremely successful high school football coach in the state of Alabama for 17 years to the defensive coordinator at South Alabama for four years. From there to the head coach at Jacksonville State, your alma mater, for one year before becoming the head coach at UAB. What do you think allowed you to move so quickly to become an NCAA Division I head football coach?**

**Clark:** I grew up in the business. My dad was a successful high school coach and all my years in high school prepared me for the next level. But one of the things that is a misnomer that more people are starting to figure out is high school football, specific to the South. I can speak on the South because that's where I've been, but especially at the upper levels, it's really gotten to be college football minus the recruiting. The numbers, the technology, etc., in high school are really getting closer and closer to what college football looks like. It was a great proving ground for us to get ready for that next step.

**UAB announced that it would end its football program after you'd been at the helm for one season. As the head coach, how did you respond personally and as a leader of so many young lives and assistant coaches around you?**

**Clark:** I've told a lot of people it was not a death, but it's the closest thing, that I've been part of, to a death since my mother passed away. It was awful; there's no way around it. The biggest thing for me was: What do I do with these players that I'm responsible for and these coaches that I'm responsible for? I tried to make sure they all landed on their feet. It's not what it was; it's different. But I wanted to make sure they were taken care of because that's my first responsibility.

## You've had major success at every level of high school and college football in your coaching career. What is your mentality when leading a football team on the field as well as off the field?

**Clark:** I think it all goes together. When I see these things spoken by other people and when we talk about family, I think there's people that say it and then there's people that do it. The only way to truly be family is to really care and to love your players and your coaches. I've said it all the time. It's just like a good parent. Loving you doesn't mean I'm always going to tell you exactly what you want to hear. Loving you means I care about you. I care more about you than just as football player or just as a coach. I care about what happens to you; what you do on the field, off the field, and in the classroom. That permeates every layer of your life and our lives as coaches. The family aspect - if you really mean that and you really believe it and you really put it together – that's what makes a successful team.

*For more great content from Bill Clark, visit
LeadershipVIP.com/BillClark*

# DOUG CRANDALL

## Author, Speaker, and Leadership Instructor at the U.S. Military Academy at West Point

**You attended and taught at West Point, where you won the excellence in teaching award for teaching leadership, advanced leadership, and leading organizations through change. You have been cultivating and sharing a rich understanding of leadership through a range of leadership experiences, including the United States Army and as Operations Manager at Amazon.com. Tell us little bit about your journey and how you got to this point in your career.**

**Crandall:** I attended West Point out of undergrad, the United States Military Academy, and largely followed in my father's footsteps through doing that. I did not come from a military family, per se, because my dad had left the army before I was born, but I knew about it because of him. I was the youngest of five kids and the only one to take that path. There were things I loved about the army. I loved the relationships, the people, and the sense of purpose. There were some other things that were not exactly what I was looking for: the time away from family and some of the other challenges. What brought me into this real focus on studying leadership - thinking about it and trying to help other people think about it - was the opportunity to teach at West Point, something my dad told me that he had wished he stayed in the army to do. The army has a great program for teaching at the military academy where they send you to get a master's degree for two years at whatever

99

school you can get into. There are some stipulations around that with costs.

I had the chance to do that and just fell in love with that job at West Point, being with future leaders and helping them think about what they really believed in and why they believed it. That took me to West Point. After that, I jumped back into an operational job with Amazon.com but really missed the process of being in a room with a bunch of people who were trying to help develop themselves as leaders and helping them through that process. I got back into that and was fortunate enough to connect with Walmart. I spent five years as a faculty member for their high-potential leadership development program, what we call Leadership Academy. I go back and forth to Bentonville, Arkansas, quite a bit and some other places, like their e-commerce headquarters out in San Bruno, California, developing a lot of their leaders. That's enabled me to go out and do a lot of that work on my own.

I'm currently connected to a coaching firm called the Boda Group and doing leader development for them as they try to branch out from coaching and developing some leadership programs and speaking. That's how I got there and what I'm doing.

**You transformed the United States Military Academy's core leadership curriculum, which was the first revision in twenty years and then moved into the corporate world where you integrated all the leadership development taught at the leadership academy at Walmart. You have written a book titled *Say Anything: How Leaders Inspire Ideas, Cultivate Candor and Forge Fearless Cultures*. Tell us a little bit more about your work and what you're currently**

# doing in the organizations with which you have shared.

**Crandall:** A lot of the thinking and studying I've done came from the work that I'm doing with Walmart. I write case studies there, where we're constantly interacting with leaders, getting their daily leadership challenges, and turning them into lessons. One of the things that popped up that's led to this book, *Say Anything*, is just that it's really difficult for people to say what they're thinking. For a follower to say what they're thinking. In fact, there's been millions of books - like *Difficult Conversations*, *Courageous Conversations*, *Fierce Conversations*, *Leading Upward* - about how people can bring up these tough conversations or even simple things with the people who are leading them. It's actually just a human condition. It's not even just a "led to leader" thing. When you're deciding with a friend where to go to a movie and your friend suggests a movie, you might think to yourself, "Boy, I'm not sure I want to see that movie, but he must want to see it because he suggested it. So, I'll go along with it." Meanwhile your friend recommended it because they think you want to see it, and you both end up going to see a movie you didn't want to see.

That little scenario goes back to a thing called the Abilene Paradox, which a guy named Jerry Harvey introduced in 1952. This whole idea we've seen in some of the organizations we're working with. Again, I'll go back to my dad, who had set a great example when I was growing up of enabling us to say what we were thinking to him and really encouraging that. We've built a book around that which has a lot of servant leadership principles. I've been out speaking on that. In fact, I was just in New York for two days talking to a number of investment banks and American Express. We'd been invited in to Gap to talk to their IT organization because they recognized they have issues - issues when people don't speak up, leading to deadlines being missed because people were afraid to say about the deadline "we weren't going make it." They knew four months out, "We're not going to make this," but they didn't want to let their boss down, and they didn't feel they could say it. That's common to a ton of organizations. I've been out doing that and continuing to do a lot of authentic leader development work with some other smaller companies. A month ago, I was with a small church team of twenty that wanted to build trust among each other and talked about this topic of saying anything.

## If a team or organization wanted to bring you in to work with them, what's the best way to go about doing that and getting in touch with you?

**Crandall:** A lot of what we do around *Say Anything* is on the Boda Group's website, so it's *BodaGroup.com*, as well as our e-mails and contact information. We do get a lot of that and it's ramping up. I think it's this idea of leaders breaking down the communication wall rather than followers figuring out how to scale it, if you will. All these books like *Fierce Conversations* - I'm not dismissing those. I have one of the best sellers, *Difficult Conversations*. I have it dog-eared, I've highlighted it, I've read it five or six times. Some of the principles in there we use in the work we're doing. But, all of that is really a way to get people to try to climb over this wall, look

on the other side, and see if they can say what they're thinking to their leader. Our approach is that you break down that wall as the leader, you set the conditions, and you do everything you can to be vulnerable, to make it explicit, and to be curious about what the people you lead have to say. You can be a great leader, and that wall's still there. So, you have to take active steps.

We are finding a lot of organizations that are hearing about this. We've been doing it for about six months. Actually, it's only been six months, really, since we put pen to paper and started writing the book. We got the book done quickly, and organizations we hear about are getting in touch with us. We're eager to share it because we think it's really meaningful.

**_For more great content from Major Doug Crandall, visit LeadershipVIP.com/DougCrandall_**

# BHRETT MCCABE

## Sport Performance Psychologist and Founder of The MindSide

# You were a very accomplished baseball player at LSU winning two NCAA National Championships, three SEC Championships, and three trips to the College World Series. You played for College Baseball Hall of Fame and U.S. Olympic Team coach Skip Bertman. Tell us a little bit about your journey and some of the leadership lessons that you learned from one of the most successful college baseball programs in NCAA history.

**McCabe:** Playing for Skip was, obviously, one of the greatest experiences of my life, but it was deeper than that. I moved to Baton Rouge when I was in eighth grade, and that was right about the start of the LSU baseball dynasty with the fan base getting excited. We used to go out to the fall games (when they used to play fall baseball games against competitions). I'd go out and watch them play. I started looking up to guys. Being a local – at that time they'd get 2,000-3,000 to a game – it was the greatest show in town. You could go, it was inexpensive, and you could get to know the players.

As I went through high school, I had a little bit of interest from different colleges. In April of my senior year, Skip called through the baseball program and they said, "Coach would like to meet with you." It was a pretty big honor. I went up, met with him, and he said, "Look, you're not good enough to play for me this year, and you're probably not even good enough to play for me next year. But, I like to take risks and take challenges. You have the body size, the frame, and you're also a smart kid from a great family." He said, "I'd like to give you an opportunity to be a part of the program; to do everything with everyone else so you're part of the program. But, you decide how much you're going to play or not based on how much you grow, how much you develop, and how much you buy into the system." It was an easy question for me. It wasn't a hard question. It was a very simple opportunity. So, I took it and redshirted my freshman year while we won the national title. I traveled with the team, threw batting practice, and I was the "scout pitcher." I would prepare as the opposing team starting pitchers would. I had some great mentors in guys like Chad Ogea, Paul Byrd, Mike Sirotka, and Rick Greene - all first round picks or major league pitchers - and learned the system.

In my sophomore year, I thought I was going to great. I ended up getting sick with mono[nucleosis] and missed six weeks of the season. I wasn't going to play. But it was that time - after I got sick with mono and had to spend time in the weight room getting stronger and healthier – that I learned what it took to put in the work and commit to a craft. I came back from the fall camp [1992] as the third starter on the baseball team.

Unfortunately, I got to a spot where – after the last intrasquad game in which I'd pitched and done extraordinarily well against our A team – I ended up having a shoulder impingement. I couldn't lift my shoulder to comb my hair. So, I was shut down for the Christmas break. I struggled during the 1993 season, a season in which we won the College World Series again. I was trying to regain the form that I had and just couldn't regain it. I really thought about quitting the game; thought about moving on because the game had passed me by, and I'd lost a lot. It wasn't until I refocused my mind and learned to work through it – what opened the door for me to be in the position I'm in today was working on the mental game. When I did that, I ended up having a lot of success. In 1994 and 1995, I led the conference in appearances and led many of the conference pitching categories, even though I really wasn't all that good at the time. It wasn't storybook, but it was pretty close to being fantastic.

## It sounds like you've experienced some adversity and had to overcome those injuries during your career. How have some of those experiences impacted what you do today on a daily basis?

**McCabe:** There's no question: I'd be a lawyer right now if I hadn't gotten hurt or if I wasn't playing ball. Being 6'5" and 220 pounds, I had a frame that a lot of scouts liked. My dream was to play professional baseball, and it wasn't uncommon for people at LSU, like me, to come in in a less-than-heralded position and be drafted. But the injury to me was the greatest thing that ever happened because, as painful as it was and as much as it made me question everything, it ended up leading me into a field of mental health and psychology. I knew that the mind had something to do with my injury and not being able to overcome it. I pitched very scared when I came back, becoming "overvalued" in my mechanics as opposed to getting guys out. If it wasn't for that I wouldn't have gone to grad school, I wouldn't have got my doctorate in clinical psychology, and I wouldn't have specialized in injury rehabilitation with medically ill patients. I wouldn't have been fortunate enough to train at one of the top two training sites in the country, Brown Medical School. If it wasn't for that injury, like I said, I'd be pushing papers as an attorney right now.

## The facility you have in Birmingham, Alabama, is outstanding. Through the platform at The MindSide you say, "The boardroom is no

**different from the golf course, the playing field, or the diamond." We all want to perform at a higher level and achieve the goals that we expect and desire. The big question is: How do we do that?**

**McCabe:** I worked in corporate for eight and a half years in pharmaceutical research. When I first got done with grad school, I had two small kids and felt like I couldn't just open up a shingle and say, "I'm going to see people." I really wanted to know how the other side of the spectrum worked: how a billion dollar drug makes it through to market, when every decision has pressure on it, more so than just, "Are we going to squeeze here? Are we going to call an off-tackle right on third and goal? What are we going to do? What's that pressure? What's the safety record of patients who are taking it out there in the world, and are they going to live or die taking your medicine?"

The boardroom is no different. The reason I say that is: Excellence is excellence. It's where you apply your trade that's different. We have to be committed to the plans that we have in front of us. We have to have a vision for what we want. We have to trust our strategy to help us get there. Then, we have to execute without fear. It doesn't matter if we're making a decision on laying off employees, making a big expansion, making an investment, or a player who's sitting on the fourth string but wants to be the starter. You've got to really clarify what you want. You've got to be willing to make sacrifices to get there. There's really no difference.

# If a company, team, or organization wished to utilize yourself or The MindSide, what would be the best way to go about getting in touch with you to get more information?

**McCabe:** If you just go to my website, *BhrettMcCabe.com*. You send in a request; that's the easiest way to do it. In today's world, we got rid of our office phone because all we got were sales calls. With direct access, everybody calls me directly on my cell phone, or my wife, who handles all my scheduling. It just works that way.

### *For more great content from Bhrett McCabe, visit LeadershipVIP.com/BhrettMcCabe*

# KEN LUBIN

## Founder of Executive Athletes and Managing Director of ZRG Partners

# You've had an extremely successful career as a competitive athlete, recruiter, speaker, and leader. What do you think are the keys to having success in so many different realms of life?

**Lubin:** I think a lot of it comes down to balance, constant learning, and time management. You know, some of the keys for me is I don't waste time doing things that aren't really propelling me forward in the right direction. Many times, many people get stuck in the entertainment world. "Let's watch a sports game," or "Let's just watch TV," or "Let's listen to the radio on a car." One of the things that I'm always doing is always looking to learn. I'm trying to learn from the best that are out there, from athletes, to business leaders, to just guys doing cool stuff, or people doing cool stuff. Another thing is knowing how to come back from minor setbacks. Those are some of things that I'm always focused on because every day we have setbacks, and how you overcome those setbacks are the keys. But, I think it comes down to balance, constant learning, and time management.

# As a champion of several national endurance competitions, what were some of the toughest obstacles you've overcome throughout your journey?

**Lubin:** Overcoming obstacles is a daily chore. There's going to be a million things that try to deter you from your trend, work, family obligations, and social obligations.

Most of it comes down to purely time. I'm always ready to go at a moment's notice, to go out for a training session, or to get a training session in. I'm always constantly looking at my calendar and say, "Hey, do I have an hour free? Do I have a half an hour free? Do I have two hours free?" Some of my favorite workouts are the fast ones; the ones that you need to do quickly, with focus, and are going to allow you to be the most successful.

So, I'm always looking for times in the day where I can sneak out and I can get my workout done, but I'm also willing to get my job done at the same time. It's not uncommon for me to be up in the mountains at 5am in the middle of winter - it's 10 below zero and blowing 20 miles an hour - to get my workouts in because I know that it's not going affect my life. It's not going to affect my wife and my kids because most of the time I'm always doing this stuff when the rest of the world is sleeping. So, I think some of the ways to overcome the obstacles is to find time when you don't have the time. There's sort of that NET time, No Extra Time. The no extra time is when you can get that stuff done.

## Is there anything that you do as part of your morning routine that you think helps you to live with this level of energy?

**Lubin:** A lot of it is getting up early. Every day, I'm up at 4:30 or 5 o'clock. I'll get up and read something inspirational for half an hour. Then, I'll do a quick core workout down on my basement to get the blood flowing. And then it's on. My kids are getting up. I'm making lunches. I'm getting everyone ready for school and getting them out the door. So, I think the keys are to get the mind prepared, to get the body moving a bit, and then you're ready to tackle the day.

## Can you tell us a little bit more about Executive Athletes, and how our audience can get in contact with you if they want to learn more about you and what you do?

**Lubin:** Executive Athletes started during the recession of 2010. It was a way for me to connect with other like-minded individuals. I figured, there's got to be other people that are athletes or professionals who don't really have a network of people to connect with within their office. Many office situations in today's world aren't really conducive to people who are going out and training, going out and racing on the weekends, and doing all that. Most people look at others and say, "You know, you're crazy. Why are you wasting so much time doing this stuff when you could be doing that stuff?"

I created this online community of individuals that share similar mindsets. What it's done is, it's turned into a community of about 20,000 people who are always sharing secrets of success or how they reach success in business and in sport. What are some of the key things that they're doing that other people aren't doing? And, on a weekly basis, I always put out a question to find out how everyone does it and how they all do it differently. That's what Executive Athletes is. It's an online community to inspire the inspired, and to push people to become better than they were before.

You can check out the website at *executiveathletes.com*. You can always find it on LinkedIn; that's where it was born and bred as a group. And then on *Facebook.com/executiveathletes*. So, you can reach me in any of those three different ways.

### *For more great content from Ken Lubin, visit LeadershipVIP.com/KenLubin*

# EXCLUSIVE CONTENT & FREE RESOURCES

# For additional content, audios, videos, links, training tools, social media and more, visit: LeadershipVIP.com

# GAME TIME
## Q&A

# LEADERSHIP DEFINED

## What is your definition of leadership?

**Gordon:** There's a number of definitions. A leader is not just one thing. To me, leaders succeed not because they're great; they succeed because they bring out the greatness in others. It's really not about your own greatness as a leader. It's what you do to bring out the greatness in others. To me, leadership is about optimism. Leaders see a brighter and better future. They rally people towards that vision and believe that they can create it and help other people believe they can create it. Bob Iger, the CEO of Disney, said, "The most important characteristic of a leader is optimism." I really believe that to be true. I believe that leadership is a transfer of belief; that's essential. But, I also believe that you have to be someone that they want to follow. You have to be someone who is filled with integrity, compassion, and someone who can connect with others. Leadership is a lot of things. It's not just one. But, you have to have these various ingredients to be a great leader.

**Janssen:** If you're interested in leadership, you definitely know John Maxwell and all of the great resources he's put out there. He talks about leadership as being influence. Nothing more, nothing less. And, it is. It's a huge influence that people can have on people. You get to choose whether it's positive or negative, but you do have influence with people. It's something that you have to earn; that influence or credibility, as we would call it. So, I would say leadership is a big part influence.

**Olson:** I'm on the John Maxwell team, and John's definition is very simple; it's influence. For me though, I believe leadership is leaving something better than the way you found it. I believe that it's taking people to a level they can't get to by themselves. In a nutshell, for me, leadership is about helping others maximize their potential so that they can help others maximize theirs. There is a legacy effect there for me. It is influence, but it's also impact. I always say this - I have some kids now, two are in college, one is in high school - when we talk about high schools it is "as the principal goes, the school goes." When you look at businesses, as the leadership of a business goes, that's how the whole business goes. I truly believe that leadership is not just a cliché term anymore. People are living and dying on leadership. Companies, organizations - I do some work with the U.S. Army Special Forces, the [Navy] SEALs, and those kinds of people. Leadership is paramount, and the SEALs have a saying: "There are no bad units, only poor leaders." I believe that too. Everything hinges on leaders, so it's very important that it's a top-down effect for me.

**Isom:** It's changed a lot throughout the years. I would've told you a few years ago that leadership was being the strongest, the most powerful, the most outspoken, the boldest, and the bravest. Through life, that definition has changed a lot.

I think the purest definition of leadership is sacrificial love. It really is seeing the organization, the team, the family - whatever it may be - as a priority. Not just leading it for the sake of your desire, wants, will, or your way. It is really seeing the family, the organization, the team; sacrificing for it; learning its needs and wants; using the skills you've been given as a leader to work all those things together for a common good. A lot of times that means a lot of sacrifice on the leader's part and doing a lot of the hard things.

That's the easiest way I can put it. I think leadership is sacrificial acknowledgment of the good of the organization and the team. I think a great leader is one who is willing to make that sacrifice and doesn't get lost in the mess of all that leadership could mean when it comes to power and privilege.

**Goldsmith:** Working within and through others to achieve objectives. The goal is the word "others." One of the great leaders that I coached said, "For the great achiever it is all about me. For the great leader it's all about them." The difference between leadership and achievement is an achiever is a person that's doing it themselves, and the leader is the person that's working with them through others to get the job done. It's really focused more on the others than himself or herself.

**White:** My definition of leadership is making everybody around you better by equipping them with the skills necessary and empowering them to reach their full potential. I want to make sure that, as a leader, I will prepare everyone for every scenario possible and know that preparation will be revealed when you go out and you do the work through the tough times and the good times. I really think it's about making everybody around you better and about giving them the tools and empowering them to believe that they can ultimately reach that potential.

**Kouzes:** I actually have two ways. The first is we do have a definition, a descriptive definition. We describe leadership as the art of mobilizing others to want to struggle for shared aspirations. Each of those words has a meaning. Leadership is an art. An art in that it is a performing art. It is something that leaders do with other people so you are performing it; it's not just in your head. Like other performing arts, including athletics, you are doing it in front of other people. There has to be a relationship between you and those people. It is mobilizing others because leadership is about getting people to move. It is getting people to go in a direction; not just "think good thoughts" but actually take some action. "Want to" is important because we want to stimulate the intrinsic motivation of people. They aren't just doing it because they have to do it, because it is their job, but because they have a great desire and will to do it. We inserted the word "struggle" in our definition because I think sometimes the way we talk about leadership makes it seem too easy. One of the things we learned from our research is there is a lot of challenge in leadership. Also, it's about shared aspirations. It is not just about what the leader wants but what the people want, whether those people are your customers, your employees, or your peers and colleagues at work. It is about a common set of values and beliefs.

So, that's our descriptive definition, and of course, as I mentioned earlier, we have five practices which we use to observe and measure whether or not leaders are engaging in the behaviors that enable them to mobilize others to want to struggle for shared aspirations.

**Elmore:** That is a word that has been defined at least a thousand times by men and women far wiser than I. The working definition we tend to use is: Leadership is simply leveraging my influence for a worthwhile cause. You and I both know people that are influential but are bad influences. They are the thermostats rather than thermometers, but they are setting the wrong temperatures. That would be an Adolph Hitler, a Saddam Hussein, a Nero, or a Stalin. We are believing that when you become an effective leader, you are leveraging the influence you become aware of that you have, but it's for a worthwhile cause. Could be for a team, could be for digging wells in Africa and getting clean water to countries that don't have clean water, it may be a cause you believe in in Asia, or it may be a company that you want to do something redemptive with. That's what we believe in. It's leveraging my influence for a worthwhile cause. So that's what we go with, and it seems to make sense to people.

**Anderson:** I really haven't found a better definition than what J. Oswald Sanders said a long time ago, that it's influence. John Maxwell has said it as well. If you can't influence people, you can't lead them. Regardless of your title, if you can influence them - even if you don't have the title - then you're demonstrating leadership. It all goes back to the ability to positively influence people in a meaningful way towards a common goal.

**Medcalf:** My definition of leadership comes back to what John Wooden said, which is, "Young people need models, not critics." I think leadership is modeling. I think people are always learning, but we're not always aware of what we're teaching them. There was a time when I went in to work with a high-level NCAA Division I program - I don't believe in using fitness as a punishment. I think that fitness is extremely important. It makes zero sense to me why we would try and negatively condition something psychologically into people's brains as a punishment that's incredibly valuable – I'd explain that [to coaches]. The next day at practice, I was observing. The coach comes over to me and he says, "All right. So what do I do? Four of my players just showed up. All of them had their shirts untucked. Typically they do some down and backs as punishment. What am I supposed to do?" I tried to be as respectful and as humble as possible, but I just said, "Can you look at you and all of your staff?" Every one of them had their shirts untucked. Let's start there.

That's what I find so often. It's like we want our kids to read, but we don't read. We want them to have true mental toughness, but we don't show true mental toughness. We want them to have beneficial and constructive self-talk, but we don't have that. We want them to have great body language whenever they're out on the court, yet our kids are scared to death. They look over every time they miss a shot or turn over the ball and see you stomping around, throwing your clipboard, or having a look of disgust on your face. To me, it's modeling. Attitude reflects leadership. You get what you allow, and you get what you model.

**Petrick:** That's a long definition. I'll keep it as short as possible. I think leadership is being the person that people look to as the go-to guy. I think the main thing to becoming a good leader is transparency. Be open and honest. Share and do things you want other people to do, and they should be able to follow in your footsteps without being ashamed of what they are doing. They should be proud and able to know that you are the person they should look up to and their friends should look up to; just an overall quality guy. Lead by example. Obviously, there are different types of leadership, but I can tell you I lead by example. I am not a "rah-rah" guy - never have been - but I lead by example. Be transparent. That's leadership to me.

**Eikenberry:** I'm not going to start with the definition. I'm going to start by saying here's what leadership is: Leadership is about a goal being reached and the people that are reaching it. Leadership is about enabling people to reach a big and valuable goal. The leader's role is to help craft that vision and help the people achieve that vision.

**Gray:** My model for leadership is that of a serving leader. So, my job is to make sure, as a leader, that I'm constantly listening. I'm like the Chief Listening Officer, and I'm finding ways to hear what people need. Identify their deep needs and then serve them well. That model is derived, as many of your listeners might understand, from a Biblical world view. I think Jesus was the ultimate serving leader.

That's what I believe we're all called to do. If everybody's asking the operative question, "How may I serve you?" imagine everybody walking around asking, "How can I help you?" The world works so much better when people have that mindset. It's less about me and more about you. And, quite frankly, you often get exactly what you want in life if you allow other people to get what they want. It's a remarkable way to approach life. I live in a spirit of abundance. There is plenty to go around. God is good. He'll take care of me at every turn. As long as I'm willing to listen and be attuned to his will, then I can be a serving leader and know that I'll be just fine as I go.

**Beebe:** Being able to get people to follow your example in whatever you're trying to accomplish. If you can do that, then you're in a leadership role. It could be anyone from a coach to a politician to just a kid walking the halls of schools today, you can be a leader.

**Brubaker:** I look at leadership like pornography. I know it sounds a little strange. It's hard to describe, but you know it when you see it. My definition - it's really my definition of leadership - but to boil it down to the basic elements, I think leadership is really communication, belief, and getting

123

people to act on that belief. Targeted, appropriate action. It's all well and good to have the best of intentions and get people to believe in what you're doing - the company's mission and what you're selling - but you've got to get them to believe in themselves first. So, really, the way you communicate that belief is through your actions, and that's leadership at its heart.

**Woodfin:** Pretty simple. It's simple but, yet, hard if that makes sense. A lot of things in life you think are really simple are not easy for people to do. It's living life in such a way that people take notice and want to follow you. I think that's leadership. It's easy to say that, but it's not so easy for people to do that because being a leader you're put under a microscope a bit more. Unfortunately, your mistakes are a little bit larger than people that are not leading. Sometimes when that happens, people don't want to follow anymore, and that's completely understandable.

**Clark:** There's so many definitions of leadership, but I think it all starts with putting others ahead of yourself. That's so easy to see. It's one thing to say it; there are tons of people that say it. There are more quotes out there than you can shake a stick at. I think people know what to say, but when I'm looking for a leader, I'm looking for the guy that works the hardest. I start with myself. I've got to work harder than my staff and put the time in. Then I can expect the same things out of them and out of my players. Once again, as a leader, if I'm putting these people in front of me and doing what I'm asking them to do or play - and the players the same way - I've got to do those things that I want them to do or ask them to do first. That's a *lead by example* method and that's where you start.

**Crandall:** It is a basic question, but you hear it all the time as you go around classrooms. I've come, quite simply, to this notion that you're a leader if people are following you. It's that simple. We have a really interesting question we ask in a lot of the leadership sessions we do, which is: When's the first time you felt like a leader? We will ask people that and get everything from, "When I was six years old and my mom had to go another aisle in the grocery store and told me I was in charge of my brother," to people who had been leading for a while but didn't feel like they were a leader.

I worked with a woman who runs the educational department in a medium security prison. She had a team of five and never really thought of herself as a leader until their budget was tripled, her staff tripled, and, all of the sudden, she was in charge of fifteen people. She said, "Wow, once I was in charge of 15 people I started to feel like a leader." The bottom line is: If someone's following you, you're a leader.

**McCabe:** That's a good question. Leadership, to me, is like defining happiness. If you're trying to be happy, you're never going to be happy. If you're trying to be a leader, you're never going to be a leader. To me, leadership is being the innate, intuitive nature of who you are to help lead to a challenge, a solution, or an outcome. It's getting other people to come together to help do that. I see so many people who try to be leaders and forget the challenge in front of them as opposed to tackling the challenge in front of them.

**Lubin:** Leadership for me is about leading by example. Showing others how things are done and collaborating with them. One of the things I have for my leadership philosophy is, "If I can't do something, I don't really expect those that I'm leading to do it. But I will ask them to try." It's always one of those things I say, "Hey, be willing to step outside of your comfort zone. Be willing to push a little bit further than you've never pushed before." If you can convince people to get outside of your comfort zone, I think that's a true leader. Someone who is always learning, someone who can lead by example, but someone who can help people become faster, better, and more efficient. Those are some of my keys for being an effective leader.

# BORN A LEADER OR TRAINED

Are people born as leaders, trained throughout their lives from experiences or mentors, or a combination of both? Is it possible for anyone to become a leader?

**Gordon:** I think it's a combination of both. I think that sometimes you're thrust into a position that causes you to be a leader and learn how to lead. I believe that some people have natural-born abilities and characteristics that help them become a leader. I think that events shape a leader. It's a lot of things that come together to make a great leader. I believe that we can learn, though, traits to be a better leader on our teams and in our organizations.

**Janssen:** I think it is a combination of both. Certainly, some people are born with certain personality characteristics. It might be a little bit more outgoing or it might be a little bit more dominant and want to get involved. That helps them. But, at the same time, with our leadership academies, we've been measuring leaders and their development over time. So, we have actual data with twenty-five different schools showing that leaders can be developed. Anybody who says a leader can't be developed: We've got tons and tons of research that would definitely contradict that. So, I think you can get better with your leadership skills over time.

Can anyone be a leader? I think anyone can improve their leadership skills. We often focus on everyone being a leader by example. Everyone can play with commitment, confidence, composure, and character. Obviously, you've got to gain that influence and credibility with other people by how you treat them, how you interact with them, and all of that. So, I do think people can become better leaders, and we've proven that at the student-athlete and coach level.

**Brubaker:** I think it's a combination of both. There's that old expression: "If they don't bite when they're pups, they usually don't bite." I do think that there are some people who are born - you see in a litter of puppies, there's that alpha dog. There are some people in their "litter," so to speak, who are born with some inherent leadership traits or abilities. But, by and large, it is a learned skill. It is something you could be trained to do, and that training takes places every day. I think everyone is a leader because we have to lead ourselves first before we can have anyone follow us. So it is a skill that we have to master and practice on a daily basis just in how we show up in the world. That is so important: how we show up.

**Isom:** I really don't see that as black and white. I would sit in the camp of people that believe it's a combination. I think that some people are born with intangible qualities that would make for a great leader. Now, you can see a lot of those people fall off the path and never put those skills to use so it can't just be a fully "only leaders are born leaders" argument. I think some people are born with intangible qualities that help leadership, but I think becoming a leader and being a leader is a very conscious choice. Even if someone doesn't feel like they possess those intangibles, they can lead in so many ways.

What's important is, first, for someone to identify who are they leading? What is the stage? Leaders aren't always the ones leading the massive ranks and the huge teams. Sometimes a leader is the unseen walk-on in the locker room that just loves his teammates well and sees that somebody's hurting and is there for them, just building them up and encouraging them. That's leading to me, honestly. I think that some people are equipped right off the bat, and they still need some guidance and some encouragement to utilize those tools while some people don't have a single tool in the tool shed that would make for a great leader. But, it is something that can be learned. It's just important to understand who you're working to lead and what the stage is. Seeing that your voice, your talent, your skills, and your position, whatever it may be, are valuable and can be used.

So, yes, I think anyone can become a leader. Some choose not to, and that's okay. Some fight hard to, and that's brilliant. It's beautiful.

**Olson:** It's funny, I'm sure you ask that of a lot of guys that are in my line of work. Just a couple of thoughts. Number one, it is a combination. There are guys who have the "it" factor. When we work with some very powerful athletes that lead people - whether it's at the pro level, college level, or all the way down to high school - it's interesting how certain kids that other kids will follow. I work with some neuroscientists, a guy named Chris Johnson, and I have asked him the same question. He says that it's a combination; that there are some innate things in there that people are drawn to. But, at the same time, once you have those things you have to be able to channel them and use them properly. I remember that I was a little bit of a pain-in-the-butt as a kid. I remember one of my report cards my teacher wrote, "He's an instigator," and I told the story when I was speaking somewhere. After the talk, someone handed me a note. On the note it read, "Isn't it interesting that the world saw you as an instigator and a problem forty years ago, but now they call you a motivational speaker and a trainer of leaders." Same gift, just using it differently. So, I think that's what's really important too, is that people have to understand; you have to really train leadership, grow it, and cultivate it because it's just not an automatic thing.

**Crandall:** Good question. The answer is that it's both, first of all, that people are born and made. To answer your last question simply: Yes, it's possible for anyone to become a leader. If you go by the simple definition I put forward – you're a leader if people are following you - everyone has led at some point. I was telling a story with a retail company just two days ago – There's a guy I know from Richland, Washington, where I just moved from a couple of years ago, named Mark Shuster who's 6'4" and bigger than life. He's smiling all the time and the most positive person you'd ever want to be around. He just makes you feel good. I've seen him coach Little League and kids are jumping all over him. When I'm with him I just feel good about myself. I would follow that guy. He's got this natural gift. I think that's what we think of when we think of people who are born leaders.

That said, all of the research, and it's fairly conclusive at this point, suggests that there are no specific characteristics that make people leaders that are common among great leaders. That's the truth. There just aren't characteristics. Mark's an extrovert, I'm sure. He's incredibly optimistic; that certainly helps him. But, some of the best leaders you'll find and books like *Built to Last* by Jim Collins, which is cited often on this topic, identifies this level 5 leader who's quiet but has fierce resolve. Some of the greatest CEOs of all time haven't been like Mark. They weren't extroverts. They were understated.

I truly believe - and I've seen it in classrooms - that anyone can lead; anyone who has a desire to lead. A lot of the authentic development research says that there are some things in common. The first one being that we have to think of ourselves as a leader. In order to lead you've got to see yourself as a leader in that situation. Sometimes our development work is what helps people see that. Then, as you go down through it, knowing what you believe and why you believe it is really core to that. If you think of yourself in a leader situation and know what you believe and where you're trying to go, that's basically the stuff that's made all of them. There's a lot of development that goes into that. People who have some of the natural gifts of leadership can constantly reflect and get better, and people who aren't born with some of those gifts can develop who they are.

**White:** I don't think it's possible for anyone to become a leader. I think that you are certainly born with something inside of you that sets you apart; whether that be a competitive fire or whether that be an instinctual ability to communicate with people. One of the best leaders that I am around every day is Tamika Catchings. She has such a compassionate way about her that allows her teammates to open up to her on a number of levels. I don't think you teach that. I think that you're certainly born with something that sets you apart. There is a fire in your gut. There is a passion. There is a competitiveness that allows others to respect you and allows you to embrace the challenge and any opportunity that you may face. Yet, I do still think that some of that can be taught. I think it has to be channeled in a direction, and that's where the mentors, the reading, and the continuing to become better allows you to channel that in the right direction.

So, I think it's a combination of both, but I also think that being a great leader is continually changing. It's a constant improvement, and it's a constant evolution. You don't just become a great leader and then stop learning. You don't just become a great leader and then stop striving for yourself to be better as much as your players to be better. There is a combination, but I certainly don't think that just anyone can become a leader. If you don't have something inside of you that sets you apart - if you don't have that fire, if you don't have that flicker - then you're just going to be a follower.

**Goldsmith:** You see, everybody I meet and everybody I work with is already a leader. So, whether they were born to be leaders or they became leaders is kind of irrelevant because they're all leaders already. The question is only can they get better? And, they can definitely get better. I wrote a research article called "Leadership is a Contact Sport." Anybody that would like a copy of it can just send me an e-mail. I'll send them a copy, or they can go to my website, *www.MarshallGoldsmith.com*, and see it. In "Leadership is a Contact Sport" we did a study with 86,000 people, and what we showed, conclusively, is leaders can definitely get better. If they get feedback, they talk to people, and they follow up, they can get better. So, whether they're born leaders or became leaders, doesn't really matter so much to me because I only work with people who are already leaders.

**Kouzes:** You have just asked the most frequently asked question that Barry and I are asked. Barry Posner, my co-author, and I probably are asked - every time we speak or do a seminar - that question. We love that question. We have done research on this, and we have determined, conclusively, that we've never met a leader who was not born. All of us are born. Architects are born, engineers are born, doctors are born, lawyers are born, athletes are born, artists are born; we're all born. The important question we think to ask is, "What do you do with what you have before you die?"

On a serious note, there is not a gene that one can identify and say, "This is the leadership gene. This person has it, and this person doesn't." It is too complex of a set of skills for it to be attributable to one gene that some people get and other people don't. It's not a birthright. Just because you might be born into a royal family doesn't make you the best leader in the world. It is not a position that people hold. There are good leaders and bad leaders at all levels in an organization. It's not something that some people get and other people don't.

In fact, you might be interested in this statistic. We just analyzed 2.5 million responses to our Leadership Practices Inventory. About one-fifth of those are leaders and the other four-fifths are observers. Only 0.0001 of a percent have ever scored leaders at the lowest possible score. For 99.9998 percent of people, leadership is something they are already doing; just not frequently enough. We make that observation for a very important reason. We often attribute leadership to a set of talents, and if you have those talents you become a great leader. If you don't have those talents you don't. What we've discovered from our research is that almost every person on the planet does some kind of leading, just not frequently enough. That's the key because the more frequently you engage in these behaviors, the more likely it is that you'll have positive outcomes, be it engagement at work, profitability, or higher performance on a team.

So, we think it is important for people to understand that all of us have demonstrated, at one time or another in our lives, leadership skills. We're just not using them frequently enough to get the highest levels of performance. Therefore, we believe, based on the data, that people can develop these skills and abilities if given the right kinds of training, role models, coaching, opportunity to practice, and the right desire to learn them.

**Woodfin:** I definitely think it's a combination. However, I do think that the greatest leaders are born or genetically wired with certain personality traits that allow them to lead in a much more effective way. I think leaders can be born, but there's no doubt that life experiences, different training, and knowledge can enhance a person's leadership skills. I do think that anyone can lead too. To which level that anyone can lead will vary, for sure, but I do think that everybody has the capacity to lead at some level, be it smaller or larger. I think the best leaders in this country definitely have the genetic makeup for that.

**Medcalf:** I don't think anybody is born anything. Jamie has a son. His name's JJ and he's almost three years old. A lot of people come up to him and say, "He's so talented and so well adjusted." He's so this and he's so that. They don't see the thousands of hours that have been put into intentionally training him and loving him and unconditionally loving him. Everything in his environment - everything that's said to him - is very intentional, deliberate, and has taken a ridiculous amount of patience and hard work from both of his parents. To me, it's ridiculous to say that, "Oh, yeah, he's just born this way." Tiger Woods had 10,000 hours of deliberate practice by the time he was twelve.

When you look at people - when you get behind the scenes - they always had something that was conditioning them. Bo Jackson used to get into crab apple fights from the time he was a really young kid. That's where he actually developed his arm strength. Does everybody have a little bit different natural disposition and different genes? Yes, but the way that those genes are unlocked is in combination with the way that we think. I believe the way that we think comes from what we read, what we watch, what we listen to, who we surround ourselves with, how we talk to ourselves, and what we visualize. I don't think any of those things are happening by accident. I think that there are different characteristics that people have inside of them, but I think that 70-80% of that comes down to the environment, conditioning, and choices that they make. That's how people are developed.

**Lubin:** I really think it is a combination of both. I also think that leaders are not afraid to throw it out there. One of the things I learned at a young age was - I was always a shy introvert (I still am a bit) – don't be afraid to throw it on the line, to throw it out there, to see what happens. I think key leaders aren't afraid of being the person who fails, and they aren't afraid of exposing themselves to others.

I think it was one of those things when you're sitting down in college or sitting down in high school, and you had to do group assignments and group work. I always thought that was the worst thing ever because I always became the one who ended up doing all the work. I didn't really trust the others to do the right thing, in order to get the right thing done. But for me, one of the things I learned was just the opposite of that - starting to trust individuals. I think that one's a major key for me, to trust individuals on the teams that you're working with to get the job done. But, in that same sense, you can't be afraid to expose yourself in front of the group as well as to give praise to the people that did really well for your team or for your effort.

**Anderson:** I believe you can be born with certain personality traits that may lend itself well to leadership. But, ultimately, I believe leadership is developed. It's not discovered. I've seen through my own experience enough errors that lost family fortunes that would serve to prove leadership isn't necessarily genetic. And, you could look at monarchies and see the same thing. You can learn how to lead better. I am a great example of that. Early on in my life, I was a good manager; I was a lousy leader. I didn't realize there was a difference between the two. And, as I started to learn what leadership was all about, I was able to develop it and improve myself. It is a skill set one can develop.

**Eikenberry:** It is absolutely both. I don't believe that anyone was a born leader. I've never seen a birth announcement that announced the birth of a leader. Yet, if you read the obituaries on any given day at any time, you would read about people who have passed from this Earth who were leaders in one way or another. I believe that inside of us is the potential to become an effective leader. That does not mean everyone will because there's work involved.

I believe it is both DNA and a lot of work. All of us will look at someone and say, "Man, they are a born leader." The reality is they have some skills, there's probably some DNA in there that helps some of those things happen, but they have honed those skills. No one came out of the womb being able to lead. Leadership is about skills. If we build, learn, and practice the skills, we get better at them. Leadership is complex so it's not one small set of skills, which means that while I believe that everyone can become an effective leader, not everyone will. Even those that work at it and become effective leaders aren't all doing it exactly the same way. Leadership is far too complex to say there's one right answer.

From my perspective, there are multiple ways to get there, and one of the worst ways to get there is to try to be somebody else. I should be learning from other leaders just like athletes learn from other athletes, but I can't try to be that athlete. I have to try to learn from them and apply that to my game. I could say, "I'd really like to be as good as Brett at that," but rather than lamenting that I can't be as good as Brett at that, say, "What is he doing and what could I learn from that to get better?" There's also stuff that maybe is hidden from me that I'm significantly stronger at than Brett is, but I'm not even thinking about that stuff.

For the most part, when people start playing the comparison game, they're the ones that lose. They're comparing themselves to other people and saying, "I'll never be as good as them at that." To go back and answer the question again, in brief: Leaders are born and made. From my perspective, it's choices that people make about how they develop those skills that, in the end, determine if someone effectively leads others or not.

**Gray:** You're asking a deeply important question. I truly believe that people are not born leaders. Everyone has within them the capacity to learn to be a leader. You see, we teach what we most need to learn. I don't have to have everything figured out about being a remarkable leader before I can start being a servant leader. I just gotta start serving, and, when I'm serving, I'm also learning about leading.

I've got a bold personality. You can hear it from my voice, the way I approach life, the cadence I use when I talk, and all that stuff. The Lord gifted me with some neat gifts, but, quite frankly, I wasn't always that way. I was a pretty shy kid. I was overweight, out of shape, and didn't have a father that was a bold leader. He was a wonderful man. He led in his own way, but he wasn't bold the way that I am. I learned to become a leader. There was a path that I took that I can talk about as we go, but I believe we all have innately within us a desire to serve. If we serve, we learn how to lead.

**Beebe:** I think anybody can be a leader, I really do. Some might disagree with that. I think some people say you're born with certain skills. Which I would agree with that. But, I always use myself as an example. I was introverted and so quiet, that for me to speak publicly in a speech class in high school or to even pray in front of my family at dinner, I struggled. That was tough for me. It was something I certainly wasn't born with. It was something that was taught to me by my parents, my coaches earlier in my life, and my family. Now, today, here I am completely the opposite. I love to speak publicly. I love to talk to people. I have become more extroverted than introverted. I definitely believe that these skills are learned from our parents, coaches, and mentors early in our lives. This is why I think it's so essential to have people in the leadership roles of today with high character because they are building our youth of tomorrow.

**Clark:** I think they can because there are so many different kinds of leadership. There are vocal leaders, leaders by example, all kinds of leaders. A lot of times we will say, especially in high school, we expect our seniors to be leaders. Here are guys that may never have been leaders in their lives. All of a sudden they're thrust into that role. That's when I always met with our upcoming seniors in high school and said, "Look, it's your time. These other guys, they've got another year. This is your year." The only way to get them to do it is to pull them into this. College is a little different because you've got a lot of older guys. We expect everybody to be a leader in different ways. But, I think everybody can. I think they could be trained to do it. Some are more natural than others, but everybody can be a leader.

**McCabe:** Absolutely. Anybody can be a leader. We've seen in today's world of technology people who are socially meek or shy get onto online platforms, and they can move mountains with people through different forms of communication. So, anybody can be a leader. But, is it born or is it trained is a great question. It's something we've always wondered. I'm an inherent believer that anybody can learn to be a leader if put in the right circumstance. We do know that certain traits are always going to be more effective in groups: Somebody who's a little bit louder or somebody who's a little bit more confident in their ability. If we go back to the clinical feelings, a little bit more of the narcissism is always better.

What leaders do is get people to believe in a common vision. I think that's inherently the most important thing: Can you get everybody to buy into the vision? More importantly, if they're not buying into your vision, are you able to sacrifice your ideals if their vision is also good? I think one of the challenges that people make is: It's my way or the highway. Being a great leader is the ability to accommodate and modify but still having a dream at the end of the road of where they want to go. I think anybody can learn. I think the most important thing about it is being willing to learn, having what Carol Dweck calls "the growth mindset." It's deeper than that. It's having the desire to believe that everybody around you gives you evidence to grow as a leader, as a person, as an athlete, or as a corporate leader. Everybody around you provides you information. It's not all or nothing.

# IMPACT

**Name a person who has had a tremendous impact on you as a leader. Why?**

**Olson:** I think that the first guy that comes to mind - a character based upon him is in the book - is Keli McGregor. Keli is a guy that I met several years ago, maybe a little bit over a decade ago. Keli, at the time I met him, was the President of the Colorado Rockies. Keli is a former football guy; 6' 8", 250 lb. tight end. Played at Colorado State, then played in the NFL for a few years. Then, was an AD at Arkansas and worked his way up. He also worked for a guy named Frank Broyles at Arkansas and had a lot of leadership lessons from him. Keli and I became very close because I led a small group of CEOs that he was in here in Denver, and I had led that for a couple of years. He and I became close, and the sad story is Keli passed away about four years ago from a heart virus. Just a weird, weird deal that caused a heart attack. But Keli was a guy that, at the end of the day, he had two things that were very important to him. Number one: you got to do one thing at a time, one day at a time. Don't get caught up in the big picture; *see* the big picture, but you have got to live for today and take care of the present. Today, we call that being where your feet are.

He had one other thing, and that was patience. He built the Rockies. When he took that organization over, they were one of the worst fiscally balanced, money-making teams in Major League Baseball. They were also worst on the field. By the time that his tenure was done, they had won the National League Championship, had been to the World Series, and was the number one money-making, fiscally responsible team in Major League Baseball. So, more important to me was his patience level. He taught and had a saying that you have read in the book – "Things that are built to last are not built fast." That's given me a lot of solace because in today's athlete, it's a fast- paced thing. We want things now. We see slow is bad and process is bad. That's how these kids and employees today view things because we are geared that speed is better; convenience is better. So, in this day and age, to be process-driven is a rarity. You've got [Alabama Head Football Coach] Saban, where all he talks about is the process. It's very important that, to stay in that mode, you have to do one thing at a time, one day at a time. You have to remember that things that are built to last aren't built fast. That includes children, marriages, and everything else. So, for me, Keli had a huge impact in those areas, along with his faith, which was off the charts.

**Woodfin:** To name one would be hard, so I'll just name a few that as I look back over my life, time periods where I felt like I've grown the most as a leader. The first is when I lived in Los Angeles. I attended a church called Mosaic, which was led by a guy named Erwin McManus. When I was at Mosaic, I felt that community of faith. Some of the pastors there, Erwin McManus, and a guy name "Goodie" Goodloe all had a tremendous impact on my leadership skills. Mosaic is where I first learned to serve others and the needs of others. I first learned that to put others before myself was one of the keys to complete happiness.

When I moved to Green Bay to work with the Packers, the head strength coach there by the name of Mark Lovat - he was a very quiet leader, different from anything that I've ever experienced before and taught me a ton about leadership. He really exemplified it through his daily action. He was very consistent in all that he did. Those are two, Erwin McManus at Mosaic and Mark Lovat with the Packers, that had a tremendous impact on my leadership skills.

**White:** Lin Dunn, first and foremost, comes to my mind. She showed me what it means to be prepared on a number of levels. Not just preparing for one thing or two things but preparing for multiple things down the road. She taught me what it means to question. We don't have to just accept things for face value. You can question the way that we do things. We can question why we've always done it that way. I hate the phrase "because it's always been done that way." I think that's the worst phrase in the human language. She challenges me and herself to change, to evolve, to be open to opinions and criticisms yet strong in your convictions, to check your ego at the door, and to improve daily. She is somebody who has been on top of the game for so long, yet she is constantly yearning and hungering for somebody to challenge her so that she can see things a different way. That's critical. A lot of people in leadership positions want others around them who don't question them, who just do as they're told, who just agree with everything that they say, and who see things through the same set of lenses. That is not leadership. Leadership is continuing to find ways for everybody to improve; it's seeing things in different ways; it's having six or eight sets of eyes that see things differently to help your franchise, your college, your players, yourself, and everyone in the organization improve. That's the biggest impact that Lin Dunn had on me. It's showing me all of those things not just by talking about it but by being about it with her actions every single day. Checking your ego at the door is huge because you have to have a certain edge about you. You have to have a certain ego to be successful, no question about it. But, you also have to have certain humility to be able to allow yourself to get to a different level.

I think we, as coaches, talk about wanting players who are coachable, but we have to be coachable. We have to yearn to get better. We have to allow others to criticize. We have to allow our players to question - not in a disrespectful way - but question, "Hey, why are we playing it this way? Could we try to play it that way? What if we did this; what if we did that?" I think that's healthy; that open dialogue is healthy. At the end of the day, as a head coach, you have to make a call and you have to live with that call. But, at the same time, the communication and the team-driven ego is more important than selfish-driven ego.

**Janssen:** Most definitely my mom, Mary Janssen. She set a tremendous leadership example for me as a mother. She's a two-time cancer survivor. Watching her go through that ordeal and how she handled that was a great example of leadership. From a hometown or local standpoint, she was the school board president of our school district for just over twenty years and had a huge impact. Helped create a new elementary school in the area. I saw her as a leader, not only on the home front but also out in our community.

She was someone who always believed in me, always challenged and pushed me to do my best. I wasn't going to be like all of the other kids. There was a higher standard set for me, and she had always said, "Hey, you are a child of destiny. You're destined for great things." I probably wasn't, but because she had fed that all into my mind for so many years, I started to actually believe that. Fortunately, I've had an opportunity to go out and share some of these leadership principles with people around the world.

**Gordon:** Abraham Lincoln is one of my favorites as a leader in terms of who you look to and what leadership is all about and what it stands for. So, one is the leadership example of Abraham Lincoln. I believe Ronald Reagan was an incredible communicator, and his optimism helped us through a very difficult time in our life, in our world, and in our society. He was very important there.

Personally, Ken Blanchard, who wrote *The One Minute Manager*, had a huge impact on me as a leader. He's a writer and he teaches leadership and just his example of the kind of person that led from the heart, led with integrity, does things the right way, and incredible compassion. I really admired him a lot as a follower and then someone who hopefully follows in his footsteps.

**Isom:** I have been under so many incredible leaders in my life. This honestly isn't meant to sound "lovey-dovey" or "froo-froo," but the few years now of knowing my husband; he really introduced a very different side of leadership to me.

When I initially met him - he commands a room when he walks into it. He's got those intangibles we were talking about - the size and the presence - but he is so gentle in nature. He's a man of few words, but when he speaks, people listen. He really painted that picture of the sacrificial leadership more so than the big, bold, brazen, loud leadership that I am so inclined to because I'm a big, bold, brazen, loud woman. I hate to rob other people in my life who've lived many more years than me. But, it was really unique meeting Jeremiah and learning about leadership and ultimately what will be leadership in our family and leadership in our marriage. It has a different nature than what the world would say leadership looks like. He leads well with great focus, he's thoughtful and prayerful, and diligent about the decisions he makes for our family. He's a total goofball half the time, but when he needs to take things seriously, he really does. That painted a great picture for me in my own life, my business, and my ministry. It's one that I really wished I had applied more and known about when I was on teams. I think it's really valuable.

**Goldsmith:** I would say that one person is Alan Mulally. Alan recently retired as the CEO of Ford Motor Company. He was ranked in *Fortune* magazine last year as the number three greatest leader in the world, behind only the Pope and Angela Merkel [Chancellor of Germany]. In theory, I was supposed to be his coach when he was at Boeing. But in practice, I probably learned about 20 times as much from him as he has learned from me. Taught me so many great lessons about leadership and about life.

**Kouzes:** My dad is probably the most influential leader in my life. He was a child of The [Great] Depression, the oldest of ten kids. He was born at a period in time when there were two World Wars and a depression in the world. He had to go out as a young man and work in the Civilian Conservation Corps and serve in World War II. When he got out of World War II, he came back to work through the GI Bill. He went to school at night, after work, to earn a bachelor's degree, master's degree, and all of his classroom work for his PhD. He started at the bottom of the ladder and worked his way up to, when he retired, Deputy Assistant Secretary of Labor for the U.S. Government.

So, I learned from my dad many things. One, of course, is the hard work. Work ethic. You've got to work hard for what you earn. I apply that every day of my life. He also was somebody who taught me about the importance of working well with other people. You don't become Deputy Assistant Secretary of Labor because you have bad relationships with people. You have to have good relationships with people. He also had a very strong faith in people. He was someone who believed in other people and always treated everyone with fairness and respect.

As I watched him – he would go to school at night after work for three degrees – he was really dedicated to continue his learning. That's something that is also very important to me. In fact, the work that Barry Posner and I are doing now is applying that to leaders and how they can be continuous learners.

**Gray:** I have to admit that Tony Dungy's leadership style has had a very formative impact on who I am as a leader. You see, I grew up in the media business. I had big budgets, a lot of employees, and a lot of influence in the world. In 2002, when I met Tony, I began to watch him and listen to him to see how he was coaching. What was it that he was doing right? This was well before he wrote his book *Quiet Strength* and when we began to look like "Hey, we can approach life by not having to be all domineering leaders in order to get things done." You know, Tony's style has really informed who I am as a person and has allowed me to have a kinder and gentler approach to my  leadership in a bold way. But, at the same time, he's a really highly effective leader that gets a lot done in any given day but, at the same time, finds a way to serve a lot of people as he goes. Hopefully, this conversation is evidence of that, trying to find a way to serve you.

I'd say Tony more than any other leader. But, because of Tony, I've gotten to enjoy a fellowship with so many other amazing people. I was with Coach Gibbs, formerly the head coach of the Washington Redskins. I was at a national event a few weeks ago and met him because of Tony Dungy. I've met so many other men that I'm able to come in contact with through my work, my vocation, and my advocation. I learned something from all of them. I can also learn from the least of these. I can learn from a homeless man on the corner, just the same as I can learn from one of my son's friends who I'm with - mentoring or engaged with - in the day-to-day life. They've all got a thing to teach me. But, if you force me to pick one, I'm going to pick Tony Dungy.

**Anderson:** I've had two wonderful mentors. One is John Maxwell, who is still a friend. John was the first one that really taught me that management and leadership were different. That leadership was a skill set at which you could get better. I was a micromanager at the time and had a lot of turnover within my organization. He encouraged me that you can get better at this. Zig Ziglar is another mentor and a dear friend who recently passed away. What Zig really taught me was that business and faith didn't have to be two separate entities. That you could live your faith out in your business. That they were complementary and not at odds with each other. I'll always be grateful to him for that.

**Elmore:** I don't know where to begin. There are so many people. That sounds like I'm about to receive an Oscar, but I'm not. I'll just say this: Besides my mom and dad, who were incredible parents and who built me into a healthy, well-adjusted adult when I turned 18, no doubt about it that John Maxwell has played a huge role in my life. I started with him right out of college, or almost right out of college, in 1983. That was really before he was this famous, best-selling author. So, he had time to pour into about three or four of us on staff, and it was incredible to get developed by him and not have to undo a lot of bad habits that, typically, we develop in our 20s because we didn't get mentored very well. I felt like I got a head start and a launch really well. So, John Maxwell. Of course, I became part of his event team and writing team, I have done books with him, and it has been such a great experience to learn under him. I totally realize that I have a different style than John but the substance of what he teaches has been so helpful. He would be one of those people I would point to and say, clearly, his fingerprints are on my life.

**McCabe:** I think the easy answer would be Skip, but I might go different than that. I was fortunate. I was an only child, and my dad was a retired C-130 navigator in the air force. He went into the air force after playing college baseball at the University of Toledo. He went into the air force as a pharmacist. He had finished his pharmacy degree, but his family couldn't afford for him to go to medical school. He had been accepted to Johns Hopkins and Case Western, places like that. He couldn't afford them and went to pharmacy school. Right about that time, the Vietnam conflict was starting to amp up in the early 1960s. He decided, "You know what? I want to choose the military branch I want to go into. I don't want to be drafted; I want to go in as an enlisted. I want to make it a career." So, he went into the air force as a hospital administrator and pharmacy specialist. After about a year and a half, he realized if you're going to be in the air force, you need to fly. He switched over, made a career transition, and became a C-130 navigator. C-130s are the cargo haulers. When he was in Vietnam, he was the forward air controller for what was called the Blind Bats. They flew missions over the Ho Chi Minh Trail and other high targets at night with no lights on. So, as a navigator, it was critically important that he knew how to navigate through the stars.

When he retired from the air force in 1983, he went back into pharmacy, working his way up as a leader through various organizations. By the time I graduated high school he was the pharmacy director at a big hospital in Baton Rouge - both hospital pharmacies. He went on to do many other things before he passed away. The reason why I've always admired what he did was because my dad had a tremendous sense of compassion for other people. Sometimes, he'd get himself in trouble because he'd trust the wrong people. He believed in them inherently. Anybody who ever knew my dad would tell you that he was the most kind-hearted gentleman ever. But, he was 6'5"; he could come across as pretty intense.

When I was playing high school or Little League baseball, he was our coach, and everybody on the team played. Everyone on the team played the same amount of innings. He was about developing each person. I think that's what leaders are: Leaders are developers. True leaders, whether it's Coach Krzyzewski, Tom Izzo, Coach Bertman, Nick Saban, or Urban Meyer, develop athletes to help them reach their goals. They don't use players. They develop players. That's what my dad did. From a leadership standpoint, he wasn't always successful in things that he did, but I always learned from him.

**Eikenberry:** That would be a long list, but I'll go back to where I started. I'll say that my father was certainly one of those people. Not just because he was my dad, but because he was also my boss. At a young age I had the opportunity to have a significant impact on our business. A couple of things that I learned were:

He wouldn't have used the word "empowerment" but he knew what that looked like. He knew how to delegate successfully, he knew how to engage people in what he was trying to accomplish, and he knew how to help people see the big picture. Those were strengths I learned from him.

Another way in which he led by example was - as a leader, there are often times when we ask other people to do tasks that are not fun. Growing up on a pig farm, you can only imagine that there were a few unsavory jobs. But, there was never a time that a job was given to me or to other people that worked for us that my dad wasn't willing to come help, if necessary or when available. One of the ways that we show support to our team is to be available to help them do the stuff that isn't necessarily fun. There are certainly things, as leaders, that we delegate to others that they may not want us to help with. I can think of a whole number of things that my team does not want me to step in and help them with because I'm not qualified to help them. But, that doesn't mean I can't. I can also be aware of when they're buried, when they've got extra stuff happening, or thinking of, say, accountants at year's-end close, where they may not want me helping them with the books. But, they might be recognizing their need for extra space, me taking other projects off their plate, me bringing in pizza when they're working late, or any of those sorts of things. I think that whole being aware of and supportive of others thing, even when empowering people, is one of the things I learned from my dad, as well.

**Clark:** It's pretty easy for me. I think starts with my father being a really good high school coach. The things that have always stood out about him to me were the things off the field. It was the players coming back to him for advice when they were out of school. We didn't have a lot of money as a high school coach's family, but he found a way to take care of these guys. Whether it was giving them gas money or whatever he could. These guys were just trying to survive. Those were the things that were more than just X's and O's. I loved the strategy, but the things that are about life - that make them better men, better people - and that family concept, that's the part that intrigued me that I love so much. That's the part I still enjoy today.

**Brubaker:** I talk about this in my book, *Seeds of Success*. The theme is: Life's a curriculum, we're all students, and everyone you meet has a lesson to teach. I think that we learn leadership lessons from everyone around us, every day. But, if there was one person that had the most profound influence on my career and my leadership ability, it's my coaching mentor, Randy Mills. He's the person that *Seeds of Success* is actually based on. What I learned from him was that everyone wants to make the big time, but there are an awful lot of people who are doing big things in small places. That's okay too. He took the road less traveled and spent 45 years coaching - college lacrosse was his sport - coaching college lacrosse on the back roads. He always said it,

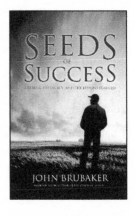

and I agree, "That's where the real work is. The real work is doing big things in small places."

What I learned from him is really the value of being a contrarian. If everyone's going in one direction and doing the popular thing, you're probably going to get your best results going the exact opposite way; so not following the crowd. I know "best practices" - it's a popular buzzword in leadership today. The problem with best practices is they're also common practices. If it's common, common isn't going to be what separates you and gets you into the 1% as opposed to the other 99% of the herd, so to speak.

**Medcalf:** John Wooden. I take it as a huge compliment - a lot of places I go, I'm told that I teach John Wooden 2.0. I had the pleasure of working on John Wooden Court three to four days a week with UCLA Women's Basketball as their Director of Mental Training. I think that he's had the greatest influence on my life. That's the person I look to the most when it comes to leadership. The second person would be Jesus. I think I look to Him more in terms of overall lifestyle and impact. Definitely, a person that I don't believe is God would be John Wooden.

**Beebe:** Without question, my dad. You know what? It *should* be your dad. For every kid out there, it should be your dad, first. My dad worked two jobs. He never missed any of my games, and you ask yourself, "Why?" Because it was important to him. I don't ever remember my dad missing work because he was sick. I don't remember my dad yelling at, cursing at, or physically touching my mom. My dad disciplined me all of the time, but I never questioned his love for me. My dad never quit anything in his life that I can remember. My dad, definitely, is my hero. These are definitely the great qualities and attributes that a great leader has.

**Petrick:** My dad. He was my coach from my freshman year through my senior year of high school. He has been through so much adversity in his life. He was born one of 15 kids. He was dirt poor and had one pair of clothes every year for school. He was stinky and dirty every day and, in turn, didn't have a whole lot of friends. He got into sports and had coaches that would take care of him. It was really inspiring to me that someone could go through that and come out being a good, quality person.

Another guy is named Lane Johnson. He was a coach; coached me in freshman basketball, football as a sophomore and junior, and basketball, again, my junior and senior year of high school. He has been a coach of mine for a long time. He was hard on me. He was a guy who would get after me and chew my fanny a little bit, but he would also pat me on the back and make me feel good. So he was a good guy, and we have become good friends. He's a quality guy; a good person to look up to, or towards, as a leader.

**Crandall:** My dad. Most of what I have thought about in terms of leadership comes from my dad. I share a story often. I'm a strong believer in something I just mentioned; that the real essence of leadership, the starting point, is knowing what you believe and why you believe it. There is a guy named Warren Bennis, a leadership luminary in the United States who died over the course of the last year. He was the emeritus professor from the University of Southern California. He has a great quote that says, "We begin to become leaders at the moment we decide for ourselves how to be." In a way, you have to reflect on that step of deciding for yourself how to be.

I tell a story, often, about my dad. He coached my soccer teams from the time I was in kindergarten until seventh grade. In fifth grade, we had this transition from recreational soccer to select soccer. Kids were going to have to try out and either be cut or picked for the team. My dad was the kind of guy who, I absolutely believed, would cut me from the team if I wasn't good enough because he lived out the integrity that he'd taken from his time at West Point. When he died eleven years ago, we put on his epitaph a phrase from the West Point Cadet Prayer – *"Choose the harder right instead of the easier wrong."* That "choose the harder right" was something he preached at the dinner table.

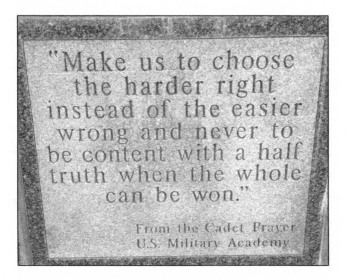

When that comes back to soccer, I just knew he was going to do this the right way. He had a group of four adults who all knew soccer pretty well that he asked. He said, "This is going to be our committee." He told all the kids, "We're going to watch you all. You're all going to have a fair shot. This isn't going to be about who's anybody's friends. The four of us will get together and pick the fifteen best players as best we can." I was nervous going to these tryouts because I figured it would be really embarrassing to get cut from your own dad's team. There had already been a higher level tryout for a premier level team that I hadn't made.

We got through the first day of tryouts. I felt pretty good, like, "I think I'm going to make this." Got a little less nervous. Went to the second tryout on Sunday. I played well again, and, as they concluded, I was watching the committee over on a track in the Seattle, Washington, area standing next to an old wooden set of bleachers. I can remember seeing them standing around talking with their clipboards. About twenty minutes later, my dad emerges with a list of fifteen kids. I looked down the list, and, about seven people down, I find my name. I feel relieved. I keep looking at the list, and I just couldn't believe it. My dad cut my best friend in the world, a guy named Eddie. We'd been friends since birth. My dad was best friends with Eddie's dad. My mom was best friends with Eddie's mom. It never crossed my mind that Eddie wouldn't make the team. I thought he was better than I was. I think there were about forty kids that tried out. If my dad took fifteen, Eddie had to be sixteen or seventeen.

We got back in the car to drive home. I can still remember; my dad had a 1979 Toyota Celica Supra. I'm sitting in the passenger seat. I'm yelling at him, "I hate you! Why don't you love Eddie anymore? I don't want to play for your stupid team!" Mrs. Baker, Eddie's mom, didn't talk to my mom for a month and a half. It was not an easy decision. Years later, I reflect back on that. That's the core of who I am as a leader. That moment and I'm not overstating it; it may sound crazy, but when my dad said, "Choose the harder right," and "You need to live your life with integrity" - I go back to stories like that. There are a number of stories like that I can point to with my dad that make me who I am. As leaders, it's those moments that shape for us who we are and what we believe. It's so important to know - Who is that person? As you ask that question: Who are those people that have made an impact on your life so you can make meaning of those experiences and develop yourself into who you want to be?

**Lubin:** I was thinking about that earlier, and I don't know if there's really any one person. I try to take leadership traits from those I'm constantly learning from or reading about.

I'm very fortunate because I interview people all day long. I interview high-level executives, high-level professionals. I interview athletes throughout my day. So, I have an amazing network of people that I can try to pull some of the best leaderships skills from. When I first started my career, I spent so much time trying to be someone I wasn't, and that caused terrible anxiety for me. So, I almost went the opposite of, "I don't want to be or want to clone any one person to be a leader." I questioned everything I did, and I wasn't being myself. I think one of the keys was, once I started to be myself, to assemble the traits I learned from others that I believe are successful. I was able to develop my own style. I'm not one who strives to be someone else, but I want to be the best version of myself.

# PHILOSOPHY AND CORE VALUES

**What is your leadership philosophy and/or the core values of your team? How do you communicate that philosophy to the members of your team?**

**Brubaker:** My leadership philosophy is simple. I like what St. Francis of Assisi said. He said, "Preach the gospel. Use words only when necessary." So my leadership philosophy is lead by example. Lead by example. It's really that simple to me. People are going to follow what you do far more than anything you say.

**Woodfin:** Our core values are:

1) Treating everyone like family. Families generally love each other; sometimes they hate each other. If they're a tight-knit family, which we try to be, we always try to talk it out. If there was an issue, bring it to that person face-to-face, always end it, and not hold grudges.

2) Hard work. It's really what allowed me to achieve most things in my life. With me leading, I really want that to be one of our core values. Working really hard at what we do, having a passion to grow, and to never be content.

3) Positivity. That's always got to be an underlying thread in everything that we do. If we want to be effective, I want to make our environment a place where people - whether coaches or players - enjoy the space we've created. I think positivity is paramount to making people enjoy coming to a place and getting better in that place.

**Eikenberry:** Our philosophy is that leadership is about helping people achieve a valuable objective, and we believe that anyone can build those skills. We come at the development of leaders from a very positive, proactive, learning-based approach. As I've said already, we believe that it's about skills. We work really hard to do the best we can, to create learning experiences for leaders, so they will not only learn those concepts and skills, but are encouraged to go back and practice them. In terms of how I lead my team, I just work really hard to continue to reinforce those messages within my own team. I find it's very convicting to be teaching leadership skills and to always realize that you're not perfect at it yourself. I always tell groups after finishing during training that my team thanks them for the chance because they get a better leader because I get to go out and teach these things myself.

**Isom:** I think some of the core values of leadership that come to my mind, the first would be attentiveness. I think that one of the core values of leading well is seeing the people that you're leading. Not just looking out and seeing the forest of trees but seeing each and every tree. Looking out and not just seeing the team but seeing the members of the team. That takes great attentiveness and honestly, it's exhausting because you constantly need to be aware and plugged in to each and every person if you want to lead well. People aren't led in a blanket manner. It's not like I could talk to Suzie and Sally exactly the same, and they're going hear and receive it exactly the same. People are unique. A leader has to be attentive and willing to be unique in their approach to leading well.

Selflessness is another big one. I think that, especially people who are equipped with those intangible qualities of leadership, they have their gut reaction, and the way they want to do things the way that they know will be successful. It's almost like we put the blinders on and just go for it. But, the fact of the matter is that a lot of people can make unbelievable contributions that maybe our brains never even thought of. Maybe we never even reached for it when it comes to solving a problem or moving towards a goal. We might've had a great plan, but hearing the input, selflessly listening, and serving the people on the team can make it an outstanding plan.

This one is going to sound a little out there because it's calling leaders to lead leaders. But, advisory is huge. Every great leader has people around them that aren't just "yes men" encouraging them, and affirming them in every idea, thought, or principle - whatever it may be. They have people around them that are honest with them, hold them accountable, and challenge them. That's what makes a leader great. We have this common misconception that leaders sit on an island; that they're this one-man show carrying a team on their back. The fact of the matter is that's not true and shouldn't be true for any of us. If we're sitting on an island, we're not leading. We're isolating ourselves. I think it's important to surround ourselves with advisory, counsel, and people who are really going to know us well as leaders, look at the heart of the situation, and be really honest and blunt with us. Those are probably the big three: attentiveness, selflessness, and advisory.

**Gordon:** I lead a team at work. I'm second-in-command of my team at home. I understand leadership and leading as a team. Our core values are love, serve, and care, from my book *The Carpenter*. We believe in loving, serving others, and showing that we care. If you do those things, you are a leader. My mission for our organization is to empower and inspire as many people as possible, one person at a time. If we inspire and empower one person at a time, then we're going to make a big difference over time.

**Anderson:** We are big on core values. We have five of them. They are very underestimated in a lot of organizations - the value that core values add to your culture and in influencing people's behaviors. Our values, we have integrity, teamwork, urgency, personal growth, and attention to detail. We also have a short description that defines each of those and what it looks like in practice. We use values as a filter for hiring. This is something we go over during an interview. We have to make sure someone can really live our values. We don't want to spring the values on them after we hire them and say, "Oh, by the way, I hope you can live up to this." It's something we measure our people by during reviews. We have a "Value of the Week" that we talk about and who lived it and how we can live it better. Our values serve a filter for decision making. I'm gone a lot so my people need to know what to say "yes" to, what to say "no" to, what to engage in, and what to withdraw from. And when the values are really clear in an organization, that becomes very easy for them to do. We also use values as a filter for firing. When you have clear values and somebody's not living them, it stands out a lot quicker and you're able to remove more quickly from the organization the misfits who don't belong there and make it difficult for everyone else.

**Gray:** I spend a lot of time and energy thinking about communication and appropriate ways to reinforce positive behavior. For me, we try to boil it down to a couple of different ways. Our big vision is to make sure that every child in the world knows the love of an engaged father. We know we'll never accomplish that. We know that's a big vision, but we talk about it a lot. What are we doing to help children know their fathers better even in a midst of a fatherless epidemic that's going on around us?

Then, I drive it down into the mission, which is to provide parenting and relational truth to men, helping them to love their families well. Give them hope. So, you move from the big vision, which you know you'll never fully accomplish, but it keeps you motivated and moving toward it. Then, we drive down into the mission, which is all about relational truth. That's all about our daily e-mails and all that we do with our websites.

We have to run big events; we have 1,200 chapters. Across America, we have 1,200 chapters where dads and kids come together, nearly 100,000 per month strong. We fill up a couple of football stadiums every month, but we do it in chapters across America, where 50-60 fathers and kids get together. They use our Tony Dungy-infused curriculum and the lessons that we teach about generosity or caring for the less fortunate. So we're constantly being missional about the way we approach things.

Finally, I have to admit that we're undergirded by a very deep purpose. We don't talk about this externally a lot, but I think it is okay for me to talk about it here, that we have a deep purpose and that's to bring glory to the Lord. We know that this is not about us. It's not about anything that I created. It's not about Darrin Gray, Tony Dungy, or anybody else. It's about how we'll advance the kingdom and make a difference to give glory to the Lord because that's what motivates us all.

So, you asked me a really complicated question, and I gave you a really complicated answer. But, with a great mission, a strong mission, and undergirded by purpose, I feel like All Pro Dad has a pretty good rhythm about it in terms of helping men to get better every day.

**Crandall:** The first core value is integrity. A lot of people will list that as their core value. I think a lot of people are sincere, but it can be seen as lip service. When you're sharing something like "My first core value is integrity," a story like the one I just told is how I communicate it. This is what it means. This is why I believe in it. Then, let's translate that to who you are and how we live that out as an organization.

A second core value is just the freedom to be authentic. For me, personally, that's huge. To be who you are - at home, at work, to bring that, to be transparent with that, and to support each other.

Family is a core value for me. I think that a lot of people say, "Well, why would family be a core value in your organization?" Well, it goes back - it connects to that integrity; it connects to that feeling of authenticity. Those are three that come to mind.

I think storytelling is essential in communicating values; storytelling in a manner that's very real, that includes the meaning that you make of those stories. I think the personal stories are important and, then, the organizations with the strongest cultures whose values are most clear. Zappos comes to mind. Zappos is a smaller company. It's relatively new, although, they're going on a decade at this point. Tony Hsieh, their founder and CEO, does a great job of explaining how right from the get-go Zappos was capturing stories. Their customer service mantra is that they "want to deliver wow." That is pretty cool. It's just two words: we want to *deliver wow*. You have to paint a picture for people of what it means to *deliver wow*, just like you paint a picture of what it means to have integrity. They have some stories about how they give out awards for their longest customer service call. One of them - that was something like six hours and thirty minutes - was their longest customer service call. They wanted to reward that and reinforce that behavior because they want their people to understand what it means to work at Zappos and what they're trying to deliver.

# LEADERSHIP IN SPORT AND BUSINESS

**Is there a correlation between leadership in sports and business? If so, what are the similarities?**

**Olson:** Yeah, no question. I spend at least once a month speaking or working with a corporation or a company. The reason they bring me in is quite simple. They said, "We want to help bridge the gap and cover the gap between leadership and motivation." What they mean by that is, we've got supervisors, we have managers, but are they coaching people? Or, are they just supervising to make sure that nothing bad happens? Are they managing things to make sure things stay status quo and just don't get worse?

At the end of the day, I got paid to win games. If I didn't, I got fired. It's very much the same in the business world. Those people are paid to make money, get results, and keep their customers and clients happy. Also, to see the trends and the future things that are starting to happen, much like we have to do as coaches. For me, it's an easy jump. When I talk to people, I tell them, "You have to quit thinking of yourself as a manager and a supervisor. Those are just titles. You have to see yourself as a coach." We say the same thing to parents. Man, it's amazing how parenting is coaching and coaching is parenting. You are trying to get them to a place where - I really won't know if I did a good job until my kids are in their thirties, have their own kids, and I watch them parent. Then, I'll know how I did. Same thing with player; I really won't know. I can win a bunch of championships, but I really won't know what type of leader I was for them until years later.

Companies are seeing the same thing. They need to connect with their people, and they need coaching tools to do that. It's more than just a life coach, where they're just trying to help them navigate the stress. What are some specific tools that you can help people and maximize their potential in the work place?

**Gordon:** That's why I love the work that I do. I get to work with both business leaders and sports leaders, and you see how they apply to both. You see how they are transferrable, same characteristics. You need to coach your team at work; you need to coach your team on the field. All the principles that I write about are transferrable and applicable to both the business world and the sports world. People say sports analogies are tiresome. There are sports analogies because they do apply. You have to be a team, you have to be united, and you have to build a great culture.

What I love about sports is you can tell whether that culture, those principles, are working in a 16-week season or in a six-month season. You know right away in sports whether those things are working. You know whether that team has chemistry and synergy. You know that that team is connected. With business it often takes a little bit longer to be able to figure that out and to be able to see the fruit of those results. But, the same principles apply.

**Janssen:** I think there is a huge correlation. I have done a lot of work with the corporate world as well. FedEx has a leadership institute in Memphis. So, there are multiple times that I would go there and get a chance to work with their frontline managers and their managing directors. I think there is such a huge similarity there. There is obviously a competitive environment. You've got that in the sporting world, and you've got that in the business world when you've got competitors trying to wipe you off the face of the earth and get your market share. You've got to achieve results through people; that happens in the sport and business world. You need to build a sense of team with a lot of different people with different personalities, different ages, and different individual goals. You got to pull them all together as one; that's obviously similar. You've got to have tremendous commitment to that common goal and get everyone on the same page.

To wrap things up, you have to have great leaders who are able to help make all of this happen. So, I think there are a lot of similarities between the sport world, the business world, the military world, and the non-profit world. Any time you're dealing with human beings, a goal, a group, and all of that, you're going to need leaders to step up and, hopefully, help make that an effective team.

**Isom:** I think it's one of the great things about kids getting involved in sports early while continuing through high school, through the college ranks, and professionally. That is an amazing way to learn leadership and learn it through the hard ways, the crushing defeats. It just makes it very black and white and tangible. The successes, the victories versus the defeats, the dynamics of the team, and listening to a coach - all of those components sing of leadership. I'm really glad that I was involved in sports growing up because now, doing what I do, I carry so many incredible lessons in leadership, in the team dynamic, and in leading well into what I do now, though it's not at all athletically related. I think it teaches the skills of working well with others, putting others before yourself, that sacrificial element that we talked about. By putting a greater goal above your own goal, realizing that you are a part of a moving machine, and that it's essential that your part works well. It also requires great trust and faith to rely on the other parts to work well also.

I see it apply in my business. I see it apply in my marriage. I see it applicable in my family unit. All of it. I really felt like I got firsthand experience by being involved in sports young, learning all those hard lessons, and celebrating with the team. It's not all just the hard stuff. Sometimes it's the amazing stuff – celebrating, growing, and improving with the team as well. It's a carbon copy for the rest of life and whatever endeavor it may be.

**White:** There is absolutely a correlation. Every lesson that we learn in sports carries over to business. From work ethic, drive, passion, competitiveness, teamwork, success, failure, bouncing back, pushing farther than you thought was possible, accountability, responsibility, communication - every lesson that we learn through sport is a life lesson that is imperative in success in business. I think from a leadership position, things constantly change. The dictatorship of the past - in coaching and in the corporate world - doesn't work anymore. People respond in different ways. Continuing to evolve, continuing to better your craft, and continuing to think, first and foremost, about the people that you have working with you - I like to say working with you rather than working for you because, I believe everybody is working for the common goal.

The people that you have working with you - if you invest in them, your product is going to be that much better. You have to invest in them first. If they feel like they're just working for you every single day and if they feel like it's product driven, they're not going to give you their best. They're not going to get better. They're not going to improve. They're not going to be confident. So, there is a direct correlation in any sort of leadership, which is why I like to try to read a little bit from the business world as well. Everybody does it a different way, and if you can take one little thing, or one little facet, or one little strategy from multiple people who have been successful leaders, it's critical to ultimate success.

**Kouzes:** There absolutely is. In fact, I have a very special affinity for athletics and leadership because our son, Nicholas, was an NCAA Division I tennis player. He played number one or number two singles and doubles all four years of his college education. Yes, we are very proud of him. I have seen how important athletics are to a young person's development, and I really appreciate the role that athletic coaches, directors, and volunteers play in the lives of our young men and women. I look for a lot of examples in sports. We had, for example, somebody who did a study using our Leadership Practices Inventory that we mentioned earlier with college athletes. They found – and I quote from that study – that "athletic participation can be understood as a leader development experience at the collegiate level because athletic involvement has a positive effect on leadership practices." In other words, those who are involved in team athletic sports, in this case in their collegiate careers, are more likely to demonstrate leadership practices than those who are not.

So, athletics does play a role in developing young men and women to be leaders. Participation in team sports, interestingly enough, fosters leadership development, not only in men but also in women, equally. It's not just male athletes that benefit from participation. Female athletes also benefit from participation. That's something we find in our research.

The leadership practices seem to be equally applicable across all kinds of industries. They are not particular to business, but they are also useful in education, athletics, non-profits, and government. They really do work in all of those different settings. I think this is a personal note because of our personal involvement with athletics. The data is very clear that we need more leaders and better leaders in the world today. Knowing that athletics can be a very positive force in developing our future leaders, we need to make sure that our coaches model the kind of exemplary leadership that's needed.

**Elmore:** Absolutely there are. In fact, I was just with the New York Giants football team yesterday; NFL team. They are launching *Habitudes* up there. These guys are young professionals. They are players who are playing a game, but they are working hard. We began to talk about how these principles, these *Habitudes*, transfer both to football and life after football. So, the concept of rivers and floods. Floods are waters going in every direction. Rivers are focused waters. They all agreed, "This is stuff I'll use as a player on Sunday. This is something I'll use as a dad when I'm 35, as a business man when I am 45 selling insurance, or whatever I'm going to do after football." So, absolutely, I think the disciplines you learn in sport - if they are transferrable - like work ethic, discipline, being punctual, maybe being early, the workouts, and the rigor. That just translates into new topics and new categories if you let it and not just be categorical in your discipline. So, I guess that's a long way of saying absolutely yes. I think they transpose it. As long as you can see how this a timeless discipline I can use in another context later.

**Anderson:** I work with people in athletics, non-profits, and businesses. I think there are a lot of correlations. It's focusing on goals. It's setting clear expectations. It's giving fast, honest, direct feedback. It's understanding the importance of accountability. Creating a culture that attracts great people; retains great people. The speed of the leader and any of those entities determines the speed of the pack. When you have problems, whether it's on a team or whether it's in a business arena, it all starts at the top. A fish rots at the head. It starts to stink at the top first. It has to be fixed there. So, I see a lot of correlations common to teams in sports or business. They share a vision, they share a mission, and they share values. They unite towards a common purpose. A number of very healthy and transferrable principles apply in both arenas.

**Medcalf:** I think almost everything that I teach and that we teach at Train 2B Clutch - it doesn't matter what you find yourself doing; everything needs great models. It doesn't matter what you have written down on a piece of paper, and it doesn't matter what you have as a mission statement. It matters what the people inside of your organization are doing. I don't think that businesses get better; I think that people do. Yes, I think that there is huge correlation because everything that we're talking about is maximizing human performance and potential. Hopefully, there's a lot of things that do translate.

One of the things that I get frustrated about and don't understand is the communication style that happens in sports. It's at some levels with people that tend to engage in more transactional leadership, but I've never understood why, in sports, people that are coaching are allowed to communicate in ways that, in any other venue, would be fired almost instantly for communicating that way. Somehow, we have this weird, sick, twisted obsession with sports where we just go, "Oh, it's high-level sports. That's what you get." I don't believe that, and I don't believe that's actually the best way to bring the best performance out of people. I think that our track record with the programs we've worked with has actually shown that over and over again. When you look at people that are really successful at anything they do, they tend to have very similar strategies, whether it's in business, sports, or in arts. The easier somebody makes something look, the more time that they've spent behind the scenes when nobody's watching.

Sometimes, people think that they're just waiting for their opportunity for the bright lights, but the bright lights tend to only reveal our hard work done in the dark. You look at people like Kobe Bryant, and in his new documentary, *The Muse*, he talks about how, if he knew everything he was going to have to go through back whenever he was twelve or thirteen, he didn't think that he would do it. Michelangelo said, "If you knew what went into my mastery, you wouldn't think it was so wonderful." Over and over again, you see the exact same thing - the guy at the top of the mountain. He didn't fall there. Ben Hogan, in golf, said, "Greatness isn't sexy. It's dirty, hard work." It's the same thing that you see over and over and over again.

We get obsessed, especially in business, and think, "We need funding, we need all this money, and that's why these companies are winning." But, I don't think that that's the case. There's a lot of different examples. The Wright Brothers didn't have government funding, yet the guy that did have government funding ended up losing and quitting after the Wright Brothers got a plane in the air for the first time. When you look at all the different companies like Facebook starting in a dorm room, Subway starting in a dorm room, Apple starting in a garage, or J. K. Rowling writing Harry Potter living on welfare in the projects after her husband abandoned her with her two-year-old child. The way IKEA was started - a twelve-year-old traveling by bicycle into Stockholm to get boxes of matches would come back and sell individual matches door to door. That's how IKEA was started.

It always comes back to two things, in my opinion. Faithfulness to the small stuff. That's why I say, "Dream big but think small." The other thing is a really ridiculous work ethic and being willing to put that work in when nobody's watching. When Kevin Martin was traded from the Houston Rockets to the Oklahoma City Thunder, he tried to be the first person into practice because he'd heard that's how Jerry Rice and Michael Jordan did it. First in, last out. He shows up to practice three hours beforehand and finds Kevin Durant and Russell Westbrook soaked in sweat in the gym already. I think that's what you find over and over and over again. The people that really take it to the next level are the ones that do those two things first. But, they're also putting hearts first, and they're really focused on being transformational, putting those first things first, and not focusing on the performance aspects. They're more focused on who they become than what they achieve.

**Eikenberry:** My experience in sports as a participant ended in high school, but my viewing of it has continued. I would say that, largely speaking, leadership is leadership is leadership. We are leaders when others choose to follow. It isn't about "I'm a leader because I was the captain." It's a leader because people choose to follow. I think the correlations are strong, and one of the great things that comes, especially from sports at the high school and younger level when well coached, is the chance to see some of those skills in action, to have the chance to be led and be a follower, and to have the chance to, perhaps, practice being a leader. As long as we realize that leadership isn't necessarily about a role as much as it is about the action. Leadership, in the end, isn't a noun. It's a verb. We get the chance to see that in athletics often. As a spectator of sports, we get the chance to see that in action often. I think that can be a very inspirational - it's one of the reasons I watch sports, we'll put it that way.

**Gray:** Of course there are. I was just having a discussion with some of my colleagues earlier this week about position coaches. Let me give you this gift. Position coaches in the league. Let's look at the NFL because that's the lens I look through, but it's the same in any pro sport. Rarely does the player have an amazing one-on-one relationship with the head coach. It's almost always the position coach like the linebackers coach or the defensive line coach. It's the one they're in contact with every day in their subgroup meetings, and so that has direct correlation to frontline leaders inside of organizations. Usually, you're not talking to the CEO of the company every day. You're talking to other frontline leaders. You're learning and you're growing.

Sports is a wonderful microcosm that you can look into to really help you figure out how you can translate that into the business world or the working world because sports careers are fleeting. Even the best athletes might play the game for a dozen years. There are a few exceptions in golf and a few other sports. For the most part, a career in the NFL is less than four years. It's the average NFL career. So, they're going to have to think about what they're going to be doing after their pro sports career. I just think that sports provide us a great lens to look through, and I think there are so many parallels. I could spend the whole hour today just talking about the parallels between the sports world and the business world. Hopefully, that position coach paralleling to frontline leader is a little nugget of truth your listeners can latch on to.

**Beebe:** I definitely think that, between sports and business, there's always great qualifications and similarities. I've always said this: What I've learned in sports carries over for me to be a better employee or an employer. I think you become a better spouse. I think you become a better parent. Most importantly, I think you become a more stable person in your faith. All of the things I learned in sports have made me a better high school coach, and, certainly, a better owner of House of Speed.

What are those traits? I can give you some of those traits I have learned. I learned to train hard. I learned to work hand in hand with my teammates to accomplish our goal. I learned to have passion for what I'm doing. People ask me all of the time, "Hey, Don, what's passion?" I think passion is training when nobody else is watching. For example, kids train today because their coach tells them to. They train because their dad tells them, "Hey, get out there and go work out." But, passion is training when nobody knows. Why? Because they just want to be great. They don't care what others think. They just want it. Lastly, what I've learned is to never, never, never give up. I believe if you give up, it would be hard to live with the result. But, if you give everything you've got, you can always – and I mean always - live with the result. Win or lose.

**Brubaker:** I am so glad you asked that question because I think right now, more than ever, there is this beautiful collision between sports and business. If you look at the top-performing executives in corporate America, who are they studying? Who are they trying to learn from? They're trying to tap into the great minds in college and professional athletics. They want to learn from the Bill Belichicks. They want to learn from the great NBA and Major League Baseball coaches. They want to learn from - how does a college coach recruit? His recruiting is sales. Recruiting is building a team. So, corporate America wants to borrow strategies from the athletic arena. In the same vein, the best coaches realize - and this is what makes them the best of their class, so to speak – they're going to get their best ideas from outside their industry.

Athletics is becoming more and more of a business. Even at the amateur level, it is a business more than ever. So, they realize there's an awful lot to be learned studying leadership in the corporate setting; studying what CEOs are doing to build a team, to attract, recruit, and retain talent. It's a beautiful collision, and this is the perfect time to be really kind of playing in both arenas. If you're not doing that, if you're a corporate leader and you're not studying what coaches are doing, you need to start doing it.

Go down to your local college; introduce yourself to the head football coach, the head basketball coach, or baseball coach. Take them to lunch, sit down, and talk with them about how they build their team. If you're a coach, find the top-performing companies in your area, sit down with those executives, and learn, "Hey, what are you doing? What's the secret to your success?" Because, I think it's not a secret. There are certain universal fundamentals there.

**Woodfin:** I think, whether it be sports or business, there are teams in everything under those two umbrellas. Sports teams; that is obvious. In business, there are small teams created to carry out certain tasks. There should be a leader within those teams. Every member of those teams should have a goal and know their responsibilities. I definitely think, whether it be business or sports, that it's all about teams: leaders of the team and the roles of each team member. If everybody knows their role and knows, "Okay, let's follow this person (or these people) and let's all move together." Then I think teams will have success.

**Crandall:** Absolutely. I think leadership is all over the place. Sometimes people struggle and think of leadership as contextual. If you go back to the definition I said - that leadership is that people are following you - those dynamics are similar, whether you're coaching 6th graders in basketball or leading an investment bank. I 100% believe that. At the outset of our book *Say Anything*, the first chapter is actually a sports story. My wife gave me some advice. I might not want to start with it because it's a story about the Seattle Seahawks. She was hoping people in San Francisco would read the book. Some other people said, "Well, is this the best way to start a book that, ostensibly, is going to be read, for the most part, by people in business?" But, the story, just to put it simply - that in the [2014] NFC Championship game when the Seahawks were playing the San Francisco 49ers - there was a moment in the fourth quarter of the game, although early in the fourth quarter, where Pete Carroll had called upon Seahawks kicker Steven Hauschka to go out and kick a 51-yard field goal that would have brought the Seahawks to within one point of the 49ers. They were down four at the time.

Hauschka looked up at the uprights in CenturyLink Field, and they were blowing in a southerly direction. He was going to be kicking into the wind. He walked up to Carroll and said, "Hey, coach, this isn't the right decision. I don't think we should kick this." The story came out after the game because it was an odd moment during the game; they actually sent Hauschka onto the field, called the time out, and later, came out and went for it on fourth and seven.

It's an incredible story to me because, if you look at Hauschka's background, he was a journeyman kicker who went to a NCAA Division III school as a soccer player. His roommate said, "Our school needs a kicker." So, he came out [for the team]. He transferred to North Carolina State and ended up kicking there for a year. Then, bounced between six NFL teams before he finally landed with the Seahawks. Those who know sports know that the kicker is, like, the lowest "status member" of the team, just about. This kicker could walk up to his head coach and say, "This isn't a good idea," was just incredible. Carroll listened to him, and he changed the play. As fortune would have it, on the next play, Russell Wilson throws a 35-yard touchdown pass to Jermaine Kearse and the Seahawks take the lead. It ended up being the difference in the game.

That's just one example. That's a powerful lesson of a leader: Pete Carroll, willing to listen to the "expert" on the team in kicking, Steven Hauschka, even though there's a huge power distance there. Even though, when we tell in the book, there were assistant coaches within earshot rolling their eyes and thinking, "Just do your job, kicker." Whether we're saying, "Just do your job, kicker," or "Just do your job, lieutenant," or "Just do your job, hourly worker," this idea of anyone in the organization being able to speak up and say what they're thinking; sports is a great venue to take a look at those things.

When I teach and speak, I draw on my coaching experiences all the time. The story I told earlier about integrity is really a sports story, but tough decisions are tough decisions, whether they're in sports or in business. Having been a guy that's in the military, that connects as well. People say there is this connection between the military and business, but, ultimately, leadership is a human endeavor. At whatever point, you're making human decisions that are filled with emotion and relationships; the lessons are translatable to all kinds of domains.

**McCabe:** I think you'll hear people say that corporations like to hire athletes. Athletes are highly competitive individuals. When it comes to leadership standpoints, you find leaders in that. But, at the same time, corporations also like to hire military. When my dad got out of the air force in 1983, the climate was different. They didn't want to hire military people because they thought they were "too stuck" in their military mentality. It's funny how things 20-30 years later have changed. But, I think there is a correlation.

I think the biggest mistake that teams and people make is having a captain. I'm great with having a captain, but you can have different leadership along the pyramid of a team. Sometimes a leader has to know when to rally the troops, get people to overcome an adversity, or be an ally for that captain. A leader can be a freshman. In business, a leader could be the person who's been in the job for six months, who's still learning the corporate culture, and has ideas and says, "Look, we don't have to follow the status quo." When I hear the words "It's what we've always done," that means there's no growth. It means we're afraid to grow. Somebody who can rock that boat and say, "Look, let's do this. Let's not do it for my own vested interest. Let's do it for what we think is the betterment of the organization or the team." Sports we have to play together because we know that highly talented teams don't always win. It's the teams that can be unified across one common vision that succeed. Things like Google, Apple, Twitter, and Facebook: why are they successful? Everybody buys in together, trying to create this model that's great. Organizations where you're just punching clocks don't work.

**Lubin:** I definitely think so. I also believe it may not just be in sport. It could be in art. It could be in music. It could be in computer programming. It could be in anything that you're passionate about.

I think one of the keys to success in leadership is to be able to be a leader outside of what you just do on a professional level. Is it raising money? Are you a philanthropist? Are you doing not-for-profit work? I think that passion that you have outside of work can always come back to the passions that you do inside of work. You can take many of those character traits - they're really mutually beneficial, both in the professional world and in the sport, or like what I was saying, in art, music, or anything like that that changes your mind. That allows you to be passionate. That allows you to be someone who you really are.

I think those similarities are there. Sometimes sport is an individual sport, or sometimes it's a team sport. Having the ability to throw it out there - to put it all on the line - is key for success both in business, sport, and whatever you're passionate about. So if you can teach someone to get out of their comfort zone, you'll forever change their lives.

# TODAY'S CHALLENGES

**What is the biggest challenge that you and other leaders are facing today? What can be learned through these experiences and adversities?**

**Woodfin:** Being consistent and having integrity in everything that I, or any leaders, do. That's what I learned from Mark Lovat with the Green Bay Packers. Day in, day out, same person, with very few gaps in what he said and what he did.

Integrity: doing what you say you're going to do and doing the right thing when nobody is looking. I think consistency and integrity are vital. There's a really small window for a character-type issue with a leader. It's just always being on guard, always being wise about the situations you put yourself in, and the decisions you make. I've been around too many really good leaders that lost everything because of a lack of judgment. It's hard to get those people back following your lead when you make a mistake of a certain magnitude like that, especially with character flaws. I definitely think that consistency and integrity are the two that I try to do my best at.

**Gray:** There's one. It's listening. People don't listen. If they do listen, they're already formulating a response before they're done listening. They don't deeply dwell upon the question and really try to understand through the lens of the person that's speaking what their deep needs are. I find myself using real simple technique like *The 5 Love Languages.* Like, what motivates people? Gifts or other rewards? Or are they motivated by language and telling them that they're doing a great job?

There's lot of ways that people are motivated. So, I try to be a student of human behavior. And I try to listen really well, be present with them, and take the time. That means a lot of long hours sometimes if you're going to invest in people. But, I think the single greatest deficit is a listening deficit that leaders face because they're time compressed. They're busy. They're in a hurry. They let that translate into not listening, and I think that has a very destructive effect on an organization. That, for me, is the one if you force me to pick one, which is what you asked. That's what I would land on.

**Gordon:** I think the biggest challenges in our world today as a leader and just people trying to make it in this world are busyness and stress. I believe that we're so busy, so stressed, we have so much on our plate, more than ever, technology, that we are forgetting to care about the people and things we're supposed to care about. We are so busy and stressed that we go into survival mode because the way our brains and bodies are wired, we're activating the reptilian part of our brain. When you activate the reptile, the reptile is all about survival. It's not about helping others thrive; it's not about leadership. It's about survival. It's about running or fighting. For me, I see it play out over and over again in this world where people are acting in ways that they don't care about others. They're acting in ways that they're not being leaders. They're doing that because of the busyness and stress.

If we can deal with this busyness and stress, if we can slow down and make relationships our number one priority, if we can focus on great communication, take the time to invest in others, take the time to be intentional, and to have clarity and be strategic about where you want to go as a team and as an organization, that is essential, now more than ever. Break through the clutter, create simple powerful steps that you can take, and act on those every day. That's the key. I think that's why my books are doing so well right now and are popular because they're so simple that anyone can apply them. You can read them in a short amount of time and then take action. I think that's the key. That's what we need today. But busyness and stress is really the biggest challenge we face.

**Janssen:** One of the biggest challenges is that there are so many things going on that are competing for people's attention. Whether it's different organizations, teams, or clubs that they can get involved in. Certainly online, there's so many different platforms and videos and such that we're constantly bombarded with. So, I think a big thing that a lot of people struggle with is, number one, really committing to a limited number of things that are going to help you be successful. If you try to be a jack of all trades and get involved in all these different things, you are just going to diffuse your energy, diffuse your focus, and you're not going to be very effective in them.

So, I think what a lot of people struggle with is really committing to a limited number of things. Whether it's your sport or whether it's your career – you name it. Then, following through, actually executing on a daily basis, and doing the things that need to be done over time to really elevate you and your team. I love the 10,000 hour rule that's been talked about so many times. If you want to be elite, you've got to put in 10 years of quality training, which is usually about 10,000 hours. I think a lot of people, nowadays, just because there are so many different things going on, it's hard for them to really commit to and dedicate that time necessary to be the best of the best.

**Olson:** I think number one is "don't chase the shiny, white object." What we mean by that is, for coaches, it's the scoreboard. By the way, we all want to win; I want to win. We want to win championships; that's why we do what we do. But, the reality is that scoreboard is a liar, and you can play well and lose all the time, and then you can play poorly and still win.

Same thing in the business world. You know what they are finding there? You can do things and get lucky and things just work out. But, what happens is that people end up chasing that scoreboard, profit margin, or just results. They chase it, chase it, chase it. We have a little thing that I'm going to end up doing in a book called *The Learning Loop*. There are specific stages that people have to go through to learn things, to be transformed, and to take ownership in skills and also leadership things. When you chase results and you're results-driven, what ends up happening is you end up skipping certain stages or you go through them faster than you should, and now, you lose sustainability.

In this day and age, everything is about trust. You know you're not going to go with someone if you don't trust them anymore. Right now, authenticity is more important to you and to me than authority is. I couldn't care less what your title is. I want to see if you are authentic. I went to a church service out in the western part of Colorado this past weekend for Easter because my kids go to school out there. The pastor got up there - I leaned over and in my son's ear after the guy talked for a while - and I go, "I like that guy because he's authentic." He goes, "Absolutely. He's the real deal."

So, for us, today, that's a huge hurdle. When we start chasing results, we become inauthentic because all we care about is being results-driven, and people can smell that a mile away. I just tweeted out last night, there's a great quote by the Duke [basketball] captain; he was on the interview after the championship game. They asked him about Coach K (Mike Krzyzewski), and he said, "You know, the greatest thing about Coach K is that he wasn't trying to win his fifth title tonight. He was trying to get us our first." That's what people are looking for. Man, if you're selfish in this world, that's a huge hurdle, and it's going to crush you. To me, that's a huge one.

**Isom:** I think one of the greatest challenges for a leader today is that it is just a noisy, noisy world. It is a noisy environment. A lot of people rise up with different thoughts, different input, different self-help, "50 ways to do this, 50 ways to do that." It's just noisy, crowded, and it's really hard as a leader to sometimes have your voice be heard with social media, with all the chaos that is the *interwebs*, and this life with resources at our fingertips.

I think that people who are looking to be led have a misunderstanding that good leadership is super accessible and easy to find. That they can just search what they need and trust what they find. When, truly, good leadership is established over time. That's a great challenge because there are so many resources out there right now. I don't think people are leaning into leadership in the traditional ways that they always have. Seeing, developing something over time, trusting all the bricks going into building the wall, and being a part of true teams; of true community. We're the most connected society that has ever existed, and I feel like we're also the loneliest.

The hardest thing for me trying to lead is fighting to have my voice heard. Trying to get my head above the masses to say, "Hey, over here. I believe we can do this well," when you have people with more resources, money, power, or whatever it may be that are filling that space and distracting. So, that's a challenge. It's really my hope that people reconnect and invest in true community, true vulnerability, true honesty, and true growth of leadership and following, rather than just the flavor of the week. I guess that's the best way to put it.

**Clark:** There are so many people out there now telling people that the things that we love and things we were brought up on aren't as important as they used to be. It's almost an "anti-team movement" in some ways. The way you combat that is by your people seeing what it's all about. What that means is when you show them what family is about, you show them what a real team does and how they work together. Maybe, the way it used to be was just do it because I said so. Now, I'm like, "We're still going to do these things because we've got to do them. That's what makes us successful, but this is why we're doing them." When a team or a person understands "Okay, this is why we're doing what we do. We still have to do it, but there's a reason behind it." I'm going to buy in that much more. When you get that buy-in, you get much more effort. The communication factor is so important.

**Beebe:** That's a tough one. Two things jump to my mind: apathy and entitlement. I think we're living in the "whatever" generation, and I want to teach kids to take ownership. We're becoming so quick to blame others instead of just taking the blame ourselves. I'm a firm believer this starts with parenting and coaching when kids are young. Entitlement is the other issue I see in kids today, especially in the athletic world. We've taken the approach that everyone deserves a trophy; that everyone gets to play or should play. I guess my question is then, "At what point in time do we teach kids to earn things in life? At what point do we teach them that disappointment is okay?" We can teach them to take those disappointments to drive themselves to become better people spiritually, mentally, and physically.

**Goldsmith:** I would say one of the biggest challenges that least successful leaders face is outlined in my book *What Got You Here Won't Get You There*. That is - we all find the challenge when we're successful, we just tend to replicate what we've done and maybe, don't become what we can become. In my own life, I met a very famous man, Dr. Paul Hersey. He got me started in the business, and I was very successful. He called me and said, "Marshall, your problem in life is you're making too much money; you're too successful. You're not really investing in becoming the person you could become." He was so true. If I had to live my life over, I'd listen more closely to that good advice he gave me. Any human or animal will replicate behavior that's followed by positive reinforcement. The more successful we become, the more positive reinforcement we get, and we fall into something called "superstition trap." I behave this way; I am successful. Therefore, I must be successful because I behave this way. The reality is we all behave the way we behave, and many people are successful. We are successful because we do a lot right in spite of doings things that are stupid. The key is always being open-minded to the fact that you can always grow, learn, and get better. Don't get lulled into that false sense of security just because you're successful.

**White:** Well, each level has a different challenge. If you're coaching for us at the pro level, one of the challenges for the WNBA, specifically, is that our players play twelve months a year. They play for us from May until September, they play in Europe from October until May, and come back. It is finding a way to balance rest and recovery with player development and team strategy. This year we're very fortunate. We have two and a half weeks of training camp before we start the regular season. In years past we might have seven days of training camp before we start the regular season. We're constantly moving and shifting with the Olympics, the world championships, and players in and out. So, I think that's the challenge of our league.

Where in college sometimes the challenge is your student-athletes. They're going to school; everybody has stuff going on in their lives. You've got to be recruiting and trying to be the coach; there's all kinds of external challenges. I think the internal challenges, the ones that keep you up at night, are when you have such an instinct gratification society. People who want the results without putting in the work to get the results. A lack of passion, drive, or desire. OR, that passion, drive, and desire is misdirected. To me, that is the biggest challenge - finding ways to channel natural talent and God-given ability with work ethic, purpose, and understanding that coaching and coaches are meant to push you to levels that you don't think that you can possibly go. We've seen an epidemic of transfers in the college game – "I don't like it here," "I don't like this coach," or "I don't like that coach." We want to just move on thinking the grass is always greener when we really have to do a lot of soul-searching as individuals. What is our passion? What drives us every single day to be successful? I have to focus on the process of getting better every single day because I can't just gain success without doing what it takes to be successful. To me, that is a coach's biggest challenge.

**Kouzes:** In the recent studies of what the challenges are in business related to leadership, the first of those is a lack of "bench strength." We don't have enough leaders in the pipeline to fill all of the leadership opportunities that are currently available and will become available. Part of that is driven by demographics and how the Baby Boomers are retiring in large numbers now and will be doing so over the next several years. There are not enough trained leaders in the pipeline to fill those roles, not only at the senior levels of the organization but middle and frontline as well. That is a huge issue. There is a lot of emphasis of developing our next generation of leaders. In fact, 90 percent of employers are now saying they like to see leadership development begin no later than age 21. That means that colleges and universities need to be looking at what they can do to train and develop leaders at a younger age.

There is increasing diversity in the workforce, which makes it important for leaders to learn how to work with differences. People with different backgrounds, different religions, different ethnicities, and different kinds of family experiences. That is a human resource challenge we are facing. Generally, the business people that we talk to are experiencing – and this is true in universities – that there is a lot of volatility, uncertainty, complexity, and ambiguity in our world today. That increases the level of challenge that leaders face.

**Crandall:** I think the way relationships are changing with social media, and that's not cliché. I'm a relationships-focused guy in terms of leader development and how we go about our business as leaders. The other thing I really believe about leadership is it's not about you. It's about the people you lead. I think it's hard to argue with that. Even if your goals are about you, selfishly, and you're trying to lead people to achieve a profit because the bottom line is going to help you make more money. In the end, the best way to achieve that selfish goal is to focus on other people and how to best motivate them. If your leadership style is that you always get in people's face and get them charged up, that's okay. I believe in authenticity. But, if that style is not pushing the right buttons for this particular individual, ultimately, it's not about you. It's about getting them to perform to their best. You've got to adapt your style to that person.

If you think about where we are and social media. I coach a basketball team of a great group of outstanding seventeen-year-old juniors in high school. Those guys all text. They text and don't want to talk to me on the phone. Maybe, I want to talk on the phone, but they don't want to. The world is changing. There are a lot of workplaces that are virtual at this point. The biggest companies are all becoming global and have operations in different places. If you're a relationship-focused leader, you've got to find ways to nurture those relationships that connect you with the people who are using a lot more technology to do their communicating as well as understanding that we're in different places and it's harder to maintain those relationships.

**Elmore:** That's a great question. I think one is - when I first started out in leadership, culture was changing but not nearly at the rapid pace it's changing today. I think one of the challenges leaders face is when you've made a very big decision on something. We need to realize we better make that decision in pencil, and the strategic plan I lay out maybe needs to be an adaptive plan. I may have to change it next year. I can't make a 10-year plan and bank on the fact that the realities of my world today will be just like this in 10 years. They won't be, probably.

A Blockbuster video store chain goes out of business because they did not reinvent themselves. Netflix kind of took the place of a Blockbuster, so I think the whole idea of reinventing and change is absolutely paramount. Whether you are a football coach, a current athlete, a business person, or a teacher - I think teachers need to reinvent their lesson plans. I shouldn't be using a lesson plan that worked in 1990. Maybe the principles are the same, but the delivery and pedagogy needs to change. So, that's one big one.

Another one that leaders face today, that's a huge issue and we don't talk about very much, is the art of making the tough call. I think we live in a world of tolerance and political correctness, and I totally understand why we do. I think we need to be empathetic toward differences and so forth and so on, but I think that whole idea of being preoccupied with "don't ruffle anybody's feathers" has made us unwilling to make a difficult decision because it's going to make somebody mad or quit. I'm not throwing everybody under the bus, I'm just saying we need to be careful, as leaders, to fully embrace the idea of, "I am accepting of everybody. But, we have a mission to do, and everybody is not going to fit into this mission."

I'd like to refer back to one of our *Habitudes*; it's called Duck Hunting. You don't go out on a duck hunt and expect to get every duck you shoot at. In fact, you can come back with a bag of 12 ducks, and you go, "Oh, that was a great hunt! Even though hundreds of ducks got away, I got 12!" That's how leadership is. Leaders learn to live with missed ducks, they're not afraid to make tough calls, they shoot a rifle not a shotgun, they know what they're aiming at, and they are okay with that. That is hard, especially for people-pleasers like me who started my career wanting everybody to be happy. Boy, I learned well very quickly that's a recipe for disaster.

**Anderson:** I do think the biggest challenge for any leader is to continue leading, especially in good times. I was on the MSNBC panel, and I was asked that question, "What do you think the biggest problem with leaders is today?" I said: "The biggest problem with leaders - whether we're talking government, family, sports teams, or business - is they don't lead. They tweak, tinker, tamper, manage, massage, maintain, administer, and preside. They sit on their rear-end and they roost most of the day. They're not acting as a catalyst. There's no vision in their organization. They're not holding people accountable. They're letting entitlement drain their culture. They're not leaving people better than they found them." There are a lot of positional leaders that when things get pretty good, they become complacent and just start to coast. We are all susceptible to that. So, the biggest challenge for leaders is to continue to lead, take mature risks, continue to work on yourself, do the right thing, change before you have to, and stretch yourselves and others. Don't slide back towards complacency. I believe that's a persistent challenge.

**McCabe:** If you have a Twitter page and a Facebook page, you're an expert. It used to be, if you got a book published, you defined some expertise. I remember being in fifth grade. Zig Ziglar came to my middle school and spoke to the families and kids. It was remarkable. Even I, as a fifth grader, was blown away. I remember my mom and dad crying in the stands. Everybody was moved, and that was a military town. Zig Ziglar was tremendous. Now, if you have a Twitter page, Facebook page, and throw something together, all of a sudden, you're the expert. All you need is a couple of people on Twitter or Facebook touting how great you are, and you're the greatest thing in the world. I see it across every spectrum. I think it's a challenge because we don't have the ability to have the traditional vetting process anymore.

I look at somebody like Jon Gordon, of whom I'm a huge admirer and with whom I'm a good buddy. Jon came up and started publishing books. He ran his work by getting out there, being completely vulnerable by publishing books, and talking his message. Now, all you have to do is have a Twitter page, retweet him a couple of times, and engage him. Now, all of the sudden, you get approval by association, and you can break away. I'm not saying that's happened to Jon, but he's the perfect example of somebody in this new generation who has done it the traditional way with tremendous success. I applaud him because I'm such a fan of him and his books. I just think he's the best. With Twitter now, you go get some followers, you create some conflicts out there in the Twitter universe, and the next thing you know – you're an expert.

**Medcalf:** I think that one of the biggest challenges is we live in a world that it's instant everything. When our internet takes 15 seconds to load a page, that's too slow for us. Ten years ago, 15 seconds for a page to load seemed lightning fast. We have so much technology around us; we have so many things that are available at the click of a button that has conditioned our society to want things immediately. What's ended up happening [for example] is that it almost caused the complete collapse of our economic system back in 2008, the Enron scandals, and all the things that happened there. I just think that we're dealing with a day and time where people want everything instant. I have people in leadership all the time who say, "Yeah, my kids just want the quick fix," and I'm like, "So do you. You don't want to do the hard work. You don't want to commit to reading. You don't want to do all the really hard stuff. You want the quick fix, and they get that from you half the time. Maybe you're not the only influence, but you're one of them." That's what I think is the biggest challenge.

Different studies have shown that the greatest predicator for future success is the ability to delay gratification - not where you came from, how much money you have, the resources that you have available to you, or the schools that you went to. The greatest predictor of future success is the ability to delay gratification. But, we live in a society that fights against that. It's had some really harmful effects when it comes to performance. I also think that it's had some really harmful effects when it comes to - if you look at the depression rates in our country or look at the amount of people on anti-depressants. For the last 100 years, our "quality of life" has done nothing but continue to get higher and higher, but so have depression rates, people on anti-depressants, and the amount of people that are killing themselves. Something isn't adding up. I think that it comes back to there are actually a lot more, deeper, greater benefits and more satisfaction and fulfillment that comes when things aren't given to you instantly. Look at people that won the lottery. Five years later, they tend to be worse off financially than they were five years before that. They'll typically tell you that it was a curse; it wasn't a blessing.

**Brubaker:** The biggest challenge is, probably the first time in the history of our country, there are really four generations in the workforce. There's the very tech-savvy, young, Millennial generation - the *Digital Natives*, as we like to call them. Then, you go all the way up to that retirement age and Baby Boomer generation and there's just such a divide in terms of how they communicate and the types of leadership that they're used to. That really resonates with those different demographics. It's the first time we've had such a wide range of ages entering the workforce and staying in it in one time.

It's finding a strategy, or a set of strategies, that appeal to all different age groups. We have such diversity in the workplace. There's no one, set authoritarian style that you can just say, "This is what we're going to." It's a combination of things. That's probably the biggest challenge. The young people today won't stay in a job very long at all if you're not making it rewarding, stimulating, and engaging for them. They're very much operating on the philosophy of "What's in it for me?" as opposed to "What's in it for corporate America?"

You look at the older generation, and they're used to staying in a job 15-20 years; starting when they go into the workforce with one company and staying in it until they're ready to retire and get their gold watch. It's just changed so much. You've really got to be able to appeal to the individual's motives, and put your people first. Your people are arriving at your company with a different mindset, from different places, and with different experiences. There's just no cookie-cutter formula. It's keeping your finger on the pulse of what's going on.

**Petrick:** I think social media and all the garbage that's on it. Social media can be great, but it can also be bad. We see stuff on the news and TV that's "trash." It's filling our kids' heads with crazy stuff. I suppose they were saying this back in the 70s, but I feel like today, more than ever, there is just trash out there. Beware as teachers and leaders that this stuff is going on and try to talk to people about it. Build a relationship with people. Don't assume that you know what's going on. Try to get into their lives, befriend them, and help them with their problems. They are getting this garbage coming in their ears from the wrong places, and kids need people with the right qualities that mean what they are saying.

**Eikenberry:** There are a lot of people that want to talk about today being different than any other time in history. They want to talk about Millennials, social media, the 24-hour news cycle, and all those things. All of those things are true, but to me, the biggest challenges are not about the new stuff. The biggest challenges are about the things that never change. The biggest challenges are, "How do I communicate more effectively with other people? How do I understand their perspective? How do I influence them more effectively?" Yes, there are some new tools, some new realities, and new contacts around us, but we're still people. Whether it was 2,000 years ago or whether it's today, the biggest challenges are: How do we communicate with, understand, and inspire people? Those are the timeless challenges that we all have to work on as leaders.

**Lubin:** I think one of the biggest challenges is finding passionate people. We live in a society with so much data and so much information that people are just becoming so paralyzed. They're not passionate about anything, and they're living in a constant fog-filled state of existence. They don't get anything done. It's amazing, you walk down the street, how many people are staring at their iPhones, or they're talking on the phone. In reality, what is that doing? It's not doing much. You can only check Facebook so much. You can only check your e-mail so much. But, that's what our society has come to; staring at your palm. Your palm doesn't really have all the answers.

I think one of the keys is to get more people engaged and energized. How do you make the work that they're doing more exciting? How do you incent them? But, I don't think the way we do it is like the way it's always been done. I think we're getting closer and closer through time and through technology.

# CAUSES OF DERAILED CAREERS

**Is there a behavior or trait that stands out to you which has derailed the career of other leaders you know?**

**Gordon:** Yes, it's ego. It's pride. It's thinking that you know it all; it's thinking that you can do it on your own; it's thinking that you are above the team or that you don't even need a team. I believe those are the biggest detriments and those are the traits that sabotage a leader. Great leaders are humble, they're hungry, they're always learning, and they're always growing. They never think they've arrived at the door of greatness. They're continually getting better every day. They're focusing on continuous improvement. They're always looking for ways to innovate their organization. They're reaching out to others. They're getting feedback. They grow themselves so that they can grow others. If you are a prideful leader, that ultimately will bring you down.

**Janssen:** I think a big thing is just leaders forgetting to lead themselves, either because they got overconfident, they think they've arrived, they're getting all this praise and they think they're God's gift to leadership, or whatever it may be. I think they forget about leading themselves. They forget about their character and making good, smart choices, knowing that everything they do is being watched especially with things being a whole lot more visible with social media. Going back to that commitment of doing all those little things that they did in the first place that allowed them to be successful.

I think that overconfidence allows them to start cutting some corners here or there and not doing what they did to get themselves to the top. So, sometimes, we can be our own worst enemy and get in our way because we forget about what we did to get us to the top in the first place.

**Isom:** Yes, and this will be getting really blunt and obvious as well. It's something I wrestle with so I'm not at all acting innocent here. It's something, though, that I've seen destroy a platform that was worked hard to be built by others and then didn't stand the test of time. It is this mentality that I think many have of putting market over merit.

I think that I've seen some leaders who've started with the best of intentions - and whether it's been the power, financial elements involved, ego behind being the head honcho, or whatever it may be - putting the value in the market of leader over the needs and the purpose of the followers. It's sad because it's so easy for us to get caught up in those ways as leaders because there's a great deal of responsibility on our shoulders. Sometimes that can just mean a great deal of pressure. It can force us, when times are tough, to seek whatever we can get our hands on to soothe the situation when, in actuality, it just requires a lot of hard work.

With great power comes great responsibility. We can't be the type of leaders that are trying to lead from afar. We have to be the type of leaders that are stepping into the messy situations, seeing the people we're leading, getting nitty and gritty, and not getting caught up in the power and prestige of our position. We have to hold tight to our merit, values, and the reason we even started trying to lead something in the first place because we thought what we had to offer was valuable. We thought we had the tools to do it well. I just think we got to go back to the basics.

I see so many leaders where the game catches them up, and they miss the players. The hype of leadership clouds their thoughts, and they miss the purpose of leadership. That'd probably be the biggest issue that I've seen. I won't name any specifics, but it's not uncommon. It's heartbreaking, but it's something we need to crawl back to the basics of. Get our heads out of the clouds and start seeing the people.

**Goldsmith:** I was interviewed in the *Harvard Business Review* and asked, "What is the number one problem of all the successful people you work with?" My answer was, "Winning too much." If it's important, we want to win; if it's meaningful, we want to win; if it's critical, we want to win; and if it's trivial, we want to win. Winners love winning, and it's hard for winners not to constantly win. Let me give you a case study that almost all of my successful clients fail. My prediction is you will fail this case study. Are you ready?

You want to go to dinner at restaurant X. Your husband/wife/boyfriend/girlfriend wants to go to dinner at restaurant Y. You have heated argument, you go to restaurant Y, but it was not your choice. The food tastes awful, and the service is terrible. Option A - you could critique the food and point out your partner was wrong, and this mistake could've been avoided if only they listened to me, me, me. Option B - you could shut up, eat the stupid food, enjoy it, and have a nice evening. What would I do? What should I do? Almost all my clients say, "I'd critique the food." What should I do? Shut up. It's very difficult for smart, successful people not to constantly go through life being right, even when being right is not worth it.

**Beebe:** In knowing some of the leaders that I've seen fall through the years, I would say the one thing that came to my mind, quickly, was dishonesty. We see it at every level, be it church leaders, government officials, and even great coaches. I think that if you keep on lying and expect to be a great leader, eventually, it's going to catch up to you. You will fail.

**Gray:** Let me tell you, the reason people don't listen ultimately is derived by selfishness. The thing that derails careers, whether it's in pro sports or in other business settings, is selfishness. It's really the root. In a Biblical context, they might call that sin. In this context, I'm just going to call it selfishness.

People are concerned more about themselves than others. Now, the behavior from selfishness is the behavior of not listening, or the lack thereof of the behavior. But, that's the thing, if you want me to boil down how careers implode. I could list to you example after example after example, both in the public and private sector, in pro sports or in churches, where leaders have been selfish. It's led to disastrous situations. They then discover the true meaning of life, which is service and serving others. They get their leadership chops back; they find a way to regroup and recover. So, it's not fatal; I'm not suggesting that selfishness is fatal and leads to ultimate destruction, but it certainly makes it tougher for people to lead well. That's what I believe we're put on earth to do. It's to lead others toward a relationship with Jesus. Beyond that, to lead them to reach their ultimate potential and, in doing so, I'll reach mine.

**Medcalf:** I think it's being transactional and focusing on results instead of focusing on people. Nordstrom's - I think they're such an incredible example. They're willing to take back anything. There are stories of them taking back tires when Sears used to be in the building that they were in and they're not there anymore. But, when somebody brings back a tire they're like, "Yes, we'll exchange it. We'll give you a refund." Their willingness to put their customers first and say, "You know what? It's okay. We might take a short-term loss here." But, they understand, once again, the long-term impact that's going to have on people.

I think that a lot of times it really comes down to cutting those corners for results, people and leadership, in sports where it's the best player on their team. They make excuses for their best player, and maybe they should have been kicked off the team. Maybe they should be kicked out of practice once a week. But, they're not willing to hold them to that standard because they say, "Well, we're not going to get the reps that we need, then we're not going to be good enough, and then I might get fired. Then, how am I going to provide for my family?" They put those results first instead of going, "No, I'm going to hold you to a higher standard because this is what you need in life."

The ironic part is that, not only does it harm the kid, but, oftentimes, it ends up backfiring on the person that's in leadership because, at some point, that's going to come out. It might be in the NCA tournament; it might be at the worst possible time. Then, what the person in leadership says is, "I can't believe that you did this after everything that I've done for you." But, you haven't done anything for them. You've handicapped them because you haven't been willing to hold them responsible. Actually, your behavior was probably selfish because you were trying to win. That's what I see a lot; that transactional type of leadership ends up backfiring at some point. That would probably be the second thing that I think is the biggest issue in leadership.

**White:** I think complacency is tough. There are a lot of coaches who have a level of success and don't strive to continue to improve or get better. The "this is the way it has always been done" mentality or "this is who I am; this is who we are." You have to change, and you have to evolve. You are either getting better or worse. You're not staying the same. Whether it be throughout a season, year to year with the influx of new players, or with the adjustment of new systems, we've seen league movement in colleges in and out. You have to change, you have to evolve, and you have to keep up with what's going on the world.

There are so many social changes that these kids are now being a part of and that they see. They want to be on the forefront of some of these social changes. How do you adapt to the new type of kid? How do you adapt to the way that the game is being played? The game is no longer a post-driven, power game. It is an uptempo, free-flowing offense with a heck of a lot of different skills than we've even seen five years ago. How do you adapt and change? So, complacency is one thing.

I do a lot of TV work as well in the winter. When you get to the NCAA Tournament and you hear a coach talk about, "Well, we're a zone team," or "we're a man team," or "we're a showing team," or "we're this team or that team." When you get to the tournament and you're playing teams that might have strengths that are your weaknesses - or might have weaknesses that are your strengths - how are you going to exploit them? How are you going to adjust? You can't just do the status quo and expect to win championships. Complacency is one of my fears, but I also think it's one of the things that you look at and you see why a leader has gotten to a certain point and not beyond.

**Kouzes:** The number one derailer of leaders is their inability to get along with others. Leadership is a relationship. Those who are poor at building and maintaining strong relationships are most likely to be derailed. The second on the list is incompetency in doing the job. You have to have the skills and abilities to do the job that you have. Other than that, the derailer is your inability to get along well with others. What we call enabling others to act is the skill set that is most required to "play the game," if you will. You can't lead if you can't really work with other people. Those who are low in that area are unlikely to succeed if they don't improve.

**Elmore:** I would say, when people ask me what's the number one lesson I learned in my 20s under John Maxwell, I think it was the art of confrontation. That's the act nobody likes, that little "come to Jesus meeting." I hated that. I did not want to have confrontational conflict with people, but I realized you cannot lead unless you're willing to do that. Nobody likes it. You're sadistic if you like it. But, the willingness to do that - I learned on a weekly basis to sit down and have, potentially, a very hard conversation that would be clarifying about the vision or the priorities that week. I think when your team knows that you as a leader are not afraid to have these conversations, it's purifying and clarifying for them to know this man or this woman is unafraid.

So, just learning to confront things that need to be confronted in a redemptive way. One of our *Habitudes* that I love is called the Velvet Covered Brick, and I love that picture. Velvet on the outside; there's empathy, there's belief, there's support, and there's love of my team. Inside, there's a brick. That means tough standards that were set and we're not going to dilute this because it seems hard this week. We're going to call you to it. We're going to call out the best. Because I believe in you, team member, I'm going to call out the best. Velvet and brick both have to be a part of leadership.

Responsiveness and demandingness at the very same time.

**Anderson:** I wrote a book called *How to Run Your Business by The Book*. It's a business book based on Biblical principles. In chapter three of that book I listed what I believe is the number one cause of management or leadership failure – it's pride. Any other extensible cause, if you peel back the onion, pride is at the core. Pride or ego gets in the way. When leaders are consumed by that, they don't give credit to others, they don't admit mistakes, they persist down the wrong path because they don't want to acknowledge that maybe it's the wrong path, they don't develop others because they put so much value on themselves, and they carry more and more of the load personally. I believe just about any aspect of leadership that you find where somebody failed, if you peeled it back, it's rooted somehow in ego or pride. Until people acknowledge it, it will keep getting them.

**Eikenberry:** A big one is when people lose sight of what their job is. In the end, our job as a leader is to serve other people in the direction of that goal as we've talked about, which isn't about being soft and squishy. It's about being very challenging of people to move into the direction of a place. The big mistake is that people make being a leader about themselves rather than about the goal and other people. If we remain others-focused and goal-focused, chances are we're headed in the right direction in terms of building our skills. When we let our own ego get more involved, when we make our leadership success about our own personal success, then we're making a mistake that may be very difficult to overcome.

**Brubaker:** We don't have enough time for this question. There are a lot of pitfalls you need to avoid, but I think the biggest pitfall that any leader needs to avoid is complacency. You reach a certain level, and you get satisfied. Or, you reach a certain level and because things are working for you, you don't want to take chances when, in reality, what probably got you to that level was your willingness, your ability to just go ahead and roll the dice, and take some chances.

I think that the best way to describe avoiding complacency - I really like what the founder of the Ferrari Motors Corporation, Enzo Ferrari, what he said. His engineer showed him the prototype for the first vehicle; it was a Ferrari convertible. This was his first look at it. He sat down in the two-seater checking every little nuance about it. They're sitting there looking at him, waiting for him to say something, and waiting for some feedback. He didn't say anything, but they could tell something was wrong. What was wrong was, actually, after a couple of quiet minutes, he reached up onto the windshield and ripped the rear-view mirror off of the windshield. Can you imagine? He just looked at his team of engineers and said, "When you drive a Ferrari, you never need to look behind you."

I think that's a great metaphor for leadership today. That is how you avoid complacency. You don't read your newspaper clippings from last week or from the last game. You don't get satisfied with your earnings from last year. It's all about what's happening next, and what can we do to get a little better every day. The reality of it is a lot of companies have taken their foot off the accelerator, and those are the same companies that end up getting left behind. Circuit City isn't around anymore. Polaroid or Kodak rather, needed to reinvent itself. It's too little too late. We're just now hearing about how the SkyMall Catalog, which has been a mainstay in the seat pocket of airplanes for many, many years, just went bankrupt. They never evolved. They didn't become digital to appeal to those *Digital Natives* in unique, creative ways. They just kept doing what they *were* doing.

**Clark:** Of course, and I say this to our players all the time. I try and use examples without getting personal, but there are so many guys that were headed down the right road. Whether it's self-destruction, following the wrong people, or hanging out in a bad crowd, all those things that are actually off-the-field issues that derail guys; they happen all the time. I hope to use examples with our guys, whether it's a week of spring break separated from your team or summer "at night" behavior: What are these things when you finish? What happens to these guys that makes them not finish or not have successful lives? That's something that happens all the time. It's just guys choosing to do the right thing or not.

**Crandall:** Yes, I think insecurity is the leadership killer. I don't know if it's a trait. It's certainly something we all experience. I have a really close friend and West Point classmate who's been incredibly successful as a leader. He's now the president at the age - I think he's 41-years-old - of one of the few biggest banks in America at this point. He just took the job a couple of months ago. I think we were sitting on his couch about ten years ago, he said this quote he doesn't even remember saying. He said that he believed that all bad leadership behavior comes from insecurity. I think there's a lot of truth to that. When we don't want to hear the opinions of those we're leading, it's because we're a little bit afraid they might be smarter than we are. Even when people ask questions, "Hey, why are we doing it this way?" There are two ways you can hear that question. You can hear it in a curious way. They just want to know why we're doing it. Or, you can hear it as, "Hey, why the hell are we doing it this way?" Our insecurity is what drives how we hear that question.

The antidote to insecurity, I think, is the self-awareness. We're all insecure in certain ways. I sing the praises of reflection and being self-aware as we go out and do our leader development work and thinking about your own thinking and thinking about your own emotions. You can't obsess over it, but you do need to understand those moments where you, maybe, just got really upset with somebody and they didn't deserve it. It was your insecurity that drove it. The down part of that answer is: What's someone to do with that? If you're insecure, what are you to do with that? I don't have an answer for how you become a more secure person. But, being really honest with yourself and recognizing where your insecurity is or manifesting themselves in creating further tough relationships. Ultimately, that is what derails people, the inability to face those and work on them.

**McCabe:** I asked this to one of the leadership guys I coach. He said, "It's when somebody makes a decision that goes against their values." He said that every great leader he's ever been around - and I think this is true - when they make a decision, the first time that flies in the face of what they perceive as their value system and how easily they can cross that line. Then, the next time is going to be easier, and the next time is going to be easier. I think we get greedy, and we abandon our value system because the short term is so much easier than the long term. We make short-terms decisions. Being a leader - sometimes it's a lot ego driven. It's great to be put up on a pedestal. But, as we've seen in every facet of our society, if you get put up on a pedestal, all they're doing is preparing to knock you down. If you contribute to that, you've got a problem.

**Lubin:** I think lack of constant education and changing with the times, both personally and professionally. There's a favorite quote that I have. "Formal education will make you a living, but self-education will make you a fortune." Many people feel that once they get out of school, once they get into the workforce, that it should be instant gratification. That once you get a job, you're there doing it for the rest of your life. I'm Gen X, I'm 42 years old, and those days are gone. I'm sort of on the tail end of that world where a lot of people thought, "Oh you came out of school. You went to State Street. You stayed there. You got your pension, you got your gold watch, and you're fine."

I think many leaders and people that are getting derailed are the ones who stopped learning and stopped educating themselves. They're being overtaken by those who aren't, and they get lost. I can't tell you how many people I've spoken with in their late 40s, 50s, and 60s who were once very influential leaders but are now on the street. They weren't willing to change with the times. They made excuses. "Why aren't you on LinkedIn to connect with other leaders? Why aren't you developing groups on Facebook? Why aren't you doing something that is going to allow you to brand yourself to become bigger than who you are?" They didn't change with the times. They lost their identities. Then, they became depressed. Have alcohol or relationship issues because they're looking for that rush or that passion that they once had. They go on a downward spiral.

# PERSONAL & PROFESSIONAL FAILURE

**How do you handle failure personally?  How do you lead your team through failure?**

**Gordon:** That's a great question because I'm an expert in failure. Personally, I've failed a lot, so I know it really well. When it comes to failure, it's not meant to define you. You have to realize that failure is meant to refine you into who you're meant to be. You have to see failure as a gift. You have to see it as something that helps you learn, grow, improve, and become stronger. You can look back on your life and realize that all your failures helped make you who you are today. When you look at the event of failure, you have to say it's an event. It's not who I am. What can I learn from that? How can I grow from it, and what actions do I want to take now?

I lost my race for city council in Atlanta when I was 26 years old. I walked door to door to 7,000 homes. I failed, but ultimately, I realized you have to lose a goal to find your destiny. I failed, I was devastated, but I picked myself back up and said, "Okay, what do I want now? What am I meant to do?" The answer didn't come to me until four or five years later as a writer and speaker, finding my calling, but that event of failure paved the way for the work that I do now. Every event where we fail teaches us, if we're willing to learn and grow from it. It's about taking our challenges and then using them as opportunities. It's about loss, L-O-S-S; it stands for **L**earning **O**pportunity, **S**tay **S**trong. You may have lost the client but learn, grow, improve from that. It's about your perspective and how you look at failure.

The pruning process is not fun. We will get pruned. When we get pruned it's actually designed to help us grow more fully. If you've ever seen a bush that's been pruned, it looks like it's been hit by a bomb, right? It's destroyed, but think about how it grows back more fully. That's our lives and that's failure.

**Eikenberry:** The way we lead the organization through it is to help people keep it in perspective. The way we lead people through adversity is to recognize that adversity is always going to come; that adversity is often a chance for us to regroup, reassess, and move forward. As a leader, we must be the one to help people find that perspective and move forward. People need a chance to grieve, if you will, but then we've got to help them stand up, dust themselves off, and move forward. If we've helped them create a compelling vision of the future, that adversity is much more seen as a stumbling block and temporary rather than permanent. If we've set the table with a clear vision and if we can help people see the perspective that says this is not final, this is not fatal, this is an opportunity for us to redirect, re-engage and learn something new, then we're in better shape. The same thing is true for us as individuals; we've got to help ourselves see the big picture, we've got to give ourselves the chance to grieve, we've got to take a deep breath, and we've got to start getting proactive about what we can learn from this and how we can move forward.

**Clark:** Failure is such a tough motivator. It's so hard, but it creates these lessons. Those are the things that I go back to in my career. Whether it's a loss or mistakes, those are the ones that I've learned from. They don't define us, but those are the things that I remember because they hurt. I use those things to motivate me; I use those as lessons for a team. I talk about them a lot. I say, "I'm going to give you a history lesson today. This happened to us before. We're going to avoid this behavior or this action which created a negative." Then you can turn those negatives into positives. But, I think those failures fuel our success.

**Woodfin:** I handle failure in different ways. I've had a lot of failures in my life from the athletic world. I was cut seven times from different teams. What I try to do is look at the failure and determine if it was something I could have done differently to cause a better outcome. Or, was it something out of my control? Based on those one or two things - that is how I handle it. If it is something I could have done differently, I really try to swallow a pill of humility and say, "Man, I completely messed that up. I've got to change it for the next time. I've got to listen to more people or whatever it may be to humble myself and get it right."

If it's something I had no control over, I always try to use the failure as a learning experience. I always try to look for the silver lining and say, "How can I grow from this?" I always look at failure, if it's out of my control, as God's plan and try to really wrap my mind around the fact that His plan is a whole lot more divine than I can imagine. Failure is a part of that plan sometimes, unfortunately. That failure can take you to bigger and better places. If you approach it the right way, you can learn from it. That's what, I think, God taught me in those seven times that I got cut from the NFL. I had a passion for the game, I loved it, I approached it with everything in my will. I kept getting cut, and finally, I learned this game doesn't define me. This is out of my control. If I can find a silver lining in these times of getting released and cut, I'll be a better person in the long run.

I was fortunate to start to learn that after the second or third cut, and it made me a lot stronger and allowed me to have a lot more trust in God's plan for my life. Now, there are a very little amount of things that could rock my boat. Playing in the NFL was a dream that I did get to achieve, but I never thought about the pain that would come with some of those cuts. After a few of them, I started dealing with it better, but I learned that this was a part of making me who I am. That's kind of how I have always dealt with failures.

**Kouzes:** It took me a very long time to learn this lesson because I was one of those – and I think it was part of my upbringing – to see failure as a personal flaw in my character. I wasn't doing something right. I have learned over time that's really more of a fixed mindset view of the world. I have learned that we are much more malleable and we can develop ourselves more than we've assumed. I learned later in my life and career to treat failure as a learning experience. I think a lot of people, like me when I first started, view failure in the same way; as a flaw in your character or a lack of competence.

Using a sport as an analogy, when a batter gets up to the plate less than one out of three times, you are going to get a hit. But, you don't approach that as if you're not going to get a hit. You approach it as, "I'm going to hit this time." So, you have to be able to treat those times when you don't not as a flaw in your character or a lack of competence but as a learning experience. Next time I get up, I'll know this about this pitcher, and I'll make this kind of an adjustment. You learn. I have learned to treat failure as a learning experience. It is a wonderful teacher.

**Isom:** Most of the time I wanted to bury my whole head in the sand like an ostrich and just hope that the moment passes. Unfortunately, when you're leading, that is not so much an option. The greatest example I can think of was when I was a goalkeeper for the [LSU] soccer team. You can play a 90-minute ball game, but if the score's 1-0 – if you've lost and you allowed that goal - you really carry that defeat as if it is all on you. Even though there's lots of soccer happening, lots of positions being played, and lots of reasons that the goal was scored, you're the last line of defense. So, when you do lose, when the goals are scored, and when the dice doesn't fall your way, it's crushing. It carries more weight because you were that final one that people were putting their hope in.

So, I guess the way that I always tried to lead my team through those failures, honestly, was really taking the brunt of that. Even if I felt like maybe our midfield broke down and I stood back there and watched the midfield break down and then the defense was out of position and all the mini factors that can cause failure or cause a goal which we see playing out right in front of us, it wasn't going to serve a great purpose to stand up on the bus and call out those players for all the things they did wrong. I think it's a bit cowardly to point the finger in a non-constructive way. There's great purpose in sitting down together and talking through how this broke down. That's really what our coach did at the end of the day - or the next day when the emotions had worn off. I wasn't going to be that player that slumped up onto the bus and started calling out who fell short. We had some players like that, and it never functioned well for the team as a whole. It stunk. I wanted to stick my head in a hole. I cried it out many nights, but I think the best thing I learned in leading well through those situations was just shouldering that - aking that defeat, absorbing it, and saying, "My bad here. I fell short too, you know. I don't need to sit here and point out how everybody else did, just know that I did. I'm sorry. I'm going to work on this." Just taking the responsibility versus trying to cast it out. Swallowing the pride and working really hard to make sure it doesn't happen again. Learning from that as opposed to just trying to dismiss it. Really working to apply that. It makes the victory all the sweeter the next time the same situation happens and you make that save. The team will pat you on the back and be much happier in that circumstance than if you had pointed all the blame on them - and made the save - but it has already killed the relationship.

I guess that's a long-winded way of saying the best way that I handled failure was by sucking up my pride, taking the brunt of it, and sitting down. Then later, when emotions have settled, things had calmed down, and people are receptive, say, "Okay guys, we're a team here. This isn't a one-person show, so as a team, let's talk about what happened. Let's break this down together." That creates a much more comfortable environment to do so. Honestly, it allows failure to be used for teaching and for growth versus for power play amongst teammates. So, that's probably the best example I can give on the soccer side of things.

**White:** My version of failure has changed over the last few years. I used to think that failure was losing, failure was missing a big shot, failure was missing a free throw, turning the ball over, or, on a personal nature, getting divorced. All of those things that don't equate to winning or don't equate to everyone else's version of success. I always felt like a failure. I didn't have the same amount of success in the WNBA that I did in college. When I retired, I felt like a failure. One of the things that I really have had to do throughout my coaching career - more importantly throughout my life and I think having children has helped me with this - is just restructure the way I think about success and failure. To me, success is not the trophies that you have sitting on your mantel or the number of times you get your name in the paper. The success that I want people to remember me by is the impact that I had in their lives, which is one of the reasons that I'm so proud to be a community project.

As I restructure my thinking of failure now, I think of failure as, "OK, I haven't prepared our team well enough for this game. We weren't prepared for what they did to us." To me, that's the failure. Did we put this player in a position to be successful? Did we put that player in a position to be successful? They're not reaching their potential; that to me is a failure. In order to lead through that failure, we constantly have to check ourselves, look ourselves in the mirror, and focus on the daily improvements that we make. We have to have a clear vision of what's expected first of all. Then, we have to see the vision in the distance but, also, see the steps that we've taken to accomplish and get to that vision. It's a much less tangible thing than it used to be. Leading through failure is about seeing the daily incremental progress that you're making. When you have a setback, reframe your mind and continue to make sure that you're focusing on the things that you can control. If you're struggling in the season and you're losing but you can get your players to see the improvement that they're making every single day; if you get your players to see whether it's tangible or not tangible. Because, in sports, we're used to seeing tangible things. We want to hold somebody to a certain percentage field goal shooting, we want to shoot a certain percentage from the field, we want to score so many points and hold them to... It's all numbers driven and it's all tangible stuff. If we can get them to see the intangible stuff, get them to see their daily improvements, and get them to focus on the process of improvement, all those other things take care of themselves. That's a huge challenge and hopefully I can stay steadfast in that belief and stay steadfast in that vision. Get our players to really rally around that and focusing much less on the end result as we focus on the process of getting to that result.

**Petrick:** I wish I had a video of me when I was 18 or 19 years old in the Minor Leagues after I struck out - what I looked like and how I handled myself - and instruct people that's not how to do it. I would do that because I looked terrible; I couldn't handle failure. That was the biggest downfall of my life. I worried so much about what other people think, and I wanted to please people. In sports, you are going to fail. I was always blessed with the ability to be good so I didn't fail a lot when I was a kid. But when you get into pro ball, everyone is good so you are bound to fail. It was tough for me to swallow. It took me three or four years to really get a grasp on the mental part of the game. Once I did, my career took off. I started putting one day behind me and take on a fresh, new day like it was. That was the biggest thing for me; flush the crap that accumulates and start fresh, start new. My faith has been big as far as going to God for well-being. So, the key for me is being able to take things as they are, not blowing them up so big in your head that it wears you down, and trying to flush all the bad stuff out so you can start fresh every day.

**Elmore:** This is a hot topic. There have been so many books written on failure, and I think they've been in response to the fact that, at least in our world today, we almost cannot handle failure. Especially the kids we're raising today, I love these kids; I absolutely love them - but parents are raising a generation of kids where we tell them they're awesome even if they did a mediocre job. It's funny. I was with the Giants and Coach Coughlin, the head football coach for the New York Giants, said, "My grandkids just got down with a game and my son-in-law said, 'You were amazing,'" and he goes, "That's not what I told them." He is a great grandpa, but he's thinking, "We are not being honest with these kids unless we're saying, here's where you can improve." So, I would say, number one, I tell myself that failure is a part of the territory. I have to not only live with it, I have to welcome it because I'm not doing anything if I'm not failing somewhere along the way at trying something new.

One question I always ask my team members at Growing Leaders is, "When was the last time you did something for the first time?" I love that question, "When was the last time you did something for the first time?" That tells me you're stretching when you're trying something brand new and not just stuck in a rut. I have to be okay with failing personally. I have to not attach it to my identity, my self-esteem. Failure is an act, it's not a person. It's not fatal; I can recover. I know this are clichés I'm giving, but I bought in. I drank the Kool-Aid. You've got to be okay with failure and not just okay. You've got to say, "If I'm going to do anything right, I'm probably going to stumble a couple of times and strike out once in a while."

**Anderson:** Our organization collaborates a lot. I still make the final decision on the big, vision decisions and so forth. But, I'm going to admit something to you. I haven't, personally, had a great idea in years. I've had some good ideas that I throw out there to the team, and the team turns them into great ideas. And, when it doesn't work out well, we do autopsies without blame. It's not about whose fault it was. It's what can we learn from this. I really have tried to create a culture here where failure is not fatal. If everything our people do is a matter of life or death, quite frankly, they are doing to be dead a lot. We learned that when we hit a wall, we want to bounce. We don't want to splatter. I tell my people all the time and I tell people in my seminars, "Listen, I still do stupid things, but they're not the same stupid things I used to do. They're new stupid things." I think that's growth. If you're doing new stupid things, it's because you're trying new things and you're making mistakes. But, you're learning and growing because of it. As long as we continue to grow, not repeat our mistakes, that's actually a very positive sign. That's the perspective I look at. Bear Bryant said a long time ago, "When you make a mistake - admit it, learn from it, don't repeat it." We're all about that here at our company.

**Medcalf:** Failure is never easy. But, when we can shift the lens and stop calling it "failure" - or as James Clear says, "Looking at it as data" - and going, "Okay, Did that work? Did it not work?" Learning from it and growing from it. Three years ago, I got knocked out by a guy in San Diego on New Year's. It was a crazy story, and I talk about it a lot. I was sitting in a hospital bed a couple of hours later with two of my close friends, and I looked over at them and said, "You know what? I'm really glad that this happened. I believe that it was in my best interest and an opportunity to learn and grow." They were like, "We took you to the wrong hospital. We should have taken you to the looney bin. Are you kidding me? There's no way this could have been in your best interest." When we start to look at events with that type of mindset, no matter what it is - believing that it's in our best interest and an opportunity to learn and grow - then we start to adopt that growth mindset like Carol Dweck talked about in her book, *Mindset*. That allows us to truly become an unstoppable force because, no matter what's happening all around us, it's an opportunity for us to learn and grow. We stop putting ourselves into a victim mindset and feeling, "Woe is me. There's nothing I can do, and I don't have the resources that I need. I don't have a good enough coach. I don't have the support of my organization or my program." Just feeling sorry for yourself instead of going, "What can I learn from this? How can I grow? What's the best that I can do with what I have right now, right where I am?" Focus on those things that are completely inside of your control.

I see it so much, even when it comes down to something simple like resources. It's funny how there are high schools that figure out ways to get Jamie and I to come out, and there are college programs that say, "Well, we don't have enough money to bring you guys out." It's like, "That's really interesting because the little high school down the road? They were able to be resourceful and find enough people that were like, 'No, this is important. This stuff is what we need. This is what we want our kids to get.'" They find a way to make it happen. Some people make an excuse while others go, "Okay, so what can we do? How can we make this work?" That's really what we try and help people realize is there is no such thing as failure. Oftentimes, if you can re-shift that lens and either double or triple your failure rate and stop running from it - changing that lens and going, "No, that didn't work, okay. What's the next thing?" and just keep going, keep iterating and keep iterating, and keep trying to learn, grow, and get better - then failure actually becomes one of your best friends. You figure out what doesn't work as well. Then, you just keep growing from there.

**Gray:** We're all going to face failure and adversity. I call it failing forward. Just because I fail, just because I run into adversity, doesn't mean that I'm a failure. It doesn't mean that I'm not worthy. It just means that I'm going to have to go back again, keep trying, and keep working hard. So, for me, the characteristic that's sorely lacking in America that I spend a lot of time teaching my employees and those I come in contact with is the principle of resilience. It's like, "You gotta be resilient. You get knocked down, what do you do? You get back up." A lot of people aren't willing to do that. They get knocked down one too many times, and they stay down. Then, it could move toward more failures. For me, resilience is the key, and it's easy to think about but tough to actually do. When you're in the midst of it, you feel like God's against you. That's not the case at all. He's just giving an opportunity to step up and be resilient.

**Beebe:** I've always told myself that I have to go through many defeats to have success, so I just keep pressing on. Everyone loses. The great ones? They just lose less. How do I want to lead my team or my business after failure? Well, personally, I want them to learn that something good always comes from every defeat. So, let's not focus on the defeat or the bad thing that happened throughout the course of that game or the meeting that we had, but let's focus on how we can get better through the adversity we faced.

**Brubaker:** I think you lead your team or organization through failure the same way that you handle failure. That is to understand that failure doesn't define you. It's not fatal. All failure is feedback. This dovetails very nicely with the last question in that you've got to be willing to take chances. There's a difference between playing to win, to borrow a sports analogy, and playing not to lose. When you're playing to win, you keep your foot on that accelerator, you keep pressing forward and taking chances. That's what is going to get you to the next level, but it isn't going to be a straight line as you're charting it on the graphs. There's going to be some bumps, and there's going to be some dips. What you need to look at, more importantly, is the trajectory long-term. You'll be on a good trajectory if you embrace failure and, in some respects, encourage it.

I really like what Google has done in that they allow a certain percentage of their employees' work week to be free time where they just spend it creating and bringing new ideas to the table. It's where Gmail was created. That's where a number of the greatest innovations were created. That never would have happened if you didn't give your people the freedom to create; the freedom to make mistakes without repercussions; then to try and tweak it, refine it, and then bring it to market.

I think you handle failure by making it - I don't want to say "routine" because that would be encouraging it and allowing yourself to make the same mistakes over and over again - but you handle it by embracing the fact that it is a reality of life. We're all going to fail at some point in some way. It's what can we learn from it? How can we improve? When you're modeling that for your team and you're willing to own some of your mistakes as a leader, now you're authentic, you're real, and you're not simply preaching. You are actually showing them the way and making it okay for them. If you're willing to do it and you're willing to try and learn from it, you need to make it okay for them to do the same, as opposed to there being punitive measures for making a mistake. In athletics, the team that makes the most mistakes is usually going to win because they're the ones that are trying to find their edge or trying to push the envelope. They're playing to win, not to lose.

**Crandall:** Great question. I take it very hard, personally. I think that I'm a people pleaser in a way, and, when I fail, I tend to obsess over it a bit. Again, this is my domain right now. I teach leadership, but the place where I'm leading or reflecting is sports. Every time I lose a basketball game, I think about it until we play again. It drives my wife crazy. Very objectively, I could have coached a great game, and we still lost. There wasn't a lot I could have done about it, but I think about every little thing I could have done differently.

That said, as a leader and looking at others' failures, I believe we have to fail and fail regularly. We have to embrace it, help people learn from it, and be really positive about it. I'm all about intentions. When you're leading, if the people you're leading are doing their best - I tend to assume they are – it's really what I focus on, is assuming they're trying to do their best work. All failure is a learning opportunity. As long as they're learning from it and driving on, it's a really good thing. It's how we get better. As much as we should reflect on our success, we should think about what we learn from doing things right. For me, there's just no comparison. The best learning has always come out of my biggest failures. It sounds kind of cliché, again, but as long as you learn from them, it's not failure.

# MOST IMPORTANT DECISIONS

**What are the most important decisions leaders make?**

**Kouzes:** I would say there are five key decisions that we make as leaders. The first of those is a set of decisions about values and standards. What do we believe in? How are we going to hold ourselves accountable? How do we develop a shared understanding of the standards we are all going to hold ourselves accountable to? I think that is the first set. It's very important that leaders be clear about values and standards. In fact, in our research we found that those leaders who are clear about that are much more likely to have engaged constituents.

The second set is around direction and vision. We have to be clear about the kinds of organization we want to create five, ten, twenty years down the road. When people talk about our organization or our team in the future, what do we want them to be saying about us?

The third is decisions about innovation and change. What can we do to continuously grow and improve? What are we doing to learn from our mistakes? What have we changed lately to make ourselves better?

The fourth set of decisions is around people. Some people say this is the most important set of decisions. Who will be on the team? How do we foster collaboration among our team members? How do we strengthen our capacity?

And the last is decisions around rewards and recognitions. How do we recognize performance, both at the individual level and the team level, knowing that it is hard work to get to excellence so that it's rewarded when we get there?

**Goldsmith:** One of the most important decisions is who to hire. It's very important that leaders take the hiring process seriously because you have to have quality coming in to get quality coming out. And, really focusing on trying to hire and get the best people we can get. The best book I know on this topic is written by friend of mine, Geoff Smart, called *Who*. It is about determining who you want to get to work with you - very important book.

My work is after you do hire them, how to coach them to make them even better?

**Gordon:** I think that leaders make decisions that are important every day and all day long. That's what leaders do. They make decisions. The key is to be very clear about your decisions, to have clarity. Once you know what you stand for, every decision you make is easy. In your decision making process, always filter through the lens of: What do I stand for? What do we stand for? Think about back to Enron. One of their core values was integrity. They obviously weren't living their values or living what they stood for. If you know what you stand for and you make decisions based on that, then it's going to be very easy to make decisions.

**Beebe:** I take into consideration how the decision that I'm making is going to affect each individual spiritually, mentally and physically. If I can keep this perspective, I believe our team and business will be more successful.

**Gray:** To love their employees and those around them well. It's a conscious decision to put others' needs first. It's hard to do; it's easy to say. But, I am convinced that it's the single most important thing that great leaders need to do. It's a Biblical principle. Love your neighbor. Love God. They asked Jesus, "What's the most important commandment?" And what did Jesus say? He said, "Love God and love others." They say, "No, we're asking for one thing." He said, "Love God and love others." They're all connected. When we love God, we love others. When we love others, we're loving God. It's all connected. So, that's what we gotta do. That's how we can improve the lives of others. And, in so doing, the natural by-product is improving your own life.

**Isom:** That could really go in so many directions. The biggest, most important decision that a leader has to make every single day when they wake up: Today, I'm going to lead well. I think sometimes we can get comfortable in our seat. We forget that it takes daily effort to build an empire. Honestly, it takes daily effort to lead a team well; it takes daily effort to be present for your employees or your teammates, or whatever it may be. It takes daily awareness. It takes daily sacrifice; daily selflessness. It's coming back to the drawing board every single morning and saying, "Okay, yesterday played out like X, Y, and Z. I need to work on this, this, and this. Today, I'm going to make a conscious effort to do that. Today, I'm not going to take the seat of leadership for granted. I'm going to take it in stride, and I'm going to lead the best that I can. I'm going to lead well." Honestly, that sounds so small, but it really has to be a daily decision; a conscious thought. Or else, our leadership becomes subconscious and an afterthought when it should be at the forefront of our thoughts because it is involving and impacting other people. That has to be our priority. We have to understand that it can't just be a passive role.

**White:** One of the most important decisions is – it's tough to say it's a decision, but it really is - what comes out of your mouth. With the types of kids that are out there nowadays there are a lot of highs and lows in terms of confidence level. There is a lot of success and defeat in everything that they do. You can build up or tear down someone with the way that the words come off your tongue. How you say things is very important, and this is something that I've not been very good at in the past. I'm really working to be better at thinking before I'm speaking. I want to be very direct with my communication, no question about it. The tone in which it is said is very important.

Your actions each day are very important, from body language to eye contact to leading by example. If your players believe in your actions, then they're going to believe in what you say, whether it's constructive criticism or whether it's praise. The people that you surround yourself with is priority. One of the most important things that I did when I became the head coach of the Indiana Fever was bring back a guy who was the head coach at Tulsa who worked with us before; a guy by the name of Gary Kloppenburg. And, to bring on Gail Goestenkors, who is a Hall of Fame coach - she is getting inducted into the Women's Basketball Hall of Fame this summer. She was a terrific head coach at Duke for a number of years, went on to Texas.

These guys are way smarter than me, and it was really important for me to surround myself with people who have tremendous experience and who are awesome in terms of skill development but who are equally as good in terms of their understanding of the game and understanding of situations. And, who have been there before. This is my first rodeo as a head coach. I feel like I'm prepared. I feel like I'm there, but there are certain things that you're going miss that they've been through. They might give me a suggestion and say, "Hey, maybe you should think about this" or "maybe you should think about that." The people that you surround yourself with on a daily basis - whether that's your coworkers or whether that's your friends – that is one of the most important decisions that a leader can make.

**Anderson:** The first one is often overlooked, and that's the decision to grow. You've got to continue to work on yourself. Another one of my mentors, Jim Rohn, said it very well – that business gets better when you get better. Never wish it were easier. Wish you were better. Growth is a choice. Just because you show every day doesn't mean you grow every day. You have to deliberately work on yourself. So, that is an essential decision. I'm going to have a personal growth program. I'm going to continue to upgrade my skills, work on my attitude, character strength, and discipline. I'm going to work on me because as I get better, I can make the things around me better. Probably the number one decision a leader has to make is to continue to work on themselves. Then, what is the vision going to be? Who's going to join the team? What do we want our culture to be like? What will our values be? These are all important decisions as well. I believe that if somewhere along the line you stop growing, none of that other stuff matters as much because it eventually fizzles out.

**Medcalf:** To read or not to read. That's almost always what it comes down to. You could have John Wooden, Jesus, Gandhi, Martin Luther King, Jr., and Steve Jobs in your inner circle and meet with them - have a staff meeting with those guys - for 30 minutes every single day. There's very few people that I meet that wouldn't take that. We don't take advantage of that because we have that opportunity with resources that they've written. I get e-mails all the time from people who are like, "I'd just really like your help," and I'm like, "Have you read my book?" "No, but I know that you –" And I'm like, "You don't want my help. You want my time. Time is the most valuable resource in the world. You want my time. If you wanted my help - I've written two books, other stuff that I've written that's in e-book form, and I've put out videos. I've put out all this stuff."

There's so many ways that we can have people in our inner circle without ever having to spend time with them. Judah Smith, my pastor, has had a huge, huge impact in my life. I've spent five minutes one-on-one with him. I've never asked him for his time. I could, but I haven't because I study his books. He speaks twice a week in Los Angeles. I'm at both services, take notes in both services, and I listen to his sermons online. He's got a thing called Jesus' music project, and I listen to it every single night as I sleep. I don't need to spend time with Judah for Judah to have a tremendous impact on the way that I think. If we were more intentional about carving out that time and space to listen to people that we respect, and we want to emulate and read their stuff, watch their stuff, and make sure that we're renewing our mind with things like that, that's going to impact all those other decisions that we have throughout the day.

I think the other one that's really important, that I wish people would do more: It's really easy to go, "Oh, yeah, we should put first things first." But, whenever it gets really tough, you're in really challenging situations, and you have people that you're responsible for leading actually trying to put first things first, that's whenever it becomes a lot more interesting. What are you going to do in those situations? I don't think it's easy by any means. You've got to put first things first in your life. That might "negatively affect our team," but that's what's most important. The question I keep trying to go back and ask myself every day, but especially around the big decisions that I'm making in my life, is: What would I do if I had six months to live? I keep going back to that, and I think more people would live their lives differently. I think a lot of people in leadership would live their lives differently if they'd start their day with that question. Would you make sure that you actually got up and spent some time with your kids before you went to work? Would you make sure that you made it home for dinner? Would you not watch as much film? Would you call your wife and tell her that you love her? What would you do if you had six months to live?

That hit home for me because I lost my little brother when I was nine years old. I lost my dad when I was twenty-three. In my life, I've watched people who have been diagnosed with cancer or had something where they knew that they had a very short time to live. I watched it drastically change how they lived their lives. I don't want to get to the end of my life and make drastic changes. I want to live my life that way. For me I try and ask myself that question every day: What would I do if I had six months to live? And, simultaneously, focusing on being grateful. At the end of my life, like Francis Chan said, "I don't want to succeed at things in life that don't really matter. I don't want to get to the top of the ladder and realize that my ladder has been on the wrong building."

**Brubaker:** I think the most important aspect of leadership – anyone, at any level, in any organization - are the people they surround themselves with. I think leadership's about having people work with you, not for you. That may sound like semantics, but there's a big difference between working with somebody and working for somebody. When you're working with somebody, it's a vested partnership. When you're working for somebody, they're just simply handing you a job description and a list of tasks that you need to deliver on. There's no sense of partnership.

My coaching mentor always used to refer to me and, over the years, all of his assistant coaches – he would always call you "partner." It wasn't just kind of like a John Wayne sort of, "Howdy, partner." He called you "partner" because he wanted you to feel like it was your program too. You were the leader as well. You weren't somebody that just had menial tasks delegated to you. It was a vested partnership. He backed that up by really listening to your ideas and suggestions and not being afraid to incorporate them. I think that if there is ever something that executives can learn from coaches and learn from the world of athletics, it's how important personnel is. Scouting or recruiting - finding the right people who fit your philosophy and fit your culture. If you don't have the right people on board, they will undo all the great things you're doing faster. It will tear down faster than you can build it up.

**Clark:** Every day, how you get up and approach the day. We've used the phrase "Win the Day" for fifteen to twenty years. I know that's become a common theme, and that's one of the ones I've said for years, going back to high school. We're just going to win today, and that starts with how you wake up that morning. Even the night before - getting a good night's sleep, physical rest, nutrition. All those things. Being an old strength coach back in the 80s, those are the things, to me, that get a guy ready to go compete or any person to go compete on that given day. What can we do today to make the day a great day? If we can do that every single day, then we've got good things happening for us.

**Crandall:** I think the number one most important decision is who to bring on the team; getting the right people for what mission you're trying to accomplish is huge. If you're bringing the wrong people, it messes stuff up. Again, that's a direct connection with sports, especially team sports. With the basketball team I'm coaching now, we've been together five years since seventh grade. This year, we had the opportunity with a lot of different kids to see what our team's doing, how much fun our kids are having together, and how they like playing together. I had a lot of enquiries about joining our team, and we really had to think about that because we've got this great chemistry. We had kids with some great skills that could have come in. But, if they destroy that chemistry and mission, that like-mindedness on the mission, then it's not going to be worth it. We brought in who we thought were the right kids for our team; two new kids out of eleven. We started practicing, and, I think, we made the right decision. Who you're bringing in. I think that when you look at studies on organizational culture, one of the driving mechanisms of how you reinforce or how you change culture - if you're going to change culture, sometimes, it's about getting rid of certain people and bringing other people in. That's a huge one.

Then, I think, a different sort of answer. On a daily basis, the micro-decisions we make on how to treat people are so, so important because they all build into bigger work climate and culture. It isn't about you. Knowing everyone you lead as much as you can and knowing what makes them tick. The decision to walk in in the morning and smile because emotions are contagious. We have to be really intentional, as a leader, about those behaviors. Yesterday, at basketball practice, a guy name Danny didn't take a shot I thought he should have taken. I said, "Danny, why didn't you take that shot?" He kind of looked at me, and I realized in the moment that my tone of voice was not *asking* him. It was *telling* him, "You should have taken that shot." But, my intention was actually to ask him why he didn't take it, so I had to back up. I made fun of myself and said, "Danny, sorry, that was a horrible way to ask that. I genuinely want to know why you decided not to take that shot." He answered me and said, "Because I want to be a team player." I was able to explain to him, "You're a team player when you're taking that shot because that's a good shot and good for the team. So, I love your answer, Danny, but take the shot." That micro-decision to step back and realize the way I asked a question – that was a really poor way to ask it - was important in building our team culture. So, not huge decisions but I think every little intentional thing we do really builds how the team operates.

**Lubin:** I was thinking about this, and I think it's knowing when to cut the cord. It happens in business, sports, parenting, and anything else that involves leadership. Once you start going down the road of hope versus certainty, you must be willing to get out.

I see it with deals that I work on, or I see it with relationships that people are in. Once they start hoping that that person will come back to them or that deal may, if we do this, be closed. At that point, it's too late. You have

to be proactive beforehand versus worrying about it after the fact, that it should have been done six months ago.

So, I think one of the most important decisions a leader can make is timing and understanding when to get out. Because you don't want to be the guy who always "buys high, sells low." You want to be the guy who "buys low and sells high." You don't want to be on the downward trajectory. You want to be on the upward trajectory.

# NECESSARY CHARACTERISTICS

**What are some characteristics you think every leader should possess?**

**Janssen:** I think every leader needs to be able to lead themselves. I think they need to have a tremendous amount of commitment. Obviously, when you're leading a group or an individual to a certain area, it's going to take a lot of time, a lot of effort. You've got to have that commitment. You've got to have that confidence that you can get to the vision that you have for your program. That's going to be important, not only to have that confidence at the beginning, but to maintain that throughout. When you're hitting those storms of adversity, you've got to have that composure when things aren't going well to maintain your poise and your focus. The character stuff. That you really have to have your own house in order and make good decisions so that people will continue to trust you.

I think the whole self-leadership thing is a big part of it. After you have that under control, then you need to know how to lead others. A big thing that we talk about in our academies is being an encourager and an enforcer. An encourager when people are doing the right things, when they are giving you a great effort, having a great attitude. We want to call that out, build on that, and let people know, "Yes, that's what we're looking for." At the same time, when they're falling below those standards, you also have to step up and say, "That's not the way we do things here. We expect more from you. If we're going to be a top team in this conference, this state, this nation, this world, this is the level that we have to train at; this is the level that we have to compete at. You're not at that level. We know you are capable of that level. We need you at that level."

Last, but not least, not just leading those individuals but then leading a whole team. Having a vision that everybody's bought in to, having some core values that everybody subscribes to and lives on a daily basis, and having those very high standards of behavior that are going to allow you to compete with the best of the best.

**Olson:** I think that number one - and I just mentioned it - is authenticity. If people don't trust you and your integrity isn't there – Look, we all make mistakes, and I'm not saying we have to be perfect. What we're looking for is people that what they say is what they do, and what you see is what you get. In this day and age, there's so many bloggers and so many guys trying to make money, or just this and that. There's nothing wrong with trying to make some money, but at the same time, they have to be authentic. As [Simon] Sinek always talks about, they have to have a clean, pure "why." We talk about, if a leader doesn't have a clean purpose statement - we call it pure fuel or clean fuel - if it's more self-motivated and they are trying to get what they want, that's really not pure fuel. Eventually, that's going to jam them up, and they're going to crash. For me, integrity, honesty, trustworthiness, and authenticity; those are pretty easy character words to throw out there, but they are extremely difficult.

I will tell you the other thing they have to have, in my opinion, is to be able to lead people. They cannot be a follower. They need to be humble and understand that they don't know it all. They have to have a teachable spirit. In my book, we talk about the four things we really want them to have. Faithful, which means they fully trust whoever they work for, and they have a strong faith themselves. They are available and accountable, meaning not only will they hold themselves accountable, but they hold other people accountable. Those people won't resent them for doing that. The last two are teachable spirit and courage. They are willing to stand up when something is not right and say something and do something about it. Those are the main ones for me.

**White:** Certainly, a drive and a competiveness because you have to continue to strive to be better as well as continue to want your kids to strive and be better. I also think compassion and humility; those are so important, especially nowadays, to really treat your players with respect. Treat your coworkers and employees with respect and humility.

Good communication skills are necessary. I don't see how, in this day and age - it annoys me to communicate through text message. It annoys me to communicate through e-mail. When you need to talk to your players, you need to talk to your players. A lot of them don't want to talk. They want that communication to be digital. Communication skills in terms of the way that you communicate, and I also think communication skills in terms of just being direct. All everybody wants is just to know where they stand.

I think attention to detail; it is important for leaders to pay attention to the details. Not necessarily get lost in the minutiae but to understand that the devil is in the details, so to speak. Details matter.

**Elmore:** Let me reach down on this one because you're asking what's a universal thing that leaders in Zimbabwe or Manila or LA all need? I would say, first and foremost, as predictable as this may sound coming from me, the art of self-leadership. I really believe Dee Hock was spot on. He was the first person I've heard say, "The first person I gotta lead is me." That's my character. That's me making a decision that, before the spotlight is on me, I'm really managing my emotions. I'm building personal disciplines in my life in private because I know they're going to pay off in public. I would say number one, I've got to build strong character.

A second one - I got four of these that I'm thinking about - the second one is perspective. I think leaders just think differently than people that only identify themselves as followers. Even though we all have leadership capacity, I think some people, you'd admit it, they just don't see themselves as a leader so they blend in rather than stand out. I had a professor when I got my doctoral degree say something, and I've never forgotten it. He said, "The primary difference between a leader and a follower is perspective. The primary difference between a leader and an effective leader is better perspective." He said it was something in the mind where I'm thinking bigger, I'm thinking before other people do, and I'm thinking beyond what other people do. I think perspective is number two. I've just got to think better and envision better so I can lead people better.

The third one is courage. This is one, when I go through this list of four non-negotiables, young leaders usually raise their hands and say, "That's the one I've gotta work on." Most of us feel like we don't have enough courage to do what we feel we ought to do. This is the kind of thing that, once you get a good idea as a leader, it gives you the guts to get up off your butt, take a risk, and do something about it. So, if somebody is listening in or reading this and saying, "Okay, that's where I'm weak," I would say begin to really take some risks; maybe start with small ones. You've gotta do something every week that you couldn't possibly pull off unless you felt like you were taking a risky step.

Number four. So, character, perspective, courage. Number four is an odd word, but it's the best word I can come up with so far for this fourth non-negotiable. It's the word favor. I believe good leaders, effective leaders, leaders that are magnetic and bring others on board, have developed the element of favor. Meaning - this is the people skill part of leadership. If you think about it, once you build character, perspective, and courage, just those three alone make you an entrepreneur, but you're not necessarily a leader. You're doing something alone, maybe. The favor element is - now I'm bringing others, attracting others, and I'm brokering the talents of others to leverage them for this great cause we decided to do together.

So, I don't think a leader has to be the smartest person in the room. I don't think they have to be the most gifted or talented person in the room. I do think they need to be the person that can somehow align people, build an aligned, clear vision, and get them moving together in that thing.

**Eikenberry:** In my book, *Remarkable Leadership*, we talk about thirteen competencies. So, that's more than a few. In the book, *Remarkable Leadership*, is the basis of pretty much what we've created in terms of leadership competencies. If I were to take that thirteen and highlight two or three, I would, number one, say that remarkable leaders must be continual learners because this is far too difficult a thing to think you ever got it figured out. If I were to pick the trait that most people might not think of is: To be a leader, we must be a learner. If I added a couple more to that, there are things that seem to show up over and over and over. That is, I need to understand how change happens, and how do I help communicate with, influence, and inspire people to change? Change is a constant force for us all. I think there are communication skills that are critical, whether those are written, whether those are oral, or whether those are listening. I'd have to probably put coaching on that shortest of short lists.

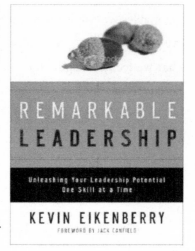

Beyond the skills, there are character and value issues. We can think of people in history who led very successfully for a while, and if you judge leadership as people choosing to follow, that were very successful for a while. In the end, there are character and value issues that are critically important in order for us to lead successfully for a long while and to make a true positive impact on those we lead and on the world around us.

**Anderson:** I'm writing a new book right now called *It's Not Rocket Science: Four Simple Strategies to Master the Art of Execution*. In that book, I talk about one of the reasons followers don't buy in to a leader's process or a leader's vision is because they really haven't bought into the leader. There are five "Cs" that I mentioned in that section that I think help answer this question. You have to have character, competence, consistency, compassion, and commitment. People are looking at a leader and saying, number one, can I trust you? That's character. Number two, do you know what you're doing? That's competence. Number three, are you consistent in both areas, or do you just have a flash of brilliance every once in a while? Because if that's the case, I can't really trust you. Number four, do you care about me or am I just another heifer in the herd? That's compassion. Do you really care about me, my future, and my growth? And then the fifth 'C' – commitment. How bought-in are you? What price are you paying? How committed are you? When I can start to see those five things in a leader, you want run through a wall for that type of leader. Those are things that we can talk about, but it's better if we live them out every single day in the trenches with our people.

**Petrick:** The number one thing that keeps coming up is transparency. I'm going to talk about that for a second. I think transparency is big, meaning be open and honest about how you are feeling every day. If you are a leader, principal, superintendent, coach, or teacher, don't try to cover things up. Be open and honest about everything. If you are having problems in your relationship with someone, talk to them about it. Don't be so vain to where you can't talk about your problems or issues. Everybody has them; everybody has things they need help with. If you communicate with and talk to people, even if you are not a leader of those people, you will gain so much more respect from them if you're not afraid to share your weaknesses. We all have weaknesses, but we can still be a leader and not hide those things.

**Brubaker:** Number 1: Leadership is about letting go. As crazy and as counterintuitive as that sounds, that is the toughest thing. It's about letting go. It's about, again, hiring the right people, trusting them, turning them loose to do their jobs, and realizing that you're going to get a better result when you do that. So, I think number one is letting go.

Number 2: Hire to your weaknesses, delegate to your strengths. Hire to your weaknesses. If you're weak in marketing as a leader, as an entrepreneur, make sure you bring on someone who has a ton of experience and marketing savvy that you don't possess. Trust them to do their job.

Number 3: Patience. Instant gratification takes too long, never mind delayed gratification. The reality is you have to be patient because progress doesn't happen overnight. Overnight successes, whether it's an individual or a company, are thousands of nights in the making to become that success. We're in the era where there's a lot of mistrust in big banks, for example. Big banks, since the economy collapsed back in 2008, still haven't really recovered and recovered their customer base from then - this is years ago - because of lack of trust. The reason there is no trust is it's manipulation, not facilitation. In the same time that big banking has taken a nose dive, credit unions have grown and expanded. Even in 2008 when we had a great recession, credit unions have seen this rise in membership and participation. Their "numbers" are looking better and better. The difference between a big bank and a credit union is that big banks, they don't have the patience. Who they really serve are the shareholders and - this is, again, playing not to lose - they make every decision based on: what do we need to do to make the numbers look right to appease our shareholders? So, they're laying people off, they're cutting back in different areas, and they're adding fees, and they're not serving the customers well or serving them right because "that next quarterly earnings report, we need to make it look good for the shareholders." Well, customers feel that and sense that. Meanwhile, credit unions are basically owned by their members. Their members are their shareholders. So, every decision they make has one focus, and that's serving their customers, serving their members. That creates a great sense of trust.

So, as a leader, if you can remember to be patient, keep your focus on the right things, and serve the right people. Over time, that's going to pay dividends financially and then also emotionally with your customer and the sense of loyalty that you engender. I would say that goes for internal customers as well. Your employees are your internal customers. How you serve them and how much trust you can engender with those relationships, those people are going to be your best recruiters, marketing, advertising, and face for your organization out in the public.

**Clark:** Once again, I think it's others before yourself. We've all got personal goals. People think ego is a bad thing. I don't think ego is bad thing. It's when an ego gets out of control, and it's not managed. It's okay to want to be good. We want people that want to be good and strive to be the best, but we've got to want to put our team ahead of ourselves and others ahead of ourselves as I'm working for these personal goals. Want to see others do well because we're talking about leadership. Leadership is trying to take others where they've never been or maybe don't want to go at that time. That's what we're talking about here is leadership. It's okay to have that personal drive, but we're looking for leaders - people that want to make others better as well.

**Crandall:** Integrity. If you don't have integrity and you're not trying to do the right things, you shouldn't lead. I personally believe that a learning orientation - so taking each failure as learning from them, constantly trying to get better, turning that back on yourself, and having a reflective attitude about your experiences. We teach in our programs that you can't learn leadership in a classroom. We believe that 100%. You can't learn it isolated it in a classroom. You have to experience it to learn. But, equally true, you can't learn leadership from experience. You can only learn leadership from the experiences you examine and reflect on. In this leader growth model, you have to have experience and you have to reflect. That requires a learning orientation and a real curiosity about moving forward.

I think that curiosity leads over into being curious about your people and what their needs are. So, integrity, learning orientation, and humility. I don't think you *have* to have it (humility). In fact, history proves you don't have to have it to be a successful leader. You can get people charging towards extraordinary missions without humility. I think, all things together, if you have all the other qualities - and the other is authenticity - and you see yourself as a leader, humility will make you that much better.

That goes back to the first question, "Can anyone lead?" I think integrity is a choice. Learning orientation - deciding I'm going to learn from failure - that's a choice. Humility - a little less of a choice but in a way, it still is something we can decide; to put others before ourselves.

**McCabe:** A clear vision is one. An inherent desire to help others is two; genuine desire. So, clear vision and desire to help others. The ability to listen to others. I sat with a guy on an airplane one day; young guy who was probably in his mid-30s who, through college, set up a computer company. He sold it for hundreds of millions of dollars and, now, has a company worth much more than that. I asked him, "How would you define leadership?" He said, "When I started my company - the new one - I put a group of people around me that could challenge me. But, the rest of the organization can't challenge me. I don't need naysayers. I need people who believe in our vision. On the board, that small group of four or five people who have had success in other areas, they can challenge me every which way they want to." You have to be willing to take coaching. Great leaders need to also understand what it's like to stand in the shadows. To have humility is important.

# ATTITUDE IN LEADERSHIP

**What role does having positive energy, positive attitude, and enthusiasm play in leadership?**

**Brubaker:** Positive energy plays a major role. It isn't everything, but I would rank it right up there. I think that the thing with positive energy is it's contagious. There's an absolutely fabulous study by a professor/researcher at Harvard named Daniel Goleman. What he did was a study on the New York City subway system. He would put people on the subway train, people who didn't know each other, and he would have them seated next to one another on a train for one stop, two stops, or maybe three. They were on the train sitting next to each other, not saying a word for 15 minutes maybe. What they found was, within the first five minutes on that train ride, three complete strangers seated next to each other, their heart rates started to synchronize to the beat of the most stressed-out person. What he found was if two of those people had a great day and were in a good mood when they got on the train, when they got off two stops later - if they were seated next to somebody who was really in a bad place emotionally, probably the person with the highest heart rate - those two people had basically caught his or her bad mood. They got on the train in a good mood. They got off 10-15 minutes later, and they were in a funk. Why? Energy is contagious. It's contagious in a positive way; it's contagious in a negative way.

I would use that subway train metaphor from Goleman's research as a great metaphor, a great example for how we show up in the workplace. If you're a leader of an organization or you're a leader of a team, people can sense your tension before you ever open your mouth. Your body language doesn't talk; your body language screams. So, what's your body language saying when you walk into a room? Is it positive? Is it negative? People feed off of energy. So, if there's one thing we need to be mindful of perhaps more than anything else, it is the kind of energy that we give off. Are you an energy giver or are you an energy taker? There are some people that brighten a room *after* they leave. We don't want to be one of those people.

**Janssen:** It's huge. The leader, a lot of times, has to be the most passionate person because everyone else takes their cues from the leader. Kouzes and Posner are two guys who have done a lot of work in the leadership realm. They said, "You can't lead a person to a place you don't want to go to yourself."

When people come to that practice, to that meeting, or walk in a classroom, they've got to see that person out in front enthused, energetic, and confident; all of those positive characteristics. You're going to have adversity hit. You're going to have some people who aren't quite as bought in to the plan or the strategy. You've got to be that person, just in how you lead yourself and the energy that you're exuding, that other people want to come to, be around, and believe in when the chips are down.

**Olson:** It needs to be positive. When I do workshops, I'll ask, in a certain point of it, "What's a coach's job? Just shout out some one word answers." People will shout out things like to motivate, to lead, to model, to challenge, to encourage, and this and that. I will say, "Is anyone going to say discipline, critique, or correct?" They will go, "Oh, yeah. That too." I will say, "You know what? If I were to ask this question thirty years ago, what do you think were the first three words that would have come out? It probably would have been critique, discipline and correct." What's interesting is that Dr. Spock wrote *The Baby Book* years ago and said, "We need to be building positive self-esteem in our children." We took that to unhealthy levels where we are giving empty praise and telling kids they are doing things well when they are not even doing it. You know, the whole "everyone gets a trophy" syndrome. So, for me, teaching positive feedback is so important. It has to be a positive atmosphere. If it's a negative atmosphere, you're not going anywhere. Your culture has to be positive.

On the other side of the coin, there needs to be truth. There needs to be correction. If you read anything on John Wooden, he spent a ton of time correcting people; I mean a ton of time. We've glazed over that and we start talking about how important it is to be positive, positive, positive. The reality is - yes we do, but we also need to critique, correct, and discipline. People will not get better if we just keep letting them do the wrong thing, or worse yet, we let them think they are doing the right thing. That goes back to parenting where there are hard conversations that we have to have with our kids – "Hey, I know everybody else thinks it's right, but we don't. We're different. I get that, and I'll wear it. You can blame us, but you know what? We're not going there." That's tough because you want your kids to like you, but what did Bill Cosby - or maybe someone else - say? Parents are concerned with having their kids grow up happy, that they don't grow them up to be tough and resilient. So, you have to be positive. Have to be heavy on the positive side along with accountability and being able to give them good, honest feedback.

**Isom:** Positive energy and enthusiasm are an important piece to the puzzle, but they're not the only piece in the puzzle of leading well. I think an optimistic attitude - I think an attitude pressed toward hope, pressed towards potential, and pressed towards growth is essential – ultimately, we're grounded in that. A leader isn't necessarily synonymous with a cheerleader because a leader has to be the one who sometimes gets real, gets raw, and gets honest. Sometimes the leader has to be the one to step up for the weak ones in the group and stand up to the ones who are bullying, overpowering, or whatever it may be. Like I said before, leadership is messy. It's like a glorious kind of messy, but it's not all rainbows, butterflies, and pompoms of "We can do this, team!" That's a great element of it, but it's not the only piece of the puzzle.

I think what's important when it comes to positive energy is that it has to be at the core of what we're doing. It has to be rooted in us so that when we have to do the messy, hard stuff, we're ultimately coming from a good place for the betterment of the team and for the betterment of the organization. But, we're able to get real, raw, and honest too. But, it doesn't have to be the constant surface level presentation to the people. When it is truly at the core - when there's consistency in how we carry ourselves and people know that's at the core, when things do have to get hard, messy, blunt, and black and white on the surface - people trust that it's coming from the right place. So, there it is. I think positive energy has to be at the core. We're leaders, not cheerleaders. Sometimes that means getting our hands dirty, doing the hard stuff, taking the blows, and moving forward. If we're rooted at a good place, that will all come in stride.

**Goldsmith:** Oh, I think it's very important. The greatest leader I've ever met in my life is my friend Alan Mulally, and I'll talk about another friend, Frances Hesselbein, who was ranked this year as one of the 50 Great Leaders in the World by *Fortune*. I've known both of them for years. I've never seen either one of them be down. Another way to look at that is "It's Showtime." I was with Alan Mulally after 9/11, and he was running Boeing commercial aircraft at that time. He couldn't have a bigger disaster on so many dimensions. You know what he said? "This is what I get paid for. Anybody can be up and positive when times are good. It's times like this that I get paid. This is when I earn the money." It's a great way to look at life.

**White:** It plays more of a role today than it has in the past. Certainly, when I was a player, there weren't a lot of coaches that had a ton of positive energy. It was mostly critique, criticism - it was much more old school in that sense. Players read into your body language. As soon as the players make a mistake they look over to the sideline. What do they see you doing? How do they see you reacting? Now, more than ever, positive energy is critical. Does that mean you have to pat everybody on the back and everybody has to be great? No, absolutely not. I think that there certainly needs to be positivity that flows through your body language, through your communication style – I think you can hear it in your voice. Are you dragging every day in practice, or are you energetic? You can have constructive criticism and it come out as positive energy in your voice. If you love what you do every single day, people feel that. They feed off of that. That is positive energy. That is critical because if you don't have it, you're not a good leader. People don't want to follow you if you're dragging every single day, you're criticizing every single day, and you're draining energy from other people every single day. You are not going to a have positive impact, and that's not good leadership.

**McCabe:** Positive energy is great. In the Disney approach, positive energy is the greatest way to go. But we also have to understand that every once in a while you can create some conflict and get people moving. Positive energy isn't the only way to go. It just may be the best way to sustain. Fear and punishment works, and that's why a lot of leaders use it. I'm not advocating for it, but it does work. Positive energy does help. Positive energy comes from the inherent belief that everybody is good, and I can help get them there. There is a problem with that belief system. Not everybody cares in your organization like you do. As a leader - as an organizational owner - not everybody cares the same way as you do.

**Kouzes:** Positivity broadens and builds. Having a positive attitude in a coach or a leader in any setting being positive towards others actually opens people up to more creativity. It also builds on itself. The whole notion of enthusiasm is that it is infectious. Other people catch that positive attitude.

The other important reason that positivity is important in leaders is that you can't perform to a negative. Somebody who is always saying "no" to you – "Don't do this and don't do that" – might be useful in terms of keeping you from making certain kinds of mistakes, but you can't improve your performance until somebody gives you a positive model of what excellence looks like. You have to have more positive to negative, the research shows, in order to have a fully engaged workforce.

The other thing is very simply this. In our research, we found that one of the qualities people look for and admire in a leader is being inspiring, upbeat, and energetic. People don't want to follow someone who's not enthusiastic, not positive, or energetic. You're modeling the kind of thing that enables people to want to follow you. Positivity attracts other people whereas negativity makes people want to run away.

**Anderson:** It's huge. It shapes a culture. It energizes a culture. You can walk into some places and you can just tell: Hey, there's something going on here. You can walk into some places, and you feel like that kid on the movie, *The Sixth Sense.* "I see Dead People." There is just nothing going on. I really believe both of those tempos start with the leader. The positive energy a leader brings is contagious. Positive attitude, positive energy, finding a way why we can do something. If they're apathetic, indifferent, or negative, then that is contagious in a very detrimental way. This is a very underrated aspect of leadership – bringing positive energy to the table on a day-in, day-out basis. Really being able to do it consistently, not just when your back's against the wall and you have to get something done.

**Gray:** I'm a passionate leader, and I speak from the perspective of a passionate leader. I do know that passion and enthusiasm can translate to short-term gains. Sometimes, if you have to climb that hill or get that project done, guys like me with great levels of passion can really help to do that. What I have to tell you is for long-term results, which really what we're all after, passion and enthusiasm are really less important. Discipline becomes much more important. It is so that you can continue to stay after it even when the passion has passed.

It may not be the answer that you wanted, because a lot of folks are like, "If I'm passionate, I'll find a way. I'll make a way." And I'm like, "Yeah, short-term. But, how are you going to do next Thursday when your passion has begun to fade a little bit and you don't have that excitement about the project? Will you keep after it? Will you continue to be a leader and a performer even when it gets tough?" That's really where I think I land on that characteristic of staying after it, persevering, and making sure that you're disciplined in your approaches. I tell you, Tony is the one that's taught me about those kinds of principles and how he's lived such a disciplined life.

**Medcalf:** This is one thing where Jon Gordon and I disagree a little bit. I'm not a huge fan of the word "positive" unless we're talking about in direct relation - as an antithesis to "negative." I think there's something much deeper than "positive." I had a person in coaching I was talking to yesterday say, "Shifting away from being a positive coach to being a beneficial and constructive coach has been so huge for me." Beneficial and constructive doesn't always mean "feel good." I think a lot of time when we talk about "positive" it falls into the definition of "feel good" and lowering standards. That's not what we're focused on. We're really focused on trying to be super beneficial and constructive in the way that we impact people's lives.

One of the exercises, or examples, I give to people is: Look, if you were in a potato sack race with somebody and you had the choice of who your partner was going to be, a positive thinker or a beneficial and constructive thinker. The only catch was that you were in this potato sack, and there's a semi-truck coming at you at 90 MPH. Do you want to be in that with a positive thinker or a beneficial and constructive thinker? Everybody always says, "The beneficial and constructive thinker" because it's a deeper level. It's not that there's anything inherently wrong with positive. I think there's something so much deeper which is beneficial and constructive.

Now, if you're talking about "positive," you're defining it the way Barbara Frederickson does, and you mean it to be hope, joy, peace, love, and kind of like the fruits of the Spirit, okay. That's fine. But, a lot of the time when we say "positive" we actually mean kind of fluffy and make us feel good. I talk about the pursuit of happiness in this country actually killing us because happiness is "me-focused." It's easy, and it makes me feel good. That's how I feel, a lot of times, when it comes to "positive" versus "fulfillment"; it's actually hard. It's others-focused, and it's the tough challenges over and over again. Because at the end of people's lives whenever you ask them, "What was the most fulfilling thing that you've done?" they say things like raising kids, climbing mountains and the biggest challenges that they conquered. Then, you ask them, "What was the hardest thing you ever did in your life?" They tell you those exact same things. Our pursuit of happiness, the easy stuff, and the "me-focused stuff" – that, I believe, is killing us in this country.

**Petrick:** Positive energy is huge. Did I tell you what I mean when I talk about flushing? It is being able to get rid of the stuff that is wearing you down. Wake up in the morning and take each day as a brand-new day. With Parkinson's, every day I wake up I don't feel like a normal person. I feel slow and can't talk very well. I try to make a conscious effort of being positive and trying to say, "Alright, let's go. My kids want daddy so let's put on a happy face and get going." Before you know it, you are having another day and being positive. That's a good thing to do. Being positive every day. That will roll off on your wife, your teammates, and your coworkers.

**Eikenberry:** It plays an important role because energy is contagious - positive or negative - and without infusions of positive energy or enthusiasm, if you will, the energy in a group will tend to degenerate, not procreate. Someone has to be injecting the energy that we want. As leaders, we must be part of that.

**Beebe:** I don't think anyone enjoys being around someone that's negative all the time. I know I don't. I think you can give someone constructive criticism without being over the top with it. We see so many coaches out there that are driving these kids – negative, negative, negative all of the time – and there is no positive feedback. It's important to create an atmosphere that athletes will enjoy and believe they can achieve their tasks. Of course, sometimes you have to "kick their cans." Do it because you care about them, not because you're mad at them. That's the difference. I think that if every coach can do that they will reach the potential of every athlete or business employee that they have.

**Clark:** I think it's a huge role. I am definitely a "half full" guy, not a "half empty" guy. We're always talking about what's going to happen; X and Y are going to lead to Z. This is what's going to happen when you do these things that are not always easy to do. This is the benefit. We're talking positively all the time. I'm envisioning great things happening. I'm envisioning positive things happening, and we're going to talk about them. My faith is very important to me, and I think there's one thing we've learned from the Bible. It is that we speak these things - we speak blessings, we speak positive energy - and I believe those things happen.

**Crandall:** It's huge. In the book *Primal Leadership* - which is, I don't know how widely read, but certainly the concepts have been spread pretty wide - has this idea of emotional intelligence, which has become a bit of a buzzword. There's lots of different sources for it, but the science shows that emotions are contagious. I'm not a scientist, but I've read enough of this incredible research to show that a boss's bad mood is going to put everyone else in a bad mood. You can't fake positivity. I think some of the reaction to that is, "Well, let's not be 'rah-rah' when it's not called for." I'd agree with that 100%. But, if you look at some of the Walmart store leaders we talk to, they all get that how they walk in in the morning - what they look like at 8:00 am when they walk into their store - the checkers are looking at that and the assistant managers are looking at that. If they look pissed off and angry, that's going to be the mood of that store that day. I'm a huge believer in this idea that leaders need to bring themselves to the table with as much of a smile on their face as they can and a positive energy. I think it's crucial.

**Lubin:** It really depends. I think it is reading people and getting a better understanding. You need to realize how members of your team react to certain things. Some members need to be pumped up, extrinsically, to get them fired up, to say "Here, let's go tackle this task and make it happen." Others just need to be calmed down. A lot of people, they start thinking way too much. Their brain goes a million miles an hour, and they sort of have "diarrhea of the mouth" with ideas. Understanding that person, saying, "Alright, let's calm down. Let's get focused on what we're going to go after." The funny thing is that some people do much better when they're really pissed off. They have something to prove; that they have to go out there and get fired up in order to make something happen.

So, I think positive energy in leadership is key to success in leadership, but I think how to deal with certain people is more key to success than that in terms of leadership and what's going to make them tick.

# HOW TO LEAD MILLENNIALS

**What style of leadership have you found to be the most effective when leading Millennials?**

**Olson:** What we found - based on our conversations and experiences - not only with the athletes at the pro level, collegiate, youth, and high school but also with the coaches - at the end of the day, the number one thing that it has to be relationship-driven. A good friend of mine, Jeff Duke, he and I worked together on the three-dimensional coaching thing. That means you have to be competent and fundamentally sound, you have to be able to motivate, but at the end of the day, you have to be able to capture their hearts.

We all want relationships today. One of the things that social media has done to us, other than also make us view speed as "anything slow is bad," it has also made us realize - how many real relationships do we truly have with people we can go to and trust? I talk about and I challenge leaders when I speak to them - Do you have a Mount Rushmore? Do you have four people in your life that you can call anytime, anyplace, anywhere, and they will speak truth into you? Well, kids and players, even the pro guys, are starving to have real relationships with people. They've got 300,000 friends on Facebook, Twitter, Instagram, and Snapchat, but how many real relationships do we have?

So, the magic sauce, the secret sauce, in this day and age, for both the corporate leader and the sports leader, is pretty simple. You need to be able to have a healthy relationship with your athletes where they trust you, they know that you love them and care about them, and you also can also critique them and they will not resent you for it. In fact, they want you to. If you can create that climate, where you can have great relationships and hold people accountable at the same time, you've got something special. We believe this too, so I'll throw this in. We teach this a lot. There are three questions every athlete asks; we all ask these three questions of everyone who leads us, especially coaches:

1) <u>Can I trust you?</u> - Are you for real? Are you authentic? Are you just in this for yourself, or are you truly here to help me?

2) <u>Are you committed to excellence?</u> - Are you going to hold me to standards, or are you going to wash them just because I found a way to win? Are you going to truly hold me to the standard and make me commit to excellence?

3) <u>Do you care about me?</u> - I love a lot of people because I have to, because that's what my faith asks me to do. But, do I like them? Do I care about them? That's different. As a coach, we talk a lot about the twenty-first century athlete; you've got to make sure your athletes are cared about. It's a very, very important part of their motivation in everything they do.

**Beebe:** You have to realize that every person that ever walked the planet wants two things. They want to be disciplined, and they want to be cared about. I make it a huge priority to set the standards and the rules and stick by them. You've got to make them very clear to each player or employee of your team. When they break those rules, I try my hardest to discipline out of care, out of love. I want every player that played for me to say that I truly cared about them. My dad always told me, he said, "Son, this is going to hurt me much more in spanking you than the pain you're going to feel." I thought he was nuts, until I became a parent and a coach.

**Goldsmith:** I think the leadership style depends upon the situation. I'm a great believer in situational leadership, and the appropriate style of leadership should depend upon the readiness level of the person for the specific task. So, when the person, perhaps, is just not motivated or lacks ability, they may need structure and direction. When a person wants to learn and needs to learn, they should be coached and taught. When the person needs support, then you can give them encouragement and support. They lack confidence? Build their confidence. Finally, if the person is motivated and confident, leave them alone.

**Gordon:** The thing with leading Millennials and also - just first and foremost - with all leaders, everyone's going to have different styles. One thing I've learned is that you cannot adopt someone else's style. You have to lead what fits you and your style and who you are. Just because it doesn't work with someone else doesn't mean it's going to work with you. You may not have the same traits. You may not be as likeable as that person and so you can't get away with some of the things they get away with in challenging and pushing people, because that person's so likeable. If you push people they may think you're a jerk. You have to find your own style that fits.

Millennials – I think this is really improving people and improving people to be better leaders because Millennials want relationships with their leaders. They want to know that you care about them, that you value them. That's a key part of leadership. People are forced to develop relationships with these Millennials. They're forced to develop a relationship with them. In doing so, it's making them better leaders.

**Janssen:** I think it's huge to be extremely interactive and engaging. Obviously, you cannot lecture anymore. That's just going to turn people off. A lot of times I've heard it called "edutainment." You have to be very entertaining but educate in the process. You involve people in doing it. You create challenges for them. We often create in our leadership academies little teams within. They will compete with each other throughout the year, and we'll have a leadership challenge with them. I think that's a really important part – make it extremely interactive, practical, and relevant. But, it hits the topics and concerns that are going on in their minds right then and there.

Partnering with them; one of the things that we do in our academies is what we call "team time," where teams get an opportunity to assess where they are, currently, through a variety of tools. What they'll find is that in every season and every week, there are probably some things that need some time and attention. So, as a group, they put some time and attention into it. Then, we'll have leaders from the other teams who are there as well and they'll throw out, "Hey, this is what we're dealing with right now. Did any of you guys have a similar situation happen in the previous year?" Odds are, when you've got multiple teams in there, "Yeah, this same situation happened to us last year. We tried this, and it blew up in our face. So, don't do that. That's not what we're going to recommend." Then, another team will say, "Yeah, we had that happen two years ago. This is what we did. We did X, Y, and Z, and it really helped solve that problem." I think the more that you can partner with them and give them a chance to interact with, engage with, and help each other, it's that much more of an impactful experience and workshop.

**Isom:** This is right up my alley. This is what I'm passionate about because this is what I have observed in what I do over time. Millennials, this generation, are led well by vulnerability and honesty. I think that we are a generation that's tired of hearing the canned speeches. I think we're a generation that's so swamped with information that it's almost numbing. I think when someone stands up before a Millennial and starts with, "Man, here's my story. Let's connect. Me and you. Let's strip it all away. Let's just get raw. Let's get honest. Know that I'm human. I may be leading you by the organization's terms. I may be your superior, but I'm just your brother/sister here. Let's just get real. Let's get honest. Let's get raw. Let's just strip away the formality." Millennials drink it up. We're in a plastic culture and people are searching for a pulse. It's like people need to know they're not the only one struggling with something. They need to know they're not going at this alone. We're at this "fake it till you make it" society. It's like "fake it till you make it" era in time and people are just walking around faking it on the outside. I was too, in my personal story. They're just dying on the inside. They're dying for something real, honest, and true.

So, I really see the best leadership come out of vulnerability and honesty. When we open the door with that, it invites someone in to sit and learn under us, be led by us, or be influenced by us. It's crucial, and I want everyone to rise up and get honest and real. That's it to me. That is tried and true.

**White:** Not sure that I completely know, yet, what's most effective because, when you're an assistant coach, it doesn't matter what you say. You are not the head coach so everybody wants to listen. One of the things that I always wanted when I was a player was – look, I don't want to guess what you are thinking. I want you to be direct. I don't want you to beat around the bush; just tell me like it is. I also think you can be direct yet be thoughtful in the way that you communicate. For example, if somebody comes out of the game, the first thing they think when they come out of the game is, "What did I do wrong?" It doesn't always mean that you did something wrong. It just means we need to get somebody else in the game; or there's been a change in the way the game is being called; or there's been a change in the substitution from the other team. There is so much strategy involved that it's not always that you did something wrong. Communicating directly, in terms of that, on the floor – look, if I want you to run harder, I will tell you to run harder. I don't have to tell everybody in a broad sense that we're not doing this. No. You run harder, you play harder, you get on the floor after a loose ball. When you hold each individual accountable and you do it with respect, they always know where they stand. I think that is important.

I also think that you have to take a second to think about what you are saying in the moment. In the heat of the moment, you can say things that might be a little degrading or disrespectful, so you have to think about that. I also think that it is really important to develop relationships with Millennials. This is a relationship-driven generation, and they want to know that you care about them. They want to know that you have their best interest at heart. They are on the forefront of all of these social changes - things that they care about - so you have to know what they care about. You have to get to know them as people. You have to find their triggers; what motivates them to be better every single day? Is it their family? Is it a vision that they have in their head of their athletic success? Is it a vision that they have of their life success? Get to know them, and that will help you understand how to communicate with them and how to get the best out of them. Not everybody is the same way.

**Kouzes:** What we've found is that *The Five Practices* – Model, Inspire, Challenge, Enable, and Encourage – work as well with Millennials as with [Baby] Boomers and Generation Xers.

You don't have to change your style of leading or the practices you use to lead when working with different generations. Demographics aren't the key factor in engagement. It's your behavior. What is important to understand, however, is the context. The content of leadership is the same across various demographic groups. However, not only age but gender, ethnicity, country of origin, can change dramatically. For example, when I am in Saudi Arabia or the United Arab Emirates doing some work, it is a very different culture, and I have to understand that context compared to Alabama or California. When we are working with particular groups of people, we have to understand the context in which they work. Millennials, for example, entered the workforce at one of the worst economic times in decades. They also grew up at a time when they saw their parents being laid off from work more frequently than in previous generations. They learned some different lessons about the loyalty of employers and developed a different set of attitudes than we did. That's part of their context. If you take my dad, he grew up in a different kind of context. So, it's a matter of understanding the context, but the practices cut across all generations.

**Elmore:** You're right, this is on the minds of corporate America and certainly, [NCAA] Division I coaches. How do I connect with these players? I yell at them, and they don't want to respond? That sort of thing. I'll say some things at first, here briefly, that may be like "duh"; you already know them. But, let me venture into these waters. First of all, I think leaders need to know that leadership operates on the basis of trust. So, if you're leading a Millennial, and they don't trust you yet, you're not done winning them over. I don't care if you've got a bad "John" and you're paying him one hundred thousand dollars a year; if there's no trust - I believe people follow you only as close as they trust you. So, trust-based leadership means I've got to build a

relationship, and I need to be credible and show some integrity. Again, I just told the coaches yesterday of the New York Giants that we must build bridges of relationship that can bear the weight of truth. What I mean by that is, if you've got to share a hard truth and maybe give harsh feedback - maybe on

a play or a performance - I think I can only do that if I've earned my right to say something hard. Say that I believe in them, and I have their back and that sort of thing. Now, I can say the hard thing. I think Millennials have to be led through relationships.

I think we need to introduce, not just put up with, but introduce change often. I think change is their middle name. The average Millennial will change jobs about every year-and-a-half. They'll have five in their 20s, post college. In fact, somebody once said the corporate ladder has been replaced by the cooperate lily pad, where they are the frog hopping from lily pad to lily pad. We need to know that's not wicked or evil, that's just a new day. We win them over, we win them to stay, by the things we do.

Another thing is the Millennials that I know - and we are in front of tens of thousands every year - but the Millennials that I know want to do a job that they believe really matters. I don't know of anybody that wants to work in a factory making widgets - nothing wrong with that - but they want to do something that they feel like is connected. The dots are connected to something that actually improves the world in some way. So, if you're employing them as a volunteer or a paid team member, you better show how this work you're asking them to do is connected to a strategic thing, a mission, not just a job or a task. They want to feel like, "Yeah, we are improving the world in some way."

Every Millennial that I know wants to feel that they're personally growing as they do their job. They don't want to stay the same. I think leaders need to give themselves to development of other people – people development and team development. At Growing Leaders every Monday, we do a lunch-and-learn where it's personal growth learning at lunchtime. We buy the food for everybody on our team; it's all free. We develop them as leaders. In addition to that, we have book reviews – everybody's reading a book and we're giving book reviews - so we take turns sharing what we're learning. We do personal mentoring of all of our interns. So, we're trying to practice what we preach. Tons of Millennials on our staff - most of our staff is Millennials - but we just believe we keep them because we grow them. So, I'll stop there, but I think that's something every leader needs to know as they consider Millennials and leading Millennials.

**Clark:** A lot of the things we were all brought up on. Being a coach's son, I was brought up on doing the little things - the right things – and continually doing them over and over. Once again, I go back to this: How did I want to be coached? The thing that stood out for me was if I knew why we were doing it. Even though I was a coach – it's not even though I knew about hard work - just knowing why. I wanted to give more effort because I felt like I had a buy-in to it. That's one of the big things I try to give to my guys is "Okay, here's why we're doing it, and here's the end result. Now, let's go do it." When that happens, you're going to see people work harder.

**Anderson:** I have three Millennials that are in my administrative staff. I work closely with Millennials every day. Here is what I have found is important with Millennials. You've got to answer these three questions; it's not just about the head issues – pay, benefits, and that sort of thing. You have to also appeal to the heart. The head is important. Financial matters matter. But, number one: What do I have a chance to become working for you? Number two: What do I get a chance to become a part of working for you? Because I want to become more, but I also want to be part of something special. Number three: What difference do I have a chance to make working in this organization? I believe with Millennials, we have to do a compelling job of understanding those three aspects are very important to them and making sure that we're purpose-driven and that we are connecting with them in a way that helps them see that those needs are being met. I believe that helps them stay engaged and involved in a positive way in moving the company forward.

**Brubaker:** Millennials operate in a very unique way. They talk kind of like they text. They're going to communicate with you in 120-character sound bites, if you will. They are very digitally savvy. I think that when you're communicating with Millennials, the first thing they want to know - and it's a lot like if anyone's a parent and had a little kid, for the first few years that that kid can talk, they're saying one thing. The kids are curious, so are

Millennials. They say, "Why? Why, Daddy? Why, Mommy? Why, why, why?" to the point where the parent just - it drives you crazy. Well, Millennials are no different. They want to and they need to know the *why*. If you're asking them to execute a strategy and you don't explain the *why* in advance, even if it's a good idea, they're going to disagree with it.

I like what the philosopher Nietzsche said: "People can handle almost any *what* if they understand the *why* involved." So, if you don't have millennials involved directly in the decision and understanding the *why* in your rationale behind an initiative, or if you're not asking them for feedback and giving them explanations, they're never going to buy into it. The great companies, the ones that Millennials are actually willing to stay at and see themselves advancing within, are the ones where their manager or leader is explaining the *why* every step of the way. Make the message so clear, not that they understand it, but that it's impossible for them to misunderstand. I think there's a big difference. When you can communicate the *why* and present a compelling future for them, they will buy in.

You have to remember, you've got to address the WIIFM – "What's in it for me?" Every Millennial's favorite radio station is WIIFM. If there's not something tangible or intangible in it for them, they're going to be disengaged. We're all operating with the same sort of software system, but they are hypersensitive to it. They can sniff it out if you've been less than genuine. So, communicate the *why* and understand they need to know what's in it for them.

**Lubin:** This is an interesting question. I think the Millennials are the key to our future. The advantage that they have over the rest of society is absolutely amazing. If you look at Generation X, Generation Y, or the Baby Boomers, what the Millennials are learning in days and weeks took us years and years to learn.

I think Millennials are going change the world in the next fifty years, change the world more than anyone else has in the last 2,500 years. I don't know if you're familiar with Moore's Law, but the Millennials are like Moore's Law on steroids. Everything's doubling. The amount of information is doubling every eighteen months. These folks are the key to our success moving forward.

With that being said, they're some of the most independent and creative people that I know. And I think in order to lead them, you have to be able to allow them to keep that independence, to keep that creativity, but to teach them process, discipline, and social interaction. A lot of Millennials in today's world are so used to just texting, using Facebook, or using means of electronics to communicate versus picking up the phone or going to see someone.

So, I think those are some of the leadership issues leaders are going to deal with in the future because people are people, and they love to communicate face-to-face. That changes. Communication styles have changed, but social interaction is going to be a key to dealing with Millennials in the future.

**Medcalf:** Once again, I think it comes back to everything we've been talking about. Modeling and the importance of modeling. Also, really making them feel loved and valued unconditionally for who they are as people. I think that once they know that you love them and that you care about them, then you can hold them to a higher standard. There's one girl on our team at UCLA, she's like my little sister, and she's probably the most talented kid on the team, if you will. She was the MVP in the McDonald's All-American game. I tell her all the time, "I'll tell our head coach to kick you out of practice. If you're not doing everything up to the best of your ability that's controllable, then I'll tell her to kick you out of practice." That's what true love is. It's holding you to a really high standard of what you're capable of doing. It's not doing that in a mean way. It's not yelling at you. It's not cussing you out. It's just saying, "Do you want to get better, or do you want to go home?" Then, if you don't change from there, it's, "You've lost the privilege to get better today."

It's kind of like what John Wooden did with Bill Walton when he showed up with facial hair to get on the bus. He was like, "Man, Bill, the facial hair looks great," and he said, "but you know you can't play on our team with that. So you've got to go figure that out, man." He didn't yell at him. He didn't do what most people today would have done, which is, "Get on the bus. I can't believe that you did this and this is ridiculous and now we have to stop at Walgreens and you're going to go in and you're going to pay for shaving cream and a razor with your own money." No, he's like, "Man, Bill, facial hair looks great. Unfortunately, you can't play on our team." He just enforced the healthy boundary with love and respect.

That's what I think this generation is desperately craving because, for a lot of them, they didn't get that at home. They got a lot of that positive leadership in terms of making them feel good, never making them do stuff that made them uncomfortable, giving them what they wanted a lot, and telling them how amazing they are. It's not that they're not amazing. It's just that we're all created fearfully and wonderfully by God. I believe that we're all created for a purpose. But, at the end of the day, I think that they want to reach their fullest potential, but they have no clue how to get there. We need to really pour into their life and help them know that we care about them so much but that we're not manipulating them. We're not trying to get results out of them. We're modeling it for them, we're putting their heart first, we're holding really high standards for them, we're enforcing healthy boundaries, but we're doing it with love and respect.

**Eikenberry:** I don't focus on that as much as some do, but I think that what Millennials want is to be engaged, to be in a place where they can make a difference, and to continue to learn. In the end, I don't think that's any different than what anyone else wants. It's just that they grew up in a time where, maybe, they thought that they could ask for more of what they wanted and get it. We make a mistake when we try to change everything to meet the needs of Millennials. I think we have to recognize that. What we're really talking about are the needs of people. If we keep that in mind, and we set clear expectations - there are some people that are spending a lot of time saying, "Well, we've got to change everything because of this Millennial workforce." We need to recognize some tweaks, but we also need to recognize that it's human nature. If there are job expectations that are required, then we need to make those expectations clear.

**Gray:** In order to lead Millennials, I believe that you have to tap into their deep desire to make a difference. So many Millennials are really hardwired that way. They're not thinking about legacy. They're thinking about what they can do to make a positive difference long before I ever was.

Early on in my career, I was just trying to make a paycheck, and to figure out what I was going to do to provide for my family. I think Millennials just have this innate sense of, "I want to do something meaningful. I want work for a charity or not for profit. I want to change the world." At the same time, I think that sometimes they can be shortsighted. I shouldn't say that with any judgmental tone, but I think that sometimes they may not take the long view about life. They may not understand that this is a marathon, not a sprint. I see a lot of them trying to sprint to the finish line, and, sometimes, they get a little tuckered out as they go. I want to be the encourager. I want to be the guy that says, "Good job!" I do a lot of pride speaking in my job, in my life, where I'm constantly telling young people "Good work! You're doing awesome! Keep it up!" But, I do find that it takes an added measure of perseverance on my part to make sure that I'm encouraging them so that they can take a longer view, and I can also make sure to tap into their deep need to make a difference. But in my world I'm constantly doing that, and I encounter communities of people that want to make a difference.

I did this yesterday with a young man. I was at a business meeting at the finest children's museum in America. We walked up to buy some food in the cafeteria when I encountered a young man behind the counter. I stopped, looked at him, and asked him a question. He felt heard. He felt encouraged. I gave him my business card and said, "If you're serious about wanting to make a difference," because he heard me talking about mentoring and the things that I'm involved in. He said, "I want to do that." And I'm like, "Okay. Well, let me listen." So I heard him, and then I gave him my card, and I said "If you're serious, be careful what you wish for, because I'm going to get you involved in mentoring. I'm going to give you people to serve, lead, and teach." I bet I will hear from this young man soon. I just hope he's willing to stay the course, take a long view, and understand that serving takes time and energy. That's my quick coaching when it comes to leading Millennials, which I've got a lot to learn. But, maybe, I have a few ideas that would help someone.

**Woodfin:** That's a great question and one that I need to get a lot better at. As I grow in this industry, I'm going to be leading more and more of these Millennials. I really haven't had a ton when I was in the NFL; most of those guys were not Millennials. Obviously, Millennials are extremely tech-savvy. They're locked in to social media like never before and everything that comes with that.

What I've tried to start doing is communicating and educating through social media. I found that's one way to lead them, whether it's leadership quotes, positivity quotes, or whatever the message is that I want to get across to my team. I know they're all on social media, so I've really started using those platforms to speak to them. Then, I'll follow that up when I see them face-to-face, whether that being training or practice, and hit them with the same messages through social media and then face-to-face.

I also think that the Millennials are looking for someone that actually does what they say they do. They're looking for people that treat them with respect. I think they like autonomy; they like the ability to make their own choices. Going back to looking for someone that does what they say they're going to do - I try to be consistent, have integrity, and follow through with every little minor detail when it comes to leading. I try to give them choices, if it's possible. Let them make some decisions, whether it be what exercises they're going to choose training-wise or any decision that I can have them make. I think autonomy is a big link to motivation. It's a big link to getting people to follow; letting them make some choices, as long as there are certain parameters on those choices. Those are a few of the things I'm doing currently to lead these guys. I'm open to all suggestions because I definitely have to continue to grow with communicating and leading those types of kids in the next generation.

**Crandall:** I'm going to go in a different direction and say I think that stuff is overblown. I think that the leadership becomes a little too much like, "I need to be a certain way." First of all, it's not about you. I agree with that, and I talked about some of the texting. You have to be cognizant of the ways they like to communicate and things like that. But, ultimately, if you go back to Bennis's quote I mentioned earlier, "We become leaders at the moment we decide for ourselves to be." He later goes on to say, "When people know that you know what you believe and why you believe it, that inspires them." They can trust you because you're an open book and have integrity. If those things are in place, then it's really not about very specific things you need to do with different groups of people. Authenticity would say that being yourself is the best way to go about it. Honestly, I don't lead the young guys that I coach in basketball any differently than I led in the mid-90s when I was in the army. I try to know what I believe, why I believe it, try to be humble, and care about the people I lead. That seems to work pretty well.

**McCabe:** That's a good question, and I think that's why it threw me when I first started my business four and half years ago, formally (I was doing it for about eight years). I was kind of passive. I wanted people to find their own pathway. As teachers, as coaches, as leaders; when a player, student, or employee has their own "aha moment" - when they figure it out – there's nothing more powerful than that. So, I held back. I would say, "Oh, you'll get this, you'll get that," and I wasn't as active. It's a challenge I always have because I believe that people need to find their own "aha moment." However, I think the style is a little bit more. People come to me, I would say, because they want help. The other thing is, they want help for the current conflict. Many times, we see the other things that we can fix down the road, but they don't care about that. They want the current conflict. So, be active, be actively engaged, give them the plan, and move them to their "aha moment." Then after that, engage to move on later to the other things.

# MANAGING CONFLICT

**Within a team, there is always some form of conflict among personalities, personal interests, or standards. What do you think is the best way to manage these?**

**Gordon:** Conversation, communication, connection. Don't avoid it. Don't let it get swept under the rug. There's the elephant in the room, as people like to say. You've got to deal with that elephant. You've got to make sure you bring things out in the open, and what you uncover and deal with could then be covered with grace, love, and an ability to move forward. Whatever issues are confronting your team and organization, deal with it and then you'll be stronger because of it.

**Janssen:** Number one - finding people who are a good fit in the first place. If you're not doing a good job either selecting, recruiting, or hiring people and you're bringing people in who do not share your vision, your values, and/or your standards, you're just asking for problems on the front end. So, number one, you've got to find people who are a great fit. You don't all have to be clones in terms of your personalities, but you do have to have that common goal.

After that, establishing clear expectations on the front end. This is what we're going for; this is what's expected of you. Have a very clear scoreboard of results of how we're doing along the way. Are we three-quarters of the way there? Are we only one-eighth of the way there? People can gauge - having that scoreboard - so they know where they are.

Lastly - communicating very frequently. When people are doing a great job, rewarding them and letting them know, "Hey, this is exactly what we're looking for. We really appreciate this." At the same time, when they're falling short, "Hey, remember, we agreed to do this. You're not there right now. What are we going to do in the next week or so to close that gap that appears to be there right now?"

**Goldsmith:** I wrote an article about this called "Team Building without Time Wasting." If anybody would like a copy they can send me an e-mail. In the article, what I suggest is that every team member gets something called "feed-forward" from the other team member. They ask him how they get better be a contributor to the team, everyone makes important behavior to improve, they develop a rigorous follow-up process, and measure change. I've done this with a myriad of teams. I've never seen it fail.

**White:** A certain amount of differentiating personalities is good. I don't know that prior to being at the professional level I would have said that. There are certain players that I watch play that I don't like their body language; or I don't like their facial expressions; or I don't like certain things that they do by watching them. But, if I have a player that's like that, I want to go to battle with them every single day because they're sacrificing for their team. I might not always like the way they go about it. Certainly, no matter what, everybody has to be "all in" for the greater good of the team. If there are selfish interests that can't be set aside for the betterment of your team, then that person just has to go.

Players live up - or down - to the expectation level that we have for them. You need to be consistent and open with your communication from the beginning, that there is no gray area. I can coach players that have different personalities. I can coach players that have different interests and different standards. But when you step between the lines, we're all in it for the same reasons. We have the expectation levels that everybody comes to work every single day. If you don't come to work for the betterment of yourself and our team every single day, then I don't want you to be a part of our franchise. Those expectations have to be laid out there to start. If somebody doesn't want to be on the bus - Jon Gordon, there you go - they can get left behind. Life is too short. Our opportunities are too short. If you've lost a chance to get better, if you've lost a chance to help our team, and you don't want to get on the bus, then we don't need you to be a part of it.

There is a certain level of handling and managing personalities and managing interest. There is a difference in whether those are selfish or unselfish in just the way that they are communicated. A lot of that stuff is open to misinterpretation. A lot of our players have grown up in different backgrounds. They have different family dynamics. They come from different socio-economic circumstances. One person may respond in one way and another responds in another. Does that mean that either of them or anyone of them are less into it for the team? Not necessarily. Again, it's how we channel that into a positive direction for our team. That's one thing that I feel like I've gotten a lot better at, is not judging the book by its cover. It's not making those first impressions on the court be those lasting impressions in your mind. Getting to know what motivates the players and getting a feel for them. If they're on the bus, we're all in together. If they're not, then we just move on.

**Kouzes:** Diversity in the workplace is increasing. There will likely be more differences in views rather than fewer. At the same time, what we know from our research is that shared values increase commitment. When there is agreement on standards, people are more successful. People are more willing to work harder, people are experiencing more teamwork and collaboration, and they feel less stressed at work. Therefore, the critical leadership variable is getting agreement on those standards against which we can all hold ourselves accountable.

So, when it comes down to a difference, we have some kind of internal compass that allows us to find our direction. We can go back and say, "One of the things we believe in is collaboration. One of the things we believe in is innovation. One of the things we believe in is accessibility." Whatever the values are and whatever those standards are. I remember one coach saying, "There is no better coach than the bench." I think that was Anson Dorrance, UNC Women's Soccer Coach. When people are behaving in ways that are outside of those standards, there is no better coach than the bench.

That's the primary strategy. Of course, it's important when we're dealing with differences and conflicts that we – as another friend of mine used to say – "grow big ears." One of the things that people want to know about leaders is that they understand and are empathetic with where we're coming from even if we don't end up agreeing. But they understand,. listening to why there are the differences, where people are coming from, and using our agreed-upon values as the decider. What will enable us to make decisions? In organizations, there needs to be a good fit between the person and the organization. One of the things that values and standards do is help us to determine whether there is a good fit.

**Eikenberry:** The first thing about managing conflict is it isn't necessarily something to avoid. You do not want an organization with zero conflict. If we're all on exactly the same page all of the time, we're missing something. You need the creative tension that comes with people having a slightly different perspective. I actually want some conflict but not conflict in a negative, emotional way. We need to be able to healthily have differences of opinion. The lack of conflict is not the right answer. The problem is when conflict is avoided, ignored, and grows to the point where it's no longer healthy. It becomes unhealthy. Our job as a leader is to get in front of that, not with the intention of getting rid of all the conflict, but making sure that the conflict that does exist doesn't become emotional, personal, and therefore, detrimental.

**Elmore:** The first thing I would say is try to cut it off before it happens. We try to hire the culture we want. I think most of the conflict usually happens because of a clash in culture, meaning somebody has different values they bring in and it doesn't align with other people or the organization. So, if you think about it, every culture has three components: values, customs and language.

If you and I traveled over to France, we would notice that they have certain customs in France, they have certain values that they have there, and they speak French. Every athletic team, every business, and every school has a culture with language, customs, and values. When you have conflict, it is usually at one of those levels. We're saying things wrong, we don't value the same things, or we just have different habits in our life. Usually, I call them back to alignment. I would sit down and confront it. I call them back to, "Where we are not aligned here?" and hopefully, it doesn't mean somebody has to leave. But, I would only keep them if they can say, "I can align here." I don't think I'm doing a service to them if I'm keeping somebody around that just cannot – they're just going to be at odds with where the organization is going or where some key people are going.

**Anderson:** I think that conflict is often underrated. Many leaders, especially the weaker ones, will shy away from it and try to ignore it rather than flush it out. I think that best form of conflict is in a meeting, not whispering by the watercooler. We have two areas in our offices where we meet. We have a formal conference area, and we have a separate area that we call the "living room." That's where we have most of the conflict. The "living room" is where we brainstorm. There's a sign on the wall that says, "None of us is smarter than all of us." This is where we really have debates about our ideas, marketing, products, and so forth. I believe that in that type of atmosphere - where everybody puts their egos aside and lives the values - conflict brings about clarity. Conflict ensures every side of an issue is being examined. I also believe that the worst decisions people make - I've done my share of them - are made void of conflict. Too much harmony, I believe, is cancerous to decision making. I believe in that type of an arena, I can throw out an issue and I can say, "Okay gang, here is what I'm thinking about doing. Shoot some holes in it." We can have a good, robust debate. Then, here's what everybody also understands: Once the decision's made, the conflict ends. The debate ends. Colin Powell said it very well. He said, "When we're debating an issue, being loyal to me means giving me your opinion whether you think I like it or not. At that stage, disagreement stimulates me. But, once the decision's been made, the debate ends. From there on, being loyal means getting out there and executing the decision as if it were your own." That's really the model we use here. Organizations where there are a lot of politics is because they don't have that open dialogue. People are talking about it in the meeting after the meeting. We want to get it all out so there's nothing to talk about later.

**Medcalf:** I typically try and have people read a book called *How to Stop the Pain*, which really focuses on observing people's behavior versus judging it. You're observing somebody's actions, and based off their actions, you're setting up and enforcing healthy boundaries versus judging their behavior. We get ourselves into so many problems and create so much drama by judging people's behavior, it's not even funny. To give you a concrete example of that: If you're walking down the street and somebody tells you - a person that lives on the street says, "You're going to burn in hell," and cusses you out and calls you all these horrible names. For most people that's not going to have a tremendous impact on their life. But, if your dad said that to you, for most people that could be a watershed moment in your life where everything goes downhill from there. People hold onto that for decades. It's the exact thing that happened, but it actually came from our internal response to it. Internally, we judge one of those to be significant, and we judge one of them not to be significant. So, really trying to let go of a lot of that judgment and really just focusing on what somebody did.

What we need to do is identify behavior and focus on the behavior versus focusing on who the person is. Once you put somebody in a box like that, then everything goes downhill from there. I think that on a lot of different teams, that's really what it comes down to. We go, "Oh, he's so selfish, he's so arrogant, he only cares about himself," and we're basically just labeling and judging everything that happens versus going, "You know what? I had $10 that disappeared out of my car the last time I gave this guy a ride. So, I'm going to not give him rides any more or I'm going to make sure that all of my valuables are secured the next time I give him a ride." Just trying to observe people's behaviors, create and enforce healthy boundaries versus judging all their behaviors. That's typically what I try and do.

I think it's a much bigger issue in female sports, in my experience, than it is in male sports. I think that males are so achievement-driven. They want to win. That's how I was. I had a fixed mindset growing up. I was trying to prove myself, and I just cared about winning. I was willing to do whatever it took to help us win, which still is not the most beneficial mindset that we can have. But, I think that type of interpersonal dynamic is a much bigger challenge when it comes to the female sports than it does with male sports.

**Gray:** Conflict will always be among us. Organizations and enterprises, especially when you've got differing styles of leadership, are always going to have some degree of conflict. I think that's okay. I think there can be healthy conflicts that really drive an organization forward.

I was in a meeting earlier today where I was addressing a very complex issue with multi-causal issues, and it really had long-term implications. We were talking about a five-year plan which, in a business setting, is a pretty long horizon to look at a particular business issue. We were debating an issue - there were men and women at the table - and I had a moment of conflict with a particular leader who had a different perspective on a matter. I just stopped and listened. I wanted her to feel heard. I edified her position. You know, "I hear that you think that," echoing back to her perspective. Then, I stopped and was able to speak and say, "But my perspective is this." By the end of the meeting, it was like we were echoing back to each other and we landed at a great outcome. We actually had a breakthrough thought that we would not have otherwise had had we not let that conflict - that uncomfortable moment - rise up and learn from it and, at the end, break through. It doesn't always work that way in meetings, but, when it does, powerful things can happen. I believe conflict can be used in a positive way.

Think about it in sports too, right? There's conflict on the field on every single play. In football, you've got eleven guys trying to do something on the offense, and you've got eleven guys on the defense trying to stop the eleven that are trying to do something. That's a pretty interesting dynamic. So, in that conflict can come opportunities to overcome, learn, and grow. So, that's the way I see it, and that's my perspective.

**Beebe:** I think it's really easy. Talk about them as a team (individually and together). It's called investment. I believe as a coach, you've got to invest in your kid's life. It shows you care, and the player is more willing to open up to you if you show them that you care about them. Then, you can find out what really makes this athlete tick. I think you'll get a whole lot higher level of play from them when you create that kind of atmosphere.

**Brubaker:** Some people look at conflict as a bad thing. I actually think conflict is a good thing. There's got to be a certain amount of tension in a relationship to get two-way communication. I look at it like we're each holding an end of a rope. The only way we can move that rope where we want it to go is if we're both holding onto it and there's a certain amount of tension on the line there. Otherwise, it's dragging on the ground, one person's trying to pull one end, and, even worse yet, the person on the other side is trying to push the rope. You can't push a rope. I think tension is something that needs to be embraced, but there needs to be professional boundaries in how we communicate.

I think the best leaders create an environment in meetings, whether it's brainstorming or a marketing team meeting. Sure, there's a CEO in the room, a CFO in the room, there are managers, vice presidents, and an array of employees of different levels in the hierarchy in the corporate structure. But, when you're in that room together, the people are rank-less. It's I'm John, you're Matt, she's Sally, and he's Bob. It's not the CEO, the CFO, the marketing manager, and you're not looking down the corporate hierarchy and you're not looking up. It's lateral. Everybody really has equal status and stature. When you have that, people have the ability to be heard and a greater ability to listen because you feel like you're on the same level. That's really the most important thing; embracing tension and understanding that instead of information traveling down from above, it needs to travel laterally.

Be willing to hear feedback from down-to-above as opposed to just above-to-down. I think that the mark of a great leader is how they treat their janitor, how they treat their groundskeeper, and to be willing to accept feedback from anybody in the company as opposed to simply delegating and giving orders. Everyone has something to bring to the table to make the company better, to make the team better. But, if you're not willing to listen - and there's a difference - you personalize something as criticism instead of accepting feedback as a critique that can improve the team. That goes back to the great collision between athletics and corporate America. When you're in the locker room, everyone's considered an equal. Sure, some people have bigger roles. Some people are captains or starters, but you're peers. You're all rowing the boat in the same direction. There's a lot to be learned from that in the corporate setting.

Dr. Stephen Covey did some great research on people from all levels of an organization, knowing the company's mission and how their role aligned with the mission. What he found was that six out of 11 people in a company don't understand how their role ties in with the mission of the organization or ties in with how a product is produced and brought to market. Can you imagine that in a team setting? That's the equivalent of six of your players on the soccer team trying to kick the ball in the wrong goal. They're trying to shoot it into their own net. That would never happen on a sports team, but it happens every day in corporate America because leadership isn't really, really, super clear about your role contributing to the end result.

I think that in every company you're going to have people doing menial jobs, and you're going to have people doing really high-profile, "important" jobs. When I say "important," I mean the perception is that it is an important job. In reality, you look at the person welding two pieces of metal together; if they don't get that right, the end product is going to have defects and flaws. The "important" job, the person that's delivering the project – that's not going to work either. One of the greatest companies that I've seen demonstrate just how important everyone's role is, is a local company (I live in Maine) in Berwick called Hussey Seating. If you've ever been in the New England Patriots' stadium in Foxborough, all the seats are manufactured by Hussey Seating. What their leadership team has done - Tim Hussey is their CEO - what's he done is a couple of years ago. They were renovating all of the seating at the University of New Hampshire's arena. They manufacture bleacher seats, bench seats, theatre-style seats, chairs, and all kinds of seats for sports venues. What he did was he took every single person in the company by charter bus to the arena to see the finished product, to see the installation, sit in the chairs, have some food, and then, later that day, I believe they even stayed and watched a game when the arena opened.

It's a great example of how you're not just welding two pieces of metal together. Here's how what you do contributed to the finished product. It helped build an arena, really. You talk about having alignment between sales, customer service, manufacturing, and really investing in your people. There was a significant expense that went into closing the shop for a day, especially when you're a manufacturing shop bussing people down one state away and feeding them. That's an investment, but it pays dividends because they get to see how their individual role contributes to the team's success. I just wish more companies would take a page out of that very playbook and show people exactly how their role aligns with the end result.

**Clark:** I think you cut those things off at the pass. We're talking about family. Brothers are going to have arguments. Sisters are going to have arguments. But, we never destroy the family and never disrupt the family. That's a constant management; cutting things off at the pass and not letting things fester. It's a daily job - seven days a week, 24 hours a day. We're always monitoring. We're always looking at our situations and our workings with our players. That's the way things don't ever get out of hand.

**Crandall:** That's a lot of what we're discussing in this book, *Say Anything*. We really believe organizations would be better off if people can say exactly what they're thinking. In the book we focus, for the sake of really making it clear and simple for people - not simple because they're not smart but simple because this stuff is complicated. We talk about "led to leader." We want the person you're leading to be able to come into your office one-on-one and say whatever they're thinking. But if they can do that and a leader establishes that climate, then within groups, that's going to carry over into the culture of that organization or the climate of that group to where people can say those things.

At the center of the book we talk about one key idea that everything rests on, this notion of positive intent. When people say things, you have to decide, despite their tone of voice or however it might come out, you've got to make the conscious decision that they're saying it with positive intent, that they're saying it to make the organization better. I think if you build that sort of trust you can get through almost any sort of conflict. Absolutely, stuff has got to be transparent. I'm a believer in talking about whatever. In groups, really getting out their true feelings. I don't think there is any downside to that if you do it correctly.

"If you're in a low trust situation, it doesn't matter how well you measure your words, the other person will misinterpret you. In a high trust situation, it doesn't matter what you say, the other person will assume you meant well."

When thinking about conflict, if you have that sort of trust, you can talk about anything. If you don't have it, you can't, and the conflict will grow into disaster.

# COMMUNICATING AT A HIGH LEVEL

**What role does communication play in the effectiveness of leading your team?**

**White:** Communication is the number one, most important component in anything that you do. On a team, in your personal life, in any organization - there has to be open and honest communication. It has to be a two-way communication. One-way, direct, dictatorship-like communication will not work.

**Isom:** Everything. It is the biggest role. I think it is one of the most important things, and I think it's crucial that a good leader listens with the intent to understand, rather than just the intent to respond. I think that it is important that a leader speaks from the right place - from a neutral ground within them, not just their opinion or thoughts, but with the group's greater goal in mind. That they choose their words wisely. Like I said when I alluded to my husband being one of the greatest leaders I know, ultimately, when they speak, people listen. That is only developed through respect, through character, and through going about all the small things the right way. So, when it's time for a big thing as a leader, people listen and you're speaking intentionally. You're listening with the intent to understand them, and you're allowing them to freely speak in many circumstances. Communication is crucial. Totally key. I really think it's one of the biggest roles in leadership and in leading well.

**Petrick:** Huge. I mean, talking about transparency, communication is so good. It has to be both ways, too. It can't just be the player going to the coach. Sometimes, the coach needs to be honest, share what he feels about certain things, and not try to keep things bottled up. Communication, in any relationship in life, is vital to the success of that relationship. I think in leadership, obviously, communication is going to play a big role.

**Kouzes:** We always ask this question in regard to communication this way, "Do you trust people more whom you know or don't know?" I trust more people that I know. That's true for all of us. I'm sure there are people you know and there are people I know really well I don't trust at all. Generally speaking, we tend to trust people more whom we know. One of the important roles communication plays is in building trust. It's that skill set which enables us to get to know other people. We sit down, we talk, we listen, we communicate, and we engage in dialogue. It also is a way for us to disseminate information about who we are, the direction in which we're headed, or why we made a particular decision in the way we did it. When people get that kind of information and when there's that kind of self-disclosure, it's empowering to other people.

Communication is vitally important, particularly in times of change, challenge, adversity, and volatility. People just need more information when there is a crisis, difficulty, or challenge than they do when things are stable and everything is going along well. Communication plays an important role in building trust and maintaining trust as well as in making people feel empowered with information to do their work.

**McCabe:** It's critical, right? Remember, it comes back to having a clear vision of where you want to take the organization. If people don't understand it, they're lost. If a general says, "Just march west. I'm not going to tell you why, but just keep marching west," people are going to doubt it every step. They don't know what they're even looking for. There are all kinds of great resources out there on the internet about coaches that have taken over teams or businesses. Whoever took over Ford way back when said, "This is what we're going to be, and it's a clear vision." You've got to continually share the vision week in and week out. It's why I hate mission statements and vision statements. It's why I hate goals. We spend so much time creating them and no time living them. I've worked in organizations where we've had two-day retreats on developing a mission statement. It comes back and sent out to everybody in an e-mail. They print out a placard, put it up on the wall as you walk to restroom, and everybody walks by it every day. Nobody lives it.

But, it's getting people to buy in to a common goal. What do they do? They consistently communicate on a platform so that everybody's aligned on a daily basis. It's amazing. We can learn a ton from looking at how religious organizations do that. It's one message. They'll stay on that message for six weeks. Then they'll move to a new message.

What do businesses do? "Hey, we're going to try this today. Oh, it didn't work. We're going to move to the next one." What do coaches do? "Hey, we're going to try this new line-up. Oh, it didn't work, so we'll try another line-up. We're trying to spark." Stick with it. Everything we do in life is a marathon; it's not a sprint. There is nothing that we do that's a sprint.

**Eikenberry:** It's absolutely critical. I've never worked in an organization that didn't think that their communication couldn't get better. I mean, everybody thinks communication is a problem and needs to get better. That's true in any relationship, in a team, and in an organization. The role it plays is paramount. You can't, ultimately, have a highly successful organization where there isn't the ability to successfully communicate.

**Lubin:** Communication is key. It's a two-way street. You need to be honest and open, but more importantly, you need to determine the best way to communicate. Like learning, people learn in different ways. Some people learn better by reading, some people learn better by writing, some people learn better by listening, some people learn better by seeing. I think communication is the same way. In order to be an effective communicator, you have to determine their communication style in order to successfully communicate with the right people, in the right mindset, and the right frame of mind.

**Clark:** I think it's everything. I think there's so many good ways to communicate now: through social media - it can be such a negative but we want to use it for the positive - texting our players, positive tweets, and positive things on social media. Taking the tools we have and use them to our advantage. I expect our coaches to be meeting with our players constantly about what's going on in their lives, their families, etc. More than just "What is this pass route?" or "What is this defense?"

**Elmore:** Well, it's gigantic. I love communication. In fact, one of our *Habitudes* books is purely on the art of effective communication. I just have a hard time separating effective leadership from good, clear communication. I think the problem is, very often, the training we receive, formally, is for us to be orators or public speakers, not communicators. The big difference there, for me, is I think a public speaker is all about, "I have this content I have to download." A communicator is more, "No, I want to make sure I'm getting through so I'm reading the people before I lead the people." One is about being polished. The other is about being personal. One is about completing the message. The other is about completing the people, if you know what I mean.

I think what people long for in communication is authencity. The way I can answer briefly is to share one of our images. It's called Windows and Mirrors. Here's what I've noticed. When a leader is up front and communicating with their team, if they would take a moment and get transparent – in other words, if they could pull back the curtain on their own soul and share an authentic story from their own life, maybe a struggle from their own life - if they'll give a window to themselves, they automatically provide a mirror for the listeners to see their own. You give them windows; they receive mirrors.

I think so often as leaders we are afraid to be vulnerable. We don't want them to see our weaknesses or our flaws. No coach wants to share what a "bonehead" thing he did or she did. I think that's what followers are wanting. They say, "Please show me that - I already know that you're not perfect - but please admit it." That sort of thing. I just think it's winsome when we communicate transparently and authentically. A number of times every month I'll get up in front of the team and say, "You know what? I really failed at this." I feel like they love me more because I'm at least saying it out loud. They all know I did. So, I'll stop there and say that we've got to learn how to be good communicators. I think transparent communication is at the top of the list of the needs of the day, at least for the Millennials, for sure.

**Gordon:** It's everything. Communication builds trust. Trust generates commitment. Commitment fosters teamwork. Teamwork delivers results. Most relationships and teams break down because of poor communication. Remember this: Where there's a void in communication, negativity will fill it. You always have to make sure you fill that void with positive communication, with frequent communication. The more you do, you don't get that negativity. It doesn't breed and grow. You don't get the gossip, you don't get the rumors, you don't get the uncertainty, and you don't get the fear. You get all the things when you have great communication that make you stronger and not weaker.

**Anderson:** I'm a big believer that the more gray area you have in a culture, the weaker it is. Performance decreases in direct proportion to the increase of gray within a culture. There's nothing better than good communication to eliminate gray areas. We have to constantly talk about things like vision, values, expectations, and mission. These are all cultural issues. We have to get fast, honest, specific, direct feedback to people so they know where they stand. If they're great, they've got to know it. If they're failing, they need to know that, too. I believe that communication keeps us on the same page with a common agenda. There's no such thing as over-communicating. People say, "Well, what if I over-communicate the vision too much?" I say, "You're never going to do that. You're far more likely to under-communicate it." About the time you're sick of saying certain things is about the time people are starting to get it. So, it's absolutely vital to keeping a culture robust and people focused on what matters most every day.

**Brubaker:** I think that communication needs to be built with a foundation of trust. Without trust, you don't have anything as a leader. You don't have credibility, you don't have two-way communication, and you don't have a relationship. Whether you're a company of two people and you're talking about your business partner, if you're a Fortune 500 company, or if you're an athletic team with a roster at 85 - a football team, maybe - if you can't communicate effectively and have that level of trust as the foundation, you've got nothing. How important is trust? There's a great study done by the Forum Company out of Boston when it comes to sales. What they found was that 99% of all sales people can equally communicate – there's that word again - the features and benefits of their product or service. This is across all industries. What they found the 1% could do better than everyone else was build trust. Trust is the quintessential aspect of the communication process. Anyone who is listening to this has invested in this product because they want to get from where they are to that next level. They want to go from being among the 99% to the 1%, and that is exactly how you do it.

You build trust with people. Take the sales process, for example. It's the difference between manipulation and facilitation. It's the difference between doing something *to* somebody to accomplish what your end game is and doing something *for* somebody to help them get what they want. I think if you can help other people get what they want, that's really leadership. Getting people to *want* to do what you want them to do and to get them on board in a way that they want to do it too, and you've aligned those goals. Building trust is the key.

**Janssen:** I think it's huge. One of the things that we do with each of our academies when we set them up is have a primary point person that we will be in contact with for a variety of things. Whether it's setting up workshops or gauging how things are going, we really want to have one primary point of contact that we're always staying connected with at that school.

Then, with coaches – a huge part of our academies isn't just working with the student-athletes. When I first started off, I would do some programs that were just with the student-athletes or just with the coaches. But a lot of times, there was a little bit of a disconnect there. So, now, our main approach is working with both groups. When we meet with the coaches, the first 10-15 minutes we spend saying, "Okay, this is what we did with your emerging leaders last night. This is what we emphasized. This is how we asked them to follow up with you. These are some simple things that you can do later on this week with them or even in today's practice." Same thing with the student-athletes. "This is what we did with your coaches. This is what they will probably be coming to you with." We want to keep all of those layers of leadership on the same page. And, obviously, need to use communication – frequent, clear, and followed up upon – so that everybody is on the same page and knows what's expected of them.

**Goldsmith:** It's very important for the leader to be an effective communicator because, in leadership, it doesn't matter what you say. It only matters what they hear. Sometimes, leaders are lost, and they think communication is that if I understand what I'm saying then they will; or no, maybe not. They need to hear the communication. Sometimes, you need to say it multiple times to get other people to actually hear it, even though you think you said it.

# STRATEGIES TO MOVE FORWARD TOGETHER

**What are some effective strategies to get all members of a team bought in and moving in the same direction?**

**Gordon:** You mean on the bus? I think to get the team and organization all moving in the same direction, you have to get them to buy in. One, you've got to be someone they want to buy in to; you've got to be someone that they follow. You're going to have to share a vision. People follow the leader first and the vision second. Let them follow you. Now, share the vision of where you want to go. Then, invite people on the bus. I believe you have to ask them to get on. That's why *The Energy Bus* is so effective. You have to ask people to get on. It's very tribal. Just by them being invited, they now are feeling like they're part of something and you're making them feel that way.

They get on the bus; they're joining you for this ride of where you're going and this journey. Then, in that process, you're making them feel like they're a part of that journey. You're engaging them, you're involving them, you're making them part of the process, and you're empowering them. When you do that, you're going to have buy-in. It's all part of sharing the vision, the relationships, the connections, and the leadership to get people moving forward. That's honestly what *The Energy Bus* is all about.

**Medcalf:** This is where I highly agree with Jon Gordon. You get everybody on your bus, and you give them an opportunity to get on your bus. Ultimately, I think that we're never going to be able to get everybody on the same page, especially as the organization gets bigger and bigger and you have more people involved. Once again, it's giving them that opportunity of going, "This is where we're going, but you don't have to get on here. But, this is the direction that we're heading." It comes down to creating and enforcing those healthy boundaries. No matter who you are, once the mission has been set - that's what we try and get people to do is to focus on creating a compelling mission for their life versus having a goal - once that mission has been set for your organization, letting everybody know about it, giving them the opportunity to get on the bus, and then, if they don't get on the bus, letting them know that they probably need to find a different bus to get on because your bus is going in a certain direction and they may not be the best fit for your organization. Because what I've found over and over again is that it's not worth having "high performers" on your bus that aren't going in the right direction because all it does is become a cancer. You're better off with having - let's call them B players. But they're all on the same page, all headed in the same direction rather than having a couple of A players that have awful attitudes, mindsets, and aren't headed in that direction. It's just not worth it at the end of the day.

I don't do a lot with team dynamics because I think that teams are comprised of individuals. Oftentimes, the hardest people to get through to are the highest performers. So, I really try and focus on them and who they are as individuals. If we can get everybody focused on true mental toughness and using their sport and using their business to become more the type of people that they want to become, then I think that the team dynamics take place a little bit more naturally.

**Beebe:** The first thing you need to do is to create team functions outside of and away from the sport itself. If it's always about football, then that can get boring. What people really want to be a part of is some form of relationship. For example, we did a father-son retreat. We had team meals at my house. Guys would come over, play games, and just hang out. We had a senior bonfire the night before the last game. The kids shared about their testimony of being a part of Aurora Christian football [where Don serves as coach]. We had team Bible studies at my house. We did a three-day getaway during the middle of two-a-days. We still practiced football during that time, but at night we played games and just bonded as players. During the last night, we had a bonfire and kids got up and poured their hearts out. That is my favorite night of the year – to see kids' lives just change and bond together. Those are bonds that last a lifetime and make them into the individuals that they become.

**Kouzes:** One of the ways I would answer that question is to use an analogy. Let's suppose that I had a jigsaw puzzle with 1,000 pieces. I brought it in, I was working with a team, I put that puzzle down on a table, and I said to the team, "Put the puzzle together." What's the first thing do you suppose they will want to know from me?

People always say, "Show me the picture on the box top. Show me what it's supposed to look like when we're done." People want to know what the end result is. We are all like that. Leaders need to be able to communicate where we're headed and what the end result of our efforts looks like in order to feel empowered and capable of contributing their best. We actually did this jigsaw puzzle research. We put a puzzle - without showing anything to anybody - on a table and said, "Put it together." We timed them, and we also asked them questions about how frustrated they were and how productive they thought they were. We did the second group where we showed only one person – "the leader" – the box top. The third group we showed the box top to everybody. What we discovered, as you can probably imagine, is that the group where everyone was shown the box top did it the fastest and they enjoyed the process the most.

We are all like that. We want to know - where does my piece fit in the puzzle? Ward Clapham, the commander of a detachment for the Royal Canadian Mounted Police in Western Canada outside of Vancouver, said, "I am the chief dot connector. I connect the dots between the strategy and the front line." I love that quote. I think all leaders should become chief dot connectors and show people where their part fits in the overall hopes. Leaders need to articulate the hopes, dreams, and aspirations for the future; where we are headed - the direction and the strategy; and then show people how they are connected to that. Here is where your piece fits in order to get the highest levels of performance.

**Janssen:** That's something that we really try to do; sit down and have everyone envision. What is it that we could be? What is it that we could achieve if we got everybody on the same page, if we got everybody working well together, communicating with each other very well? What's possible for this program? I think co-developing that vision of what we could do if we really hit on all cylinders.

Then, what are the values that are going to dictate the commitments we're going to ask from each other, how we're going to treat each other, the positive vibe we want to have, how we're going to value results, and how we're going to value relationships?

Lastly, what are our standards or expectations? What is it that we need to do to give this vision the best possible chance of happening? If we can set our standards at a level that's going to maximize that vision and stay in alignment with our values, then we're going to give ourselves the absolute best shot to get that vision that we all want to have.

**Goldsmith:** The more you can include them in establishing the vision, the more likely they are to commit to the vision. The more the vision is externally imposed, they don't feel like they have any say in it. Somebody's just telling them what to do and how to do it. They're going to be much less likely to be motivated to achieve the vision to the degree that they're part of the vision and they buy in to the vision. They're much more likely to be motivated to achieve the vision.

**Woodfin:** It's simply communication. When I got to UAB, I tried to go to every single sport coach I could, communicate with them, let them know that I value their sport and what they do. I think it's highly important. How can I make you guys better? To hear them say that has never happened before was alarming. We've got a lot of room to grow, and we can make this thing awesome. Communicating is key, and that is what Coach [Bill] Clark is really good at. Find a common thread among all the people that you're communicating with, getting them on board.

Everybody obviously has different goals, different personalities, and different needs. To find a common thread amongst them, run with that, and get everybody pushing in the same direction is key. It doesn't sound hard, and it's not hard if you're willing to put in the time and you actually do care about everybody involved. That's what we really tried to do at UAB, and that's what I'm trying to do at Southern Miss. Communicate with everybody. Make sure we're all on the same page; make sure we're all pushing in the same direction to reach our goals.

**Anderson:** First of all, you have to make sure that they're bought in to you. Buy-in is never automatic, and it can never be assumed. If they're not really bought in to the leader's character, competence, consistency, compassion, and commitment, they're going to be skeptical. They may comply because they want their job and they want a paycheck. They're never going to commit. Once that happens, when we're really clear about where we're going, they have to understand the why. I believe people buy in more when they understand this is why it is important and this is what it means to me. Here's where we're going, here's why it's important, here's my role in it, and here's what's in it for us when we get there. If we're not doing a good job of communicating and addressing those aspects, we'll never have the buy-in that we'd like from our people.

**Clark:** It starts early. The very first day; these are our goals – there aren't a million of them. These are our goals, and this is where we're headed. Players see honesty. When I say we're going to do something, we're going to do it. Or, let's not say it. Let's limit the number of things we tell them, good things that we're going to do, and then we're going to stand by them. These are the few rules we've got, and we're going to enforce them whether it's the best player we've got or the worst, based on ability. It doesn't matter. These are the things we do. Teams understand that; they believe in that. It's a constant. It's a never-ending job. Starting with an early vision and then staying with it.

**Lubin:** I think it's having a clear vision, goal, and outcome. Have a clear vision of where you want to go. Like a pilot, they spend 90% of the time off-course and making corrections along the way, but they always land where they're supposed to. I think that's the key. Know the end result.

The road is going to be long and curvy. You're going to have mountains and valleys you need to overcome or go through, but I think having the vision of the end result is the way to be successful. Have that predetermined in their mind. If you can get the vision, communicate it to the people you're working with so they know where they're going. I think that's the key.

There are so many teams out there that just have meetings upon meetings, and they don't really know why they're having meetings. They may be doing it to get over one piece of the puzzle, but they don't see the clear vision. They don't see the end result. I think the end result - and drawing the end result - is the key for success. It's getting to home plate or it's getting across the finish line at the marathon. Those are the ways that you can get a team bought in and moving in the same direction.

**Elmore:** One - I think vision needs to be repeated. Do not ever be afraid of finding fresh ways to repeat the same vision. Vision leaks; it just leaks. So, we need to know that we need to keep putting it in the containers because it leaks out.

Another one, that is a second cousin, every Monday morning at Growing Leaders we have a stand-up meeting with our entire team. Our stand-up meeting - we call it stand-up because we *stand up*. That keeps the meeting short; it's 15 to 20 minutes, not two hours. But we will stand next to a white wall, where we have written our top priorities for the week. We've got several categories, and we say that these are our priorities this week. By the way, every Monday, we look - did we scratch off the priorities, having accomplished them from the last week? We are looking at priorities. Here are the big rocks that we want to put on our container this week. Here are the priorities; here is the vision. I feel like that's a recall back to the vision every single week with, "Are our tasks this week aligning with the mission of the organization?" It's been a purifying exercise that seems to work.

Then, one more thought. Years ago, we started doing something at Growing Leaders that I actually learned from Jack Welch when he was CEO of General Electric (GE). When he first sat down at GE, they were on the demise; they were going down. They decided to write down - they as in he and his executive team - wrote down every product that GE produced. One-by-one they did an exercise. Looking at each product one-by-one they asked themselves, "What needs a facelift, what needs an overhaul, and what needs a funeral?" Facelifts were, "That was a good idea. We just need to give it a fresh look for 2015." Overhauls were, "That's a great idea, but we need to completely overhaul the way we're going about that idea." Funerals, quite frankly, are the toughest. Maybe that's a service or product we offered at one point, but it worked in 1990. It doesn't work now so we kill it. We kill a book that we had written or we kill a service or product. So, I think that facelift-overhaul-funeral thing is so good at keeping everybody fresh on mission with what we were trying to pull off.

**White:** One of the things is that you just have to appeal to each individual's internal or external motivations. You don't know what those are until you get to know your players. Getting to know your players defines what those motivations are. Then, you'll sort of know what buttons to push. You have to share your vision, and you have to share your expectation level. Those who want to be a part of that journey, believe in that vision, and who have that same vision, will work towards the common goal. Those that don't will reveal themselves. I don't think you can beg or persuade someone if they don't believe in the vision, they don't trust in you, or trust in the vision. I don't think you can persuade those people to get on board. Building trust is so important in anything that you do. Building trust within your players, for a team, then building trust in one another.

One of the things that I've always disliked in sports is when coaches use the term "you and us." No, it is not you, it's "we" – it's we coaches, we within the team. It's not you have to do this better, it's we have to do this better. When you use just little verbiage like that and the players believe and know that you have their back, then they're going to have your back. I think that is really critical, especially when it comes to sports.

**Isom:** I think that just takes a great deal of creativity. That's where leadership really gets fun. If you've seen the people that you're serving, the people that you're leading, and you know them well, you really get to sit back as a leader and get creative about how to get this group fired up. The language and culture you can create within your team, within your organization, it's going to be perfectly unique to you because somehow it resonates with everybody. That's where things get fun. To name five things off the top of my head would be challenging, but one is just to be creative in group organizations.

I think that a lot of the time, getting people bought in is first letting them know that you're bought into them. That's investing your time and your energy. Sometimes doing things outside of the work or the sports realm to let them know that you love them and that you value them.

One of my greatest examples would be with LSU soccer. We were a team that competed hard on the field and gave it everything we had. It was all business most of the time. Sometimes we would lace up our cleats and be ready for practice, and our coaches would have a bus pull up and we get to go bowling and just be a team, be friends. When you can create a true culture within your team and an environment that lets people know that they're seen, valued, and loved, it makes standing up on the soapbox and saying, "Okay guys, let's buy into this, this is the goal, this is the focus," they're going to be so much more apt to stand up with a rally cry and join you because they then know, love, and support each other.

So, I think the best ways are the things outside of the business, work, or sports realm. Just understanding that you're a team. You're leading these people and you create a community and you create honesty, vulnerability, and true friendship. People buy in when they know others are bought in for them first. That's probably the best way to get people moving in the same direction.

**Eikenberry:** A crystal-clear picture of what that goal is and why that goal is important. I mean, that's ultimately what it is. Do people understand what the goal is? Why does it matter for us, for individuals, for our community, and for our customers when we reach that? What will it look like?

If you take John F. Kennedy in the early Spring of 1961, he said, "We're going to send a man to the moon and bring him home safely before the end of the decade." Clear. Clearly described. Very large. Many people thinking there's no way we could achieve it. But, clearly described, not just "We're going to the moon" but "We're going to the moon and bringing a man home safely." Crystal-clear and reasons why.

The biggest reason that we went to the moon was to beat the Soviets. There were other people involved in that project that had other reasons why it was compelling. For the scientists that might not have anything to do with the Soviets. For the scientists that might think about the pure discovery reason. For some people, it was about the investment, the economic value that came from all of that scientific research. Other people could have different reasons why, but those "why's" have to match up with what that clear goal statement is.

We want to engage people in a goal and in a direction. People need to know exactly what it is and what's in it for everyone to get there. If that reason "why" is strong enough, we're going to get there or get as close as is humanly possible to it.

**Gray:** Unified approaches are so important. You've got to make sure that no one's left behind. You can have a great vision as a CEO. At the end of the day, if everybody's not bought in, you're not going to get the best possible outcomes. I just look for ways to unify people.

We do a lot at All Pro Dad and Family First. We have team picnics. We have weekly Bible studies on Mondays where we come together. We have a weekly prayer service on Thursday morning before the workday starts. We actually have a person on staff - she's awesome, her name is Vicki - and she's the queen of fun. It's, like, in her job description, literally, to plan fun things each quarter. So, we have "Froyo Fridays" where we all go get frozen yogurt together. It sounds like simple things. You know what? They're simple, but they're important. So, we find ourselves trying to plan fun and make sure we're all stewarding our time well so that we can set aside time for others. It's hard to do, but we just stay after it and make sure that we're all on the same page to the best of our ability. We all understand what the mission, vision, and purpose is. When you've got all those things in alignment, it's not as hard as you think to stay on the same page, get work done, and do it with excellence.

**Brubaker:** I look at it like a team of any kind is like building a high-rise. You can't build the penthouse until you've already built a solid foundation and everything in between it. That's your construction project. You have to start with the basic elements as a leader. The basic elements are - again, I'll go back to the personnel you recruit, the personnel you select, and creating a compelling vision for them. What's in it for them? I think the most successful teams with the greatest leadership are the ones that the leader lets go. He lets his people or her people shape the core values of the organization. He lets them create, innovate, and exchange ideas that actually get executed. It's not the anonymous employee suggestion box that doesn't get read for months at a time or gets thrown in the paper shredder. It's taking that input.

The key to the team is that people support a world that they help create. So, again, the process of letting go and allowing your people to have significant input. Probably the greatest challenge in leadership is letting go. When you have the ability to do that - you have the right people, in the right roles, with the right goals, moving in the same direction - that same direction will be a natural by-product of trusting them and allowing them to put their thumbprint or fingerprint on the project and culture of the organization. Now, they're invested. They see that, "I'm listened to. I'm valued. My suggestions work." They will support that world they helped create. That's really the key to outstanding performance in any organization.

The corporate pyramid: I think for many, many years - and most companies have this backwards - they've got the pyramid pointing up. The CEO is at the top, the people spread out across other departments are in the lower end of the pyramid, and the manager is in the middle. In reality, that pyramid should be upside down. Your people should be at the top, and you should be a servant leader CEO at the bottom, willing to do all the little things and willing to lead by example.

Probably the greatest example of that I can give is an organization in Providence, Rhode Island, called Turfer. Turfer is a division of CleanBrands Company, and their CEO is Gary Goldberg. Gary is a friend of mine. What Gary does every day is he goes around from office to office – every single day if he's not on the road – and he empties out his employees' wastepaper baskets into a big garbage can that he pushes. Then, he'll take that out back. Now, what does that do for Gary, but also for his people?

1) They see him as a servant leader.

2) For Gary, he gets to check in and put his finger on the pulse of how each of his employees are doing every day and have some dialogue, some two-way communication.

3) Big picture. What this does is it sends a very subtle, very silent but powerful message to every single person. That message is that there's no job too small or too dirty for me to do. The CEO, the very man that founded the company and signs my paycheck, is willing to empty out my garbage and take all the garbage out to the dumpster every day. When he asks you to do a project, how could you say "No" if he's willing to get his hands dirty with you? I don't think people work *for* Gary. I think they work *with* him. There's a big difference. He's modeling exactly what he wants to see. He wants to see people going the extra mile. He listens, and he sets a great example.

**Olson:** Number one is clarity of purpose. Where there's high clarity, there's high performance. Where there's low clarity, there is confusion and performance diminishes significantly. It's a simple way to say that they better know exactly what you want from them all the time. There better be high clarity. For me, I just remember my first team meeting, I have to galvanize those guys and get them bonding together, which means that I need them all pulling in the same direction.

We have always said that there are thirds to a team. There's the top third, which is like the 10%; they're all-in already. Whatever you tell them, they are in; they're going to do it. Then there's the lower third. These are the cancer guys or potential cancer guys. They are a very small percentage also. There's a big third in the middle - about 70% - that are trying to figure out which way they are going to flip. We call them "the fish" – which way they are going to flip on any given day? They are either going to go with the 10% of the high-performance guys, or they are going to be pulled into the cancer guys. As a coach, my job was, instead of pushing people, I needed to pull them in the right direction. A lot of things that we did, spent a lot of time on number one, clarity. What do I want out of you guys? I want great attitudes, give us great effort, and you better be a "we" guy, not a "me" guy. If you are selfish here, you are gone! Then, we had to defend those standards. That means that older people take care of younger people; they don't haze them. Younger people listen to older people; they're not arrogant. We had to create a climate and a culture where, much like a family, certain things weren't allowed and they needed to be enforced. Certain things that were expected were rewarded, so that would continue to happen more. That would get everybody on the same page, if that makes sense to you.

The second thing we would do is we would spend a lot of time making sure that we're putting them in situations where we are developing a culture. Where it is a "we" attitude, a selfless attitude, versus a selfish attitude. A good friend of mine, Steve Shenbaum, has his company called *game on Nation*. Steve spends a ton of time - he works with us with the Pirates, he and I have done some corporate things together, he's been with the Lakers, the Yankees, Kentucky, everybody. You've seen him on ESPN - using improv to teach communications leadership. What he really does is he teaches how to laugh *with* each other, not *at* each other. In this day and age, that's probably the biggest thing. Everybody's trying to catch somebody doing something bad and embarrass them. Then, that person looks better for having embarrassed that person. Steve does a great job of using situations and trainings with the team to build cohesion. It's team building, but it's a different way to do it. So, that's one way. We used to play games with the guys. I used to look at *Whose Line is it Anyway,* and we would play games with each other and just have fun together. I always used to say this, and this is one more thing that is really important. You need to have what we call a "quality use of a waste of time" workout. Everybody goes, "What are you talking about?" I say, "Well, we are going to waste time, but we are going to do it together. It is going to be a quality use of that time." I used to do things with my football teams where, on a Friday night in the offseason, I would get them all together and divide them up into two teams. We give each team a video camera and say, "There are 30 things on your list or 20 things on your list; it's a video scavenger hunt. Go get them, and whoever finds them first, wins!" Another thing that we did was we would play no-dribble basketball with the guys. We would get them out of the element of the game that they played and have them do something else that was still team oriented and highly competitive but also fun. Those were our rules. Those kinds of things to pull a team together are very important to me. The elite coaches in the world don't just spend time with their teams during practice. They also make sure they build leadership counsels, and they talk with those counsels weekly.

There are so many different things but the biggest thing to me is high clarity, make sure everyone knows what the standards are, and defend and uphold them so that everyone gets on equal footing. The second thing is find ways to really develop cohesion during the in-between times. That's huge for teams; teach them how to laugh with each other, not at each other, so that they'll care about and take care of each other. That's huge.

Part of what we teach coaches, to your point, what we teach coaches to in that learning loop, and master teachers have known this since the beginning of time. You really don't know something until you have to teach it. The other thing that we teach is, in order to keep that guy from becoming selfish, if he is one of the best players, we are going to start having him teach other players. We are going to give him, what we call them is micro sound bites of teaching, where he is going to be over for a minute or two, teaching a younger player and we are going to force him to be selfless. We're going to put him in situations where he is imparting his knowledge on other people. Sooner or later, he is going to find out they are going to keep making me do this; I need to get good at this. Then he really starts understanding that,

"Wow, this is really difficult for some guys, even though it's easier for me." Or "I remember when it was difficult for me," and that helps bring them back to reality a little bit. That is one of the tools and techniques we use because you are right, that is a brutal deal when guys start thinking they are all that.

**Crandall:** Number one is helping every single one of them see how they contribute to achieving that goal. I keep going back to sports, but I'm doing that right now. I've got a team full of eleven guys. Every one of them is the best kid at his high school. Now, they've come together for spring and summer basketball. Some of them who were all-conference players are the eighth man on this team. But, we're going to accomplish some great things this season. It's our final season. We've come a long way, and we've got some big games to win. But, every guy has to feel like that's worth it and being part of this journey together is worth it. Whether you're running retail stores, restaurants, or banks, help the people you lead to see how they contribute to that.

Then, making it real clear where we're going. There's a lot of stuff out there on the topic of vision and being able to paint a picture. Storytelling is so important, and it's interesting it came up. It's hard trying to master the ability to tell stories about the past and where we came from to explain your values. You can usually come up with some stories in the present, things that happened within the last few weeks. It's hard to tell stories about the future. How do you make up a story about the future? Some people have done it real effectively. Henry Ford. There's an old quote about how he painted a picture of what it would look like, someday, where there are no more horses and buggies, and there's a car on every road. The vision is important to say, "This is what it looks like when we get there," to get everybody bought in.

Then, giving people ownership. That's, again, going back to this book we wrote, *Say Anything*. When people are able to contribute their ideas, even if their ideas are inside their head and they're thinking, "This is a crazy idea."

But, when they get it out there, you don't have to take their ideas and use them every single time. When people have input, when they feel like they're being heard, they're bought in. I think those three things: Everyone knows where we're going because we painted a good vision. Everyone has had an opportunity to provide input into where we're going. Then, once we're going there, everyone feels valued in the journey.

# MILLION DOLLAR QUESTION

**What do you know now that you wish you knew then?**

**Gordon:** It's definitely relationships. Years ago, I owned some Moe's Southwest Grill franchises. I look back and I would have been a much better leader if I would have done then what I know now. I would have invested more in relationships back then. I would have spent more time cultivating the relationships with my managers and my employees. I was such a hard charger. I think people liked me, but I didn't take the time to invest in the relationships. I was so busy doing so many things that I never sat down and really connected with people. If I could do it again, I would have connected more with my team, developed a stronger relationship, and I believe that would have been better in the long run. The business still was successful, but I would have been a better leader if I would have done that.

**Goldsmith:** One simple lesson in life is find happiness and contentment now. Not next week, not next month, not next year. The great Western disease – "I'll be happy when, I want to get that money status, BMW, and condominium." We all have the same "when." A learning point from old people is learn to find happiness, meaning, and contentment now.

**Janssen:** Over twenty years of doing this, what I really learned is the more you can put your ideas and process into a very practical system - that can be done in bite-size chunks over time and is developmentally based - it's going to have some long-term impact. There needs to be a method to the madness and a system to it. I think that's what we've come to with leadership development. That's what we've come to in building a championship culture.

Whereas, when I first started off, I was just doing a bunch of "hodgepodge," one-at-a-time workshops. Those things would have a little bit of impact here and there and were good, but they didn't build off of each other like a real system does. Over time, we've learned that lesson and continue to perfect, tweak, and evolve that system so that it does make sense and it does achieve the results that everyone is looking for.

**Olson:** Two things. Number one - it has to be about other people; it has to be. Zig Ziglar said it: "If you help other people get what they want, you'll get what you want." Which means you have to care about other people; you have to and put others before yourself. By the way - all the normal answers, hard work, relentlessness, grit – that's huge, but I knew that back then. I knew I needed to work hard. I needed to have grit. I needed to out-work people. I needed to be tough. I knew that. I didn't know that I needed to care about others more than myself.

The other thing that I didn't know is that passion drives everything. Stay with your passion. Don't get caught up in the money. I keep telling my own kids to just follow your passion. My oldest is going to be a bilingual sports psychologist, so he's a Spanish psych guy. I said, "Don't worry about the money. The money will follow your passion. Stay with your passion." Same thing with the game; just keep being passionate about the game. When you lose your passion for the game, then it's probably time to stop and do something else. Same thing in the corporate world. If you're not passionate about it, then don't do it. Don't stick a round peg in a square hole; it will be absolute torture for you, and you'll put yourself in a dungeon. There's no reason to do that. So, follow your passion, trust that everything else will follow it, and care more about other people than yourself.

**Isom:** Jesus. Honestly. I think one of the greatest things that I've learned about leadership: I have learned to leap fearlessly because I've learned to follow faithfully. That involves religion in the mix, and some people aren't so crazy or apt for that. But, it's an important component in our lives. The example of how to lead well was set for me. I believe it, and I see that sacrifice made for me. It really just encourages and inspires me to love, lead, and sacrifice for others as I was already loved, led, and sacrificed for, in the grander scheme of things.

That's really where it comes from now. That's when I started valuing the position of leadership - valuing the purpose in other people - was when it became more than just about myself. It became about a greater story that was being told, a greater purpose, and a bigger picture.

**White:** I think one of the biggest things is just to realize that it is a process. It's not finite. The failure is not fatal. Success is not the "end all be all." The highs and lows of when you feel like everything hinges on your performance, and everything hinges on every decision that you make. I wish, as I was younger and going through this, I would have focused more on the daily improvements. I wish I would've enjoyed and embraced the moments because a lot of times, as an athlete, you win a game then you move on to the next. You win a Big Ten championship; you move on to the next. You win a national championship; you move on to the next. You win WNBA Championship; what's the next thing I can accomplish? You don't really enjoy those things. It's interesting because people always ask me, "What was winning the national championship like?" I'm like, "You know, I really don't remember."

As soon as we won the national championship - I had an injury, and I was focused on rehab and the WNBA draft. As soon as we won the WNBA Championship, we turned our attention to the next year. I really wish I could have reminded myself or go back and focus on that process. Embrace those moments and use those moments to fuel more passion in me as opposed to using what I hadn't yet gotten to continue to drive you. Ultimately, then you're always searching for something that you don't know that you're ever going to get. Then it becomes about success and failure again. So, for me, just enjoying the process and realizing that it is a process.

**Kouzes:** Another lesson I learned late. Like a lot of people, I started out with these images of these famous leaders in my head and thinking leadership is about the leader. In fact, leadership is not at all about the leader. Leadership is about the constituents. One of the leaders we interviewed very early on, now over 30 years ago, was Don Bennett. Don Bennett was the first amputee to climb Mt. Rainier (14,410 feet) - on one leg and two crutches. I asked Don, "What was the most important lesson you learned from that climb?" He said, "You can't do it alone. If it weren't for my wife and seven kids, I never would have made it to the top. If it wasn't for my team, I never would have made it to the top or been able to do that. You can't do it alone."

I think that's probably the single most important lesson I've learned over all the years of researching leadership. Leadership is a team sport. It requires everyone to get us to the top. There may be one person who is responsible for providing the direction, initially, for making sure that they're the spokesperson for the values and beliefs, making sure that everyone is heard and considered, and making sure we're focused on improvement. But, it takes a team effort in order for all of us to be successful. I think that's a critical lesson for all emerging leaders to learn. It's not about you, the leader.

**Anderson:** I wish that I had known earlier that management and leadership were two separate skill sets, and that the most common tendency is to over-manage and under-lead. This is what I learned from John Maxwell

- management is the paperwork part of your job; leadership is the people work part of your job. They're both important. You have to have good management systems, processes, forecasts, scheduling, inventory - the whole bit. But, you have to also get it done through people. I was really good with the stuff; I wasn't very good with the people. Because of that, I micromanaged the people. I did way too much myself. And, when I started to learn that management and leadership are not synonymous (they are two different skill sets), when I started to develop the leadership aspect, it started to change everything – the momentum, morale, my credibility, and results. It, unfortunately, took me a couple years of booming around as a manager to figure that out. I abused a lot of good people in the process.

**Medcalf:** That we're all building our own house. I think, a lot of times, we think that we're building somebody else's house and that it's about our team. That it's about our relationship, our girlfriend, our boyfriend, our boss, or our company. But in any given situation, we're all building our own house. If we would focus on that and realize that it doesn't matter what somebody's doing to us, and it doesn't matter how tough our situation is. It doesn't matter any of those things. We're all building our own house. If we would focus on that and focus on using that experience that we find ourselves in to develop the personal characteristics that are important to us, then our levels of success would just dramatically increase over our lifetimes because we'd be preparing ourselves for everything that we're going to do in the future.

**Petrick:** I had this crazy idea; I always wanted to be the best. I would watch NFL Films and those awesome players. I would watch Major League Baseball highlights and dream of being the best, being a star. As I grew up, I started becoming a star in my own community, so that fed my ego. I had this crazy idea that people were always looking at me or thinking about me when that was not the case. My vanity blew up. I wasn't a cocky person. I was very humble, but inside I was vain, and I was worried about what other people thought about me. I wish now I would have not let that happen. If I could have changed my inner being and how I thought about myself, I would have enjoyed things and relaxed a lot more.

**Eikenberry:** I really wish I figured out a whole lot earlier to be a lot less selfish. I think I said earlier that leadership is not about us – it's about other people. I think that being selfish has gotten in my way in many parts of my life. As I continue to work on being more selfless, I am happier, healthier, and more successful.

**Woodfin:** Serving others and being generous. I didn't have either of those things coming up, really, until I was in my mid-twenties; not too long. Knowing the joy, the energy, and the excitement that generosity and service give me now - if I knew that a lot younger or a long time ago, I think I would have been on to something. I'd probably have been a lot happier and not wanting everything for myself earlier on in life.

**Gray:** I'm going to give you this thought. The Lord doesn't just call the highly credentialed, He credentials the ones that He calls. If I could unpack that - it's like He had a calling on my life a long time ago, but I kept feeling like I had to be highly credentialed. I had to go after, I had to learn more and do more, before I could really lead on a grand scale. What I didn't realize is that He was credentialing me as I went. He was training me and teaching me in the cauldron of business and media that I was in so I could do the work that I'm ultimately called to now, which is strengthening families and leading them.

I went to some interesting places across the country, having worked with 18 of the 32 NFL teams. I've worked with hundreds of different NFL players, coaches, and alumni. I have interacted with some fairly influential people so that we could influence culture in a positive way, make a difference, find a way to transform the lives of others, and all those things. All that wouldn't have been possible if I would have not allowed the Lord to credential me as I go.

But, imagine if I would have that thought a little bit earlier in my life? Imagine if I would have had more confidence early on? To not wait for that time in the future, that distant land that might get here someday, but to have more confidence in myself and my calling earlier in life. I think that would have made a difference in who I am and what I've become. I trust that God had a time, purpose, and plan for all of those things, but I do think that it would've helped me if I would've had that message earlier. If I would've had a mentor that would have spoken the truth into my life in just the right way, that could've given me that truth and allowed me to become the leader that I was called to be even sooner.

**Beebe:** I've talked about my faith enough, but that's who I am as a person. One thing that I learned is if I could go back and do things, I would become more of a God pleaser than a people pleaser. I was always trying to please others, and their opinions affected my play as an athlete. It seemed like I could never satisfy my coaches, my teammates, the fans, or the media enough. They always wanted more. But with God, He just wanted me, and I wish I would have known that a long time ago.

**Brubaker:** This is a great question. I think it's a question everyone should reflect on. The one thing I know now that I wish I knew back when I got started is the very thing that my book, *Seeds of Success*, addresses. That is that the best ideas you will get, you'll always get from outside of your industry. I think that coaches have become such students of the game, whatever their game is, and executives and leaders of organizations have become so insular. They study their industry, they want to see what the best are doing, and then they go copy what the top-performing company in their industry is doing. All that will ever get you, if you're copying the top performer in your industry or if you're an athletic team - take a look at football and Bill Walsh in the NFL; he was the coach years ago of the San Francisco 49ers - everyone copied his West Coast Offense. Well, basically, that mode of thinking, all that will ever get you is a runner-up trophy in whatever industry you're in.

To get to the next level you need innovating. You need to get ideas from outside of your industry. Southwest Airlines is a great example of this with their CEO Herb Kelleher. They used to be a tiny, little regional jet line that  was in small markets in the Southwest. One of his friends invited him to go to a NASCAR race one weekend. Kelleher wasn't a NASCAR fan, but he decided to tag along. He became fascinated watching the pit crews perform during the race. He wasn't so much interested in the race, but he was watching what was going on in the pits. That's where a lot of the action is, if you've ever been to a race. He was watching how fast they were able to change the tires, fuel the vehicle back up, get the driver a hit of water, wash off the windows, and then get that car right back on the track in a matter of seconds.

He came away from that weekend thinking, "That's what we're going to do with airplanes. I can't afford additional jets to get more planes in the air. I can't afford to have a position in the major airports, major cities, and markets in the U.S. But I can increase my revenue by getting the few planes I have up and down faster than our competition." At the time, it was about a 60-90 minute turnaround. What I mean by "turnaround" is by the time a plane lands, let's say, in New York City, to the time they de-board everyone – get the luggage out, clean it up, refuel it, get the new crew and pilots on, get the new ticketed passengers on, get the luggage loaded, and get them up in the air to their next destination. It took an hour to an hour and a half. What

Kelleher decided was what he was going to do was he was going to treat, from the time they landed to the time they took off again, like a pit stop.

If you've ever flown Southwest you'll see the pilots come out of the cockpit – if you're one of the last ones off the plane – and you'll see them go up and down the aisle with the flight attendants picking up garbage to help ready the plane for the next crew or for the next takeoff. They get up and down now inside of 20 minutes. In the industry they call it "the famous 20-minute turnaround." The industry standard is 60-90 minutes. They were getting their planes up and down in 20. So, they were able to maximize revenue, create faster flight schedules, and become more efficient, which then allowed to them grow later. Their fastest turnaround – they got it down at one point to 12 minutes. It's just a great example. That was the million dollar answer for Kelleher. Take an idea from outside of my industry and apply it to my industry. That put him in the 1%. Coincidentally, Southwest Airlines is the only airline in the United States that's not in Chapter 11 bankruptcy. Coincidence? I think not.

**Clark:** I think I did go in with my eyes wide open. I don't think any of us realized just the amount of work that was going to go into doing this job. I tell people all the time, "Everybody thinks they want to be a coach, but to do it, and do it right, it's going to involve so much time." I would say that just to understand the workload that goes into it, even though that didn't shy me off or scare me. I would say, really just seeing the amount, the volume of work going in, that's what it takes. I don't know that there's really anything different than that, but I think it is something that we all need to understand going into this line of work.

**Crandall:** When I left the army – I'd been in the army for thirteen years – I interviewed with all kinds of different places from Teach for America to McKenzie Consulting to a bank in Cleveland. I was exploring lots of different options. A gentleman who I consider a close friend and had done some publishing with – a really great guy – and I were talking. I was telling him about an interview with one of the organizations and how I thought that went. I was looking at these interviews as trying to sell myself to all these companies, and he said, "Hey, just remember, you're interviewing them as much as they're interviewing you." I nodded my head because I really trusted this guy, but inside my head I was a little cynical. I was thinking, "Yeah, but I need a job, and that's kind of goofy. They've got the power; they can hire me or not." I look back now, and I think that was such a wise, wise thing of him to say. It relates to leadership in the sense that the essence of leadership is knowing what you believe and why you believe it as well as being comfortable in your own skin and who you are. That will carry you to your passions, it will carry you to your very best, and you'll be the best leader possible because you're doing the things you believe in. I look back at that phrase – you're interviewing them as much as they're interviewing you. That should have been so true, and I believe that now. Not just in seeking out a job but in seeking out the decisions you're making. Ultimately, it's got to come from within.

I don't know that I could have learned that much earlier in life. You've got to experience things. The sooner you become self-directed in who you are as a leader, the better off you're going to be. I think that's been really valuable to me over the last four or five years; making decisions that are based on my core values. Saying, "No, I'm not doing that," or, "Yeah, I am doing that," or, "We're doing this." "This is about the kids." It's about the mission or the organization and having a lot of clarity in things like that. Going back to middle school; it's almost like becoming immune to peer pressure. But, it takes a long journey to get to that level of self-understanding and self-confidence.

**McCabe**: One of the biggest challenges, to me, is patience. Patience is tough. When I teach people – for instance, somebody calls me and says, "I'm struggling." I've got a professional golfer who calls me and says, "I need your help." They want an immediate fix. To me, it always gets better before it gets worse. The learning cycle is that, first, you have this honeymoon period where everything gets easy. Then, as you get away from the coaching impact – the leadership impact – it moves into what I call "the fog": the difficulty, the depth. Where you get really, really frustrated and really, really confused. If you're willing to be resilient through that time and persevere, you can maneuver through "the fog" and go to mastery. For me, patience has always been a tough thing because I think "I do it, I want to get it done right, I want to go, and I want to do it." Sometimes, A plus B should equal C, but it doesn't. A plus B with some factor of time, opportunities, and luck before it ever breaks through. That's the challenge.

I think a generation in college after me was right about the time when everybody started getting the "dot com" booms. Everybody had immediate hits, and we lost patience in this society. In today's world, we can't pay attention very long because everybody is on their phone immediately. Or, if you have a question, you don't search for it through your mind; you search for it through Google. You lose that ability to recall and pull in information. Patience is lost. Patience is tough for me. I want it; I want it now.

**Lubin:** Don't be afraid to take chances and be yourself. I spent so much time doing what I thought was the right thing versus being myself. I wasted a ton of time out there trying to tell myself I need to be a doctor, a lawyer, or an Indian chief. I wasn't allowing myself to be who I really wanted to be. Once I started going down that road, adopted my own style, and continued to learn and educate myself, that's when I started to become significantly more successful.

# HOT SEAT

**Fire Away!**

# BELIEF

**Isom:** Faith.

**Gray:** Faith.

**Beebe:** Faith.

**Crandall:** Faith.

**Lubin:** Passion.

**Eikenberry:** Paramount.

**Brubaker:** Contagious.

**Petrick:** In yourself.

**Woodfin:** Jesus Christ.

**Olson:** Faith in God.

**Clark:** Believe in each other. Faith.

**Anderson:** A conviction worth fighting for.

**Kouzes:** If you don't believe you can do it, you won't even try.

**Medcalf:** Jesus unconditionally loves you and me and gave his life for you.

**Janssen:** Confidence. Even though things don't look easy, you can still – with a lot of effort, time, and attention – make it happen.

**Goldsmith:** Frances Hesselbein. The woman that is my wonderful mentor who demonstrated that when she was a CEO of the Girl Scouts every day.

**White:** The first thing that comes to my mind with belief is just confidence. Confidence in yourself, confidence in your teammates, building confidence in our players.

**McCabe:** Desire. Belief is the desire to achieve something. It's something that you really want. It can be belief in a person, belief in self, belief for the system, belief in the outcome, or belief in the world around you. It's how it matches in that desire.

**Gordon:** You have to be an over-believer if you want to be an overachiever. Let me say that again. You have to be an over-believer if you want to be an overachiever. [Clemson Head Football Coach] Dabo Swinney said to me, "Jon, people often call me an overachiever. I say, 'No, no, no. I'm an over-believer. And that's why I'm an overachiever.'"

**Elmore:** I believe that leaders are going to be pretty helpless and powerless unless they have strong belief in who they are and what they're doing. I think it goes beyond that. Faith plays a huge role in my life. That faith is transcendent of me. Certainly, I got to believe in who I am and what I'm doing or – good luck with that because Monday I'm going to shut down because life is hard.

# CULTURE

**Gray:** Values.

**Crandall:** Critical.

**Beebe:** Create one.

**Lubin:** Collaborative.

**Isom:** Counter-Culture.

**Medcalf:** It drives your organization.

**Petrick:** Put yourself amongst quality people.

**Eikenberry:** The way things are done around here.

**Brubaker:** Beats strategy every day of the week.

**Woodfin:** How you feel when you walk into a place.

**Anderson:** It dictates behaviors; those behaviors determine the results.

**White:** Priority. Number one. Creating your culture and sustaining that culture.

**Janssen:** Absolutely critical. It's impacted by the leaders. They've got to set that up.

**Kouzes:** The underlying assumptions that are passed along in the organization and taught to new members.

**Clark:** We create it. Our coaching staff creates the culture that our players are going to live in.

**Goldsmith:** My friend Alan Mulally who totally changed the culture at Ford Motor Company by having clear rules that he established and maintained in turning Ford around.

**Olson:** Culture eats vision for lunch. Culture is 90% what people experience and only 10% of your signage and what people say. It's all about what they feel, experience, and see in the body language.

**Gordon:** It's everything. You have to focus on investing in the root if you want the fruit. Focus on the fruit, the outcome, and the numbers – but ignore the root, your tree will die. But if you invest in that root, you'll always have great fruit.

**Elmore:** Culture trumps everything. I think strategy is important, vision is important, no doubt about it. But, the culture that a leader cultivates on a team will trump everything. Culture works like the tide. When the tide goes up, all the boats go up. I just think it trumps everything.

**McCabe:** It sets up the playground for where you can be successful. Culture is important. I think, unfortunately, culture has to be organic. I've been brought in a lot to create cultures. I tell coaches all the time – when they ask me to come in and develop a culture – I can help guide them in the right direction, but it has to be organic. It has to have something that happens in a dugout, on the bench, on a bus, in a corporate lunch meeting, or else something that's created.

# COMMITMENT

**Gray:** Understanding.

**Crandall:** Difficult.

**Lubin:** Essential.

**Gordon:** A committed team becomes a powerful team.

**Kouzes:** Values drive commitment.

**Beebe:** Essential for success.

**Brubaker:** Two-way street.

**Medcalf:** Much more important than a wish list.

**Isom:** Let your yes mean yes, and your no mean no.

**Woodfin:** Following through; being consistent the whole way.

**Clark:** It's every day; every second of every day. You've got to have it.

**Goldsmith:** My belief in trying to help people have a little bit better life.

**White:** Willing to do the dirty work; willing to sacrifice on a daily basis.

**Petrick:** When you are doing something, you are going to do it all the way until it's done.

**Anderson:** Pledging yourself to something. Being willing to pay a price on an ongoing basis.

**Eikenberry:** Commitment is about so many different things. So, for commitment let me just say, it is powerful.

**McCabe:** Willing to sacrifice. When you're committed, you're willing to sacrifice other things in order to be committed to the outcome.

**Janssen:** Commitment level is being forgotten and watered down. The follow-through isn't there and you need time and attention to it.

**Elmore:** There's no such a thing as a half-hearted kamikaze. You're either on mission, flying that plane into a weapons arsenal or whatever, or you're not. I think you cannot be a leader unless you're absolutely committed to a cause. I just believe it's a non-negotiable.

**Olson:** Truly being all in means that you are "burning the ships." You truly have an entrepreneurial spirit that you are going to dig, and dig, and dig, even though you may not know what is around the corner. When you do see what's around the corner, you'll keep following it and trust the people that lead you.

# COMMUNICATION

**Lubin:** Vital.

**Crandall:** Stories.

**Gray:** Branding.

**Kouzes:** Grow big ears.

**Anderson:** Fast, honest, clear, specific.

**Beebe:** Ideal for great chemistry.

**Brubaker:** Can't take place without trust.

**Medcalf:** Very important in relationships.

**Eikenberry:** It's really about message received.

**White:** Paramount. Communication is paramount.

**Woodfin:** Every little detail with every single person involved.

**Isom:** Listen with the intent to understand, not just the intent to respond.

**Goldsmith:** That's one of the most important things any leader needs to do.

**Janssen:** Essential. You've got to have all the different moving parts and moving pieces on the same page working together.

**Petrick:** Be open, and don't be afraid. It's not going to kill you. Talk to your wife, talk to your kids, talk to your players, talk to your coaches.

**Clark:** Critical. We've got to communicate every way we can – with our players, with each other, with our staff. It's critical.

**McCabe:** It's the key to everything. Let me know how you feel, let me know how you think. Has to be authentic, has to be true, and has to be full of integrity.

**Olson:** 55% percent is body language, 38% is tone of voice, and only 7% is verbal. For the last month, that is what we have been teaching. That's the latest research on communication, and it's powerful.

**Elmore:** You cannot separate leadership and communication. If you've got a great idea but you cannot somehow relay it to your team, you will abort. You have to develop your communication skills, verbal and non-verbal.

**Gordon:** Communication, one-on-one, is essential. Most leaders communicate in groups, but you have to have that one-on-one communication to develop the relationships that build strong teams and strong organizations.

# ACCOUNTABILITY

**Gray:** Discipline.

**Isom:** Vulnerability.

**Eikenberry:** Is about ownership.

**Crandall:** Having good friends around you.

**Lubin:** The most important piece of success.

**Kouzes:** Do what you say you will do. DWYSYWD.

**Beebe:** Critical. Everyone needs to be held to the same standard.

**Brubaker:** Accountability isn't everything; it's the only thing for a leader.

**Woodfin:** Not letting your teammates down; not letting yourself down.

**Anderson:** Protects your culture, and it tells someone you care about them.

**Medcalf:** More important for those in leadership than those enacting accountability.

**Gordon:** You have to be accountable to yourself first, and then you have to hold your team accountable. If you do those two things, you're going to have a strong team.

**Janssen:** Responsible for me, accountable to you. Being accountable to a team is absolutely critical if you're going to have any success as a team.

**Goldsmith:** Accountability is the process that I can teach you that takes two minutes a day, incredibly easy to understand, and almost impossible for most people to do.

**White:** When I think of accountability, I think of accountability to something greater than yourself. It always brings me back to my playing days and my accountability to my teammates. Wanting to be better for them.

**Petrick:** Be ready to pay for what you are doing. Do right because you will be accountable for the things you don't do right. Try to stay in good graces amongst your leaders and peers.

**Clark:** It starts at the top. You've got to have it. It starts with the head coach. Player to player, player to coach, coach to player, coach to coach. You've got to all have it amongst the whole family.

**Olson:** It's the key to everything. You can't have accountability without trust, and you can't have trust without accountability. Accountability to me – the special coaches, the special leaders have relationships where they can hold people accountable including themselves. Those people don't resent it.

**McCabe:** If it is to be, it's up to me. Accountability, to me, is a building block of responsibility. I'm responsible to the world around me. But in order to be responsible to the world around me, I must take care of my own actions. I'm no good to my organization, my team, or my clients unless I'm good for myself.

**Elmore:** I would be out of business without accountability. I think leaders can grow into a place where there's very few people in their lives that can ask them hard questions and hold them accountable. I have maintained in my life two individuals – that I respect greatly – that ask me hard questions on a regular basis. Accountability has saved my life; to make sure I'm staying on the right path as a good husband, good leader, good father, and good man because I would deviate very quickly if I didn't have it.

# MOTIVATION

**Isom:** Passion.

**Gray:** Powerful.

**Eikenberry:** Is internal.

**Crandall:** From within.

**Lubin:** Moving forward.

**Goldsmith:** Should come from your heart.

**Woodfin:** That one thing that makes you tick.

**Medcalf:** Not nearly as important as equipping.

**Brubaker:** Motivation is the fuel that drives people to exceptional results.

**Kouzes:** Internal motivation is significantly more powerful than external motivation.

**Janssen:** Drives everything you do. It's essential if you're going to be successful.

**Gordon:** You have to share it. Even if you're an introvert, you still have to find ways to motivate your team.

**Anderson:** It's an inside job, first. It has to start from within. Any external motivation is just a plus.

**Beebe:** I once heard a coach tell me, "I want players that are self-motivated, not players that I have to motivate."

**White:** What drives you to be your best? What is it that drives you to be your best every single day? I think it's different for every person. For me, it's competitiveness. Competing motivates me.

**Elmore:** I love what Zig Ziglar said about this. That's what I would say about this too. Motivation is necessary, just like taking a shower is necessary. But, you have to take another one tomorrow. So, I think you have to be re-motivated every day. Get a fresh shower; get re-motivated.

**Clark:** You've got to be self-motivated, and that's something we work on all the time. What is our motivation for the day? That's what we talked about "winning the day." Start the day off right, being motivated to have a great day.

**Petrick:** Both ways. You want to be motivated; I think that's an important thing in life. You always want to be motivated so look for other ways to be motivated whether it is reading a motivating statement every day or if it is watching a video or show that motivates you. Go for it.

**McCabe:** Motivation, to me, is that inherent desire. It comes back to belief; that inherent desire that moves us. People have different levels of motivation. We can't assume that everybody is motivated the same way. As a psychologist, we study motivation in many different ways. There are a lot of really good theories of motivation. The truth of the matter is, it gets down to: What do you want?

**Olson:** It all starts with "why." You've got to find out why that person does what they do. Are they driven by money? Are they driven by this or that? You have to connect at that level to see what their core motivation is and start from there. You can't tell them what to do until they know why to do it. You don't know how to tell them why to do it or how to do it, if you don't know what their motivation is and how you can teach them so that they'll receive it. It's all about knowing what their "why" is.

# INTEGRITY

**Isom:** Honesty.

**Eikenberry:** Personal.

**Gray:** Principles.

**Lubin:** Absolute necessity.

**Gordon:** You have to have it.

**Beebe:** Without it, you have nothing.

**Crandall:** The foundation of everything.

**Goldsmith:** Should come from your heart.

**Medcalf:** Without it you're destined to fail.

**Woodfin:** Doing the right things when no one is looking.

**Olson:** Honesty. Authenticity. Very difficult. It's a day-by-day thing. You have to work on it every day. Never take it for granted.

**White:** Compassion and knowing that each decision and action that you make you can't compromise that integrity.

**Kouzes:** Credibility is the foundation of leadership. If you don't believe in the messenger, you won't believe the message.

**Janssen:** Lots of things are needed for leadership, but, if you are going to isolate one of them, I think you cannot be an effective leader if you don't have integrity for the long term.

**Elmore:** Because leadership operates on the basis of trust, I can't gain any change in my pocket and any trust among the people that I lead unless I exhibit integrity. For me, integrity doesn't mean I'm perfect. It just means I'm one. I'm one person. What I say and what I do are alike.

**Anderson:** Doing what you said you would do, when you said you would do it, how you said you would do it, and doing it without excuse, regardless of the cost.

**Petrick:** A quality person. Someone who talks a good game and you know is backing it up. You know that is a quality person.

**Brubaker:** Integrity is what matters at the end of the day. Who you are, not what you do. Who you are is your value system.

**Clark:** It's who you are when nobody's looking. Who you are when nobody's around. "The mirror doesn't lie" was an old saying my dad always told me. When you look back in the mirror, don't lie to yourself. That's the thing. Integrity is doing what you say you're going to do, all the time.

**McCabe:** Something that we're missing a lot in business in this field. Integrity is doing what you say you're going to do, when no one else is watching. Integrity is critical because if you do things with a lack of integrity, it will eventually catch up to you.

# SELFLESS

**Crandall:** Jesus.

**Woodfin:** Jesus Christ.

**Gray:** Integrity.

**Lubin:** Keys to success.

**Eikenberry:** The basis of true success.

**Isom:** The true definition of love and leadership.

**Goldsmith:** Putting other people's needs ahead of your own.

**White:** Sacrificing for something bigger than yourself.

**Medcalf:** I believe in it, but at the same time, enforcing healthy boundaries.

**Beebe:** Rarely seen in today's sports, but it's definitely a sign of great leadership.

**Clark:** I think that's huge in athletics. Specifically, team athletics. It's putting others ahead of yourself.

**Janssen:** Challenging for many people because of ego but necessary if a group is going to be effective.

**Kouzes:** We're not remembered for what we do for ourselves. We're remembered for what we do for others.

**Anderson:** Subordinating your own comfort and preferences to what's best for the team. Serving.

**Petrick:** Giving yourself. In life, there are so many people that are out for "What can I get for this money?", "I need more money so I can do this" instead of saying, "What's out there for me to help someone else? What can I do to better my community, my friends, or family? What else is out there for me to do?" Not in it for myself, in it for others.

**Brubaker:** Selfless/selfish. What I mean by that is I think that every great leader, selfishly, you're trying to lead everyone to a greater result because that's what we all want. People join the team because they want to win. To lead them to a great result you need to be selfless.

**Olson:** The key to everything. It's the key to living in this world. It's the key to leaving a legacy in this world, and it's the key to leaving this world. I would say that selflessness is the core of an elite performer.

**Elmore:** I think leaders eat last. That means I've got to demonstrate to my team I'm willing to pay the price. I'm willing to, in our office, maybe pack up some boxes of books and help ship them. Even though I'm the president, that lets an intern know, "Wow, he's just as selfless as he's asking us to be and do the grunt work." So I think you've got to model that.

**McCabe:** I'm going to change it on you a little bit. It's not selfless. It has to be selfish, in my mind. It can't be self-centered. I want players or employees that are selfish. What I mean by that is: I want them to look at the mirror every day and say, "What do I need to do to be great?" Self-centered is, "What can I do in order to take away from everyone else on my team?" As an organization, to be great, I have to be phenomenal myself. Selfish is important to me. I don't want them self-centered. I want them fulfilling. I tell moms all the time – moms are so selfless, they get worn out and exhausted – be a little selfish. Take care of yourself, and your kids will respond appropriately.

# VISION

**Gray:** Togetherness.

**Eikenberry:** The reason we work.

**Medcalf:** More important than goals.

**Lubin:** Having the end in mind.

**Kouzes:** Vision trumps everything.

**Isom:** Vision-casting. The ability to cast that vision.

**Woodfin:** Futuristic. Someone who can see a lot further than most.

**White:** Necessity. I think vision is necessary to have your direction.

**Crandall:** Difficult to communicate but critical to communicate.

**Brubaker:** Victory. If you don't have a vision, you're never going to have a victory.

**Beebe:** You've got to have it. Without it, it becomes too confusing, and definitely leads to failure.

**Anderson:** A specific direction that unites and inspires a team towards a common goal.

**Clark:** Any great leader has to have a vision: Where am I headed? What are my goals? What am I working towards?

**Janssen:** Something that leaders need to put in place, with the help of their team early on, so that everyone is clear about the direction we are going.

**Goldsmith:** The ability to look into the future and see something that everyone in the world hasn't already seen.

**Olson:** Without vision, people perish. If a leader does not have vision, then complacency is going to come in. Complacency is the single, most dangerous thing for a successful organization. For me, you have to make sure complacency doesn't come in.

**Gordon:** It helps you see the road ahead. If you can see it, you can create it. If you have a vision, you also have the power to make it happen. Every organization needs a vision of where they're going, why they're going there. They need a North Star. Then, every great leader points their team towards that North Star, towards that vision.

**Elmore:** Without vision, I'm just going to wander. Vision is like a target in front of me and a bull's-eye in front of me. Maybe a better metaphor is like a blueprint before I build a house. Without a blueprint – wow! Good luck on those 2x4s, you know? You're just guessing, but it's the big picture that helps me stay on track and make sure I get where I want to go.

**McCabe:** You have to see where you want to go down the road. I don't think you need to have a vision thirty years down the road. That writes great books, but I don't think that has great practical ability. I think two to three years down the road is all you really need. Where do you want to be?

**Petrick:** Vision is important because any person who has aspirations of being something someday, they need to have a vision in their head of seeing themselves in that position. I heard Mark McGwire talk the year he hit all those home runs. Yes, he was allegedly using steroids, but it takes a lot of skill to hit the ball. He talked about how good his vision – mental vision – was. Every time he came up to bat, he would envision himself putting a perfect swing on the ball. That could be related to any part of life; visualizing yourself being successful.

# LEADING BY EXAMPLE

**Isom:** Sacrifice.

**Gray:** Serving leadership.

**Eikenberry:** The best way to do it.

**Medcalf:** Of the utmost importance.

**Crandall:** Can't succeed without it.

**Lubin:** It's the only true way to lead.

**Kouzes:** You either lead by example, or you don't lead at all.

**Woodfin:** Hard, yet highly effective.

**Clark:** I think it's huge. That's the kind of leadership that I like the most and we need the most because that is what's going to make us go.

**Goldsmith:** Is being a role model for living the values that you're preaching to others.

**Anderson:** You go first. You work hard first. You live the values first. You get results first.

**White:** Honorable. I think you can't just talk about it. You have to be about it in everything that you do every single day.

**Beebe:** This is me as a person. You don't always have to be a talker to be a leader. As a matter of fact, I enjoy the ones that don't.

**Brubaker:** It's the silent assassin. It can kill your results, or it can be that awesome lethal weapon that takes you to the next level.

**Gordon:** George Boiardi, my book *The Hard Hat*. He didn't say much, but he led by example. Benjamin Franklin quote – "Well done is better than well said." If you do that, you're a leader.

**Janssen:** The absolute first part of being an effective leader. All leadership starts with self-leadership. If you cannot lead yourself, please don't try to lead someone else.

**Elmore:** I think the number one management principle in the world is – people do what people see; not what they hear. We can't lecture or preach our way; we've got to lead by example. I just think people do what people see so I better show them before I tell them.

**Petrick:** I think it goes back to integrity when you are leading by example. Just being a quality person. I'm not saying I'm a quality person; I can't talk very well. When I talk to someone on my team or say something to somebody, it's hard sometimes. I try to make sure that I'm behaving and acting in a way that shows a person who has been somewhere at a higher level and how you behave when you are a pro. Just try to set an example of how it is supposed to be.

**McCabe:** I saw an interview with President Bush one time, and he said, "People aren't going to judge me in the next fifteen years. They're going to judge me in the next sixty years. Maybe, they'll look back and think that we made the right decisions." He said, "I lead by doing what I feel is right, not what everyone agrees I need to be." I think leading by example is that. Leading by example is doing it by saying, "I'm willing to do, sacrifice, and be. I'm not doing it for any inherent reason. I don't need your approval. I'm doing it because I think it's what is right." I think people will learn from that.

**Olson:** I still think that it's proven that modeling is still the number one learning style on the planet. What I mean by that – there is auditory, kinesthetic, and visual. We are still getting it wrong in the classrooms. We're standing up in front and speaking to kids, which is totally a twentieth-century model. Kids want to experience, which means they also need it modeled for them. Even John Wooden, back in the day, he would explain it, model it, and then have them do it. It's just like parenting. If I can't model it, then it's not authentic. Then, why should I do it? If I've never seen it, it's a lot harder for me to learn and implement it into my own life.

# THE
# CONCLUSION

# RECOMMENDED READING

## What books or resources would you recommend to anyone looking to improve their leadership abilities?

**Janssen:** The *Team Captain's Leadership Manual*, which is a 10-module program designed for the captains. The new one that I mentioned as well, *The Team Captain's Culture Manual*. Another one that Greg Dale, who's over at Duke, and I did is called *The Seven Secrets of Successful Coaches*. We looked at really successful coaches, but not just ones that won. They won because they won their athletes' respect, and people would run through a wall for them.

One that I really love that I recommend to coaches and student-athlete leaders is called *The 2R Manager*. It's by Peter Friedes. He boils things down to saying leadership is really about doing two things well – relating to people, being able to connect with them and requiring things of them and making certain demands and upholding certain standards. Great leaders can do both of those things well and know when one is more called for than another. So, his *The 2R Manager* is the ability to relate and require to people. Just an excellent resource to boil the complex topic of leadership down into something that makes a lot of sense.

**Olson:** I'm reading one right now that is pretty crazy. You would never expect a coach to be reading it. It's called *Love Does* by Bob Goff. It's a very simplistic way to implement caring about other people and being selfless.

Another one is *Legacy*. I think he spent about four years with the All Blacks, the number one sports team of all time. Over a hundred years, they have won over 90% of their matches in rugby. It's a great book. It's a little more technical, but it talks about culture.

A very simple one, but it is John Wooden's *You Haven't Taught Until They Have Learned;* that's a very easy one. The last one for me that I think is powerful – there are so many little books out there – *The Go-Giver* is a very powerful book to me. *Training Camp* from Jon Gordon. Those are just excellent books, if anyone wants a quick read. Anything that Jon Gordon writes like *The Carpenter.* He's a good friend. They are simple but very good.

**Isom:** There are so many great resources out there and so many people talking about the topic of leadership and speaking about it well. I know that one of the books – it's not directly about leadership – but one book that really got me thinking about other people, other ideas, and other individuals in my life as important and as valuable was the book called *Crazy Love* by Francis Chan. It's challenging, honest, and it really gets you thinking about the things that you're doing, saying, and why you're doing the things the way that you are.

Jon Gordon is another incredible author who writes about leadership and does an amazing job at that. He's a good friend and a good mentor, honestly.

I think that another would be any of the books by Tony Dungy. *Quiet Strength* was one of his first and a New York Times Bestseller, but he's actually written many more than just that. He really embraces the same idea of leadership by sacrifice, leadership through selflessness, and that quiet leadership that commands attention and respect.

So, those are three great sources right there: *Crazy Love* by Francis Chan, any and everything by Jon Gordon, and any and everything by Tony Dungy. I just look up to those men a lot and lean into their truth.

I, additionally, just signed a book deal, actually a two-book deal, so you will be hearing from me in written word for a couple of years' time now. That book will come out in, probably, late summer 2016. Late summer, early fall. It will be called *Wreck My Life: A Journey from Broken to Bold* and will be another one that is not black and white specifically about leadership but just has so many leadership elements woven throughout it, especially when it comes to embracing failure, adversity, struggle, and suffering. You can jump on and pre-order that or buy that when it releases. That would be awesome.

Again, just another resource would be my website too, *moisom.com*. I'm always writing about interesting ways that we can look at this world differently and current events that we can look at from a different view – a more selfless, more withdrawn from emotion, and just honest and raw view. So, *moisom.com*, there's a resource. Any of those books are awesome. My book in the future would be great.

I think that wherever you're looking or searching for resource for leadership, I would challenge you first to look who is writing it or saying it; who is leading. That will probably give a lot of answer of whether that advice is worth following or listening to.

**Goldsmith:** I would recommend my friend Frances Hesselbein's book *Hesselbein on Leadership*. My friend Jim Kouzes's book *The Leadership Challenge*. Those are two books that I always recommend aside from my own books.

**White:** I love Joshua [Medcalf] and Jamie [Gilbert] stuff. I love *Burn Your Goals*. I'm in the middle of reading *The Impractical Guide to Becoming a Transformational Leader* right now. I love Jon Gordon's stuff. We read *The Energy Bus* as a team last year. I read *Training Camp* before our training camp last year. I just read *The Carpenter* on a flight to the Women's Final Four; I love it. I love all of his stuff. One of the books that Joshua [Medcalf] and Jamie [Gilbert] suggested to me is *Mindset* by Carol Dweck. I saw myself all over that book. I think that's an awesome book for everybody to read, not just people in leadership positions.

I certainly love all of John Wooden's leadership books. John Wooden because he was way ahead of his time in terms of the process and in terms of his compassionate service leadership. So I like reading a lot of his stuff. I read Steve Jobs' book, and I really had a hard time reading that book. I would like to try to read it again with a fresh mindset because I do like reading a lot from the corporate world as well.

I just got a book *Start Something That Matters* by Blake Mycoskie, the guy who did TOMS shoes. I'm really looking forward to reading that as well. I'm really into a lot of stuff that helps you with your vision. I don't take everything from every book. Just like whenever I say – if I'm speaking somewhere, I can leave people with just one thing that they can take from whatever I say that can help them be better. That's what I try to do with a lot of these books that I read as well.

**Elmore:** This is a book that I don't hear recommended a lot. It's like the first book I give to young leaders as they start their journey. It's simply called *Leadership and Self Deception*. It's by a group of psychologists, The Arbinger Institute. This book is a narrative; it's a parable. It's brilliantly written. It's one of those page-turners about a guy who learns to live out of the box rather than in the box. It's a book on how we are naturally selfish as leaders and how we need to learn to get out beyond ourselves. I highly recommend that book. I read it in one sitting, *Leadership and Self Deception*. Fantastic book.

**Anderson:** I wrote *Up Your Business: 7 Steps To Fix, Build, or Stretch Your Organization* that has been extremely helpful to people all over the world. Then, John Maxwell's, *The 21 Irrefutable Laws of Leadership*. I believe it's just a leadership classic, and, regardless of where you are on your leadership journey, it'll help you.

**Medcalf:** We actually have a leaders reading challenge that's available on our website. There's about 45 books that we have in order that we suggest reading. You can take the challenge and just sign up for it and go through it or just take the books and read them at your pace. But if you went through it, I think that you get through all the books in about a year and a half, two years. We just get e-mails almost every day from somebody that's doing it and the transformational impact it's had on their life.

**Petrick:** To be honest with you, I can rattle off leadership books, but what I do on a daily basis – I started this before I wrote my book – was a blog site that I write called *Faith in the Game*. It's really empowered me. I have a Facebook page called Faith in the Game, and I get quotes off of Twitter, search the internet, or have friends give me daily quotes. I try to find one or two of the most inspiring or motivating quotes of the day and post them in my *Faith in the Game* blog so I can share it with others. Reading things like that keeps me in check, like reading the Bible. For me, it is trying to keep yourself in tune with being a leader and having positive, motivating thoughts.

**Eikenberry:** Well, all of mine, of course. *KevinEikenberry.com*. We'll go from there to *Remarkableleadershipbook.com* and *budtoboss.com*. You can't go wrong if you read Ken Blanchard, you can't go wrong if you read Jim Kouzes and Barry Posner, you can't go wrong if you read John Maxwell, and you can't go wrong if you read Peter Drucker. If you start there, it's a pretty good place to start.

**Gray:** The ultimate leadership book is the Bible. But, I can tell you a couple of other great ones. Jim Collins' work with *Good to Great* and all that he created with that is just an amazing form of leadership. I'm currently reading a book called *Culture Care* which is a great model about how to lead in some creative ways. There are so many wonderful books that have been written to help others get better in their leadership. For me, I'm just trying to break things down and understand the root causes of what motivates people. I mentioned a book earlier, a strategy earlier, called *The 5 Love Languages*, so I think I'm going to reinforce it right now. That's a great book. It's one that I've used for many years both personally and professionally. My wife and I talk about it often, but I use it in a business setting as well. Let me recommend that to your listeners as well.

**Beebe:** The Bible; it's all you need.

**Brubaker:** I'd love to shamelessly self-promote all of my own books, but I'll tell you what I told one of my clients. He's read all my books. He has his people try and follow them to the letter. They've created a book club, each year, around a different book of mine. As flattering as that is, I told him: "Ted, that's really flattering, but look at it this way. You're the book your people read. You, as a leader, are the book your people read. They read you every day, and they read you cover to cover, so to speak." So, really it's about the example you're setting. Having a book club's great. Having written resources and audiotapes just like this (dating myself a little bit there, "audiotapes") – having audio, books, and materials is wonderful. But at the end of the day, the go-to resource for every leader is the example they set because your people are reading you like a book.

**Woodfin:** Some of my go-to books are by people who you have had the privilege of speaking with. Definitely, Jon Gordon. Everything that he's written is just gold to me. John Maxwell has awesome stuff. A guy that I mentioned earlier who had a big effect on my leadership skills, Erwin MacManus. Erwin has written several books; you can just Google his name. A quick story about Erwin, I'm pretty sure Erwin MacManus led Jon Gordon to Christ, which is something I didn't know until I was having dinner with Erwin in San Francisco. We were playing the 49ers, and I was talking about Jon Gordon's books and he made the connection. Erwin MacManus has some really powerful stuff.

A book that was really unique – yet effective – to me was called *Leadership and Self Deception.* The Arbinger Institute put that out and was a really good book for me. Those are a few guys, through reading, that have had a big influence on my leadership.

**Clark:** I would always say the Bible first because I think there are so many great examples. Beyond your faith, there are so many great examples of leadership. I would say this to any young coach. Get your hands on as many great, successful leaders and not just coaches. Whether it's military leaders or whoever, you can take one or two things. We're going to all have our own style. Don't try and be somebody else, but I think there are so many good things you can borrow out there. A good leader, a good coach, anybody that's willing to lead people; that's what you need to do. There is so much out there that you can look at.

**Crandall:** I, very genuinely, recommend that everyone pick up a copy of this book we just put out, *Say Anything,* which you can get on Amazon. I wrote it, in lot of ways, because I receive that question a lot: What book would you recommend for your grassroots, on-the-ground, frontline leaders? I think it is super valuable, and it is tough to find books out there that really speak to leaders. We wrote it as a letter to leaders. It's on a specific topic of getting the people you lead to say what they think and contribute within that context. The underlying message is a bunch of leadership questions through stories, some of the well-grounded research that we did over two years, and a lot of other people's research that we've read.

I actually think there are a lot of really good movies. Anyone who is really interested in leadership and developing themselves should watch the movie *Glory* (1989). It's got Matthew Broderick and Denzel Washington, and it's about the Civil War and Matthew Broderick's journey leading what they called, at the time, the colored regiment. It's a phenomenal study in one man's journey to develop himself as a leader.

**McCabe:** As I said earlier, the Jon Gordon series is great. I would always highly recommend his books. But I tend do it differently. I don't read a lot of leadership books or sports psychology books because, to me, there's a lot of circular arguments – meaning, the best part of those books are usually in the first half of the book or first third of the book. After that, it's all about validation. I read biographies, and I like to read books of great people, people who have failed and people who have bounced back. Then, pull out the lessons from them. Early on, I was a huge proponent of *The Lone Survivor* book. Now, it's a big movie, and everybody is on it. I loved *Unbroken* when it first came out. There's a book called *Presidential Courage* that I read – a great book about what it takes to make hard decisions. When we read biographies, people who have firsthand accounts, or an author's account of the decisions, trials, and/or tribulations they've had – first of all, it normalizes them. Secondly, it shows us that they are vulnerable. We need that as leaders.

**Lubin:** I'm a big fan of the Seth Godin and Malcolm Gladwell books because they're all about thinking outside of the box. In today's world, it's less and less so. We don't have to do things the same way we did things before. If you look at Kickstart, social media, and all these different ways to raise money, be successful, or get the information you need. Thinking out of the box now is becoming more of the norm than it ever was in the past, but we're not even close to where it is. But I like how Seth Godin and Malcolm Gladwell books are always constantly getting you to think outside of the box. Think a little bit different. Think a little bit on the edge because the key to success in your career is that you own your career. On the bottom of my e-mail I've got another quote that says, "You don't own your job, but you own your career." I think that some of the keys is taking ownership in what you're going to do and how you're going to be successful down the road.

# THE FUTURE OF LEADERSHIP

## Where do you see the future of leadership training going in the next 5-10 years?

**Janssen:** I think it's really exciting. Eleven years ago, North Carolina was really the first college athletic program to create a Carolina Leadership Academy. We were at the forefront of putting this together. Now, over a decade later, you have about 50 different colleges that have created leadership academies. That's an exciting thing to see. It has evolved and developed over time. I think, much like some of the other disciplines of strength training and athletic training, hopefully in five or ten years, you're going to start seeing people specialize a little bit more with teams. So, in an athletic department, you may have either some people in-house or bringing in outside consultants, especially in the power five conferences, where they may have their own leadership development person they work with and a very specific program that they work through, not only throughout one year, but it's a four- or five-year evolutionary process.

That's what I think will happen over time because coaches, ADs, and student-athletes see how important leadership development is, not only for the short term with their teams but as they go out into the business world and the work world. They're going to have those leadership skills that they can rely on as well.

**Olson:** I believe sports psychology and mental conditioning is going to be like what strength training was thirty years ago. Everybody's going to have one. The other piece for me is people are going to need to have coaching development. That's where you've got ADs and GMs are going to have to start training their coaches on how to deal with everything they deal with – not just the players but also their own lives and how much they have to deal with.

**Goldsmith:** I think more and more focus on leadership training is going to be about demonstrating that actually produces positive long-term change. The movement toward more and more coaching has become great in the last five years. Many more people have coaches, and coaching is now seen as much more helping successful people get better than fixing people that were seen as losers.

**McCabe:** That's a good question. Leadership platforms and leadership training – I think you're going to continue to see the influx of the military leaders coming out. Let's take a look at the Navy SEALs for a minute. The SEALs have the greatest organization in the military, so we believe. So we've been told. My dad's brother is retired navy, and so is my cousin. The navy did a tremendous job of marketing, and it started with *Top Gun*. They realized that, after *Top Gun*, they got so many new pilot applications. They started becoming pretty great marketers. There's no question; the SEALs are the best of the best. But, the air force has the Air Commandos and the Pararescuers. You don't hear much about them. I think what we're going to continue to see individuals that come out of these unbelievable leadership organizations of the military coming out to train organizations. Why? Let's take the SEALs. We know more about them than anyone else. There's more books written about the SEALs than maybe anyone else. They create chaos on a daily basis, and either you know how to function in chaos or you don't.

Leadership – I think we try to put a little bow on it too much. I think we try to make it too good, and we try to make it like "everybody can do this." The 10,000-hour rule – it's like "Hey, if you just work hard enough you can be successful." No, you have to be uncomfortable. You have to be vulnerable. Leadership is easy when everything is going right. Leadership is hard when it's all hitting the fan. A sign of a leader is somebody who runs into the fire, doesn't run away. How do you know who's going to run into the fire? You have to put them into high-intensity circumstances. I think leadership training over the next couple of years is going to be more involved with that. You can give me a book with ten leadership principles, and I don't know if I understand any of them. But you put me in a chaotic situation where I see a leader rise up, I can remember one or two of those.

**White:** The biggest change is because now we're starting to see a lot of former players get into coaching. The dynamics of communication between athletes and coaches is going to continue to change. One of the things that is really profound when you look at somebody like Greg Popovich. Watch how many times he is communicating on the sideline with Tony Parker. How many times has Tony Parker, after a free throw, go over there and talk with Greg Popovich? I highly doubt that every time he goes over there Popovich is telling him what to do. I truly believe that Tony Parker is saying, "Hey, I've seen this. I've seen that. What if we try this? What if we try that?" That dialogue is critical. I think we're going to see more open two-way communication. I think we're going to see it at the collegiate level as well.

I was really impressed watching the evolution of Mike Krzyzewski this year after watching the national championship game and after having his time with USA Basketball. The last five minutes of the national championship game this year was all high pick and roll offense. That's pro offense. Typical Mike Krzyzewski has been ball movement, setting screens, using screens, ball reversals. This is a guy who – all of his sets and motion offenses really dominated the game for a long time. Look at what he did this year to win the national championship. High pick and roll the last five minutes with Tyus Jones. He changed, he adjusted.

I think on the court, before too long, we're not even going to see a true back-to-the-basket post player. I think that's going to change. Off the court and in the business world, I think we're going to see more open communication, more dialogue. Again, that's where it all goes because we don't get better by ourselves. We get better by listening to the people that are around us every single day. By taking parts of their ideas and making it our own. I also think we get better by surrounding ourselves with people that are better than us. I really challenge young leaders, specifically, to do that.

**Anderson:** I see live seminars and workshops getting more focused. Covering less material but going deeper into that material. Less of a buffet and more of – let's really get down to the things that matter most. I see more interaction and the creation of action plans within the classroom. So, when people get back, they get off to a faster head start. I also believe more of it is going virtual. 24/7. People can get on and continue to improve their leadership. More intense workshops and an ongoing support and reinforcement through virtual training.

**Gray:** It's what I talked about early on. The future of leadership training is just staying grounded in the basics. Listening well. Teaching employees about resilience, overcoming obstacles, and being unified. I feel like over the course of the last few minutes together with you, we've touched on a lot of principles and values that I lean upon in my personal and professional life. But, as for leadership and training, I really think it comes down to people having a deep desire to improve. If they want to improve as an employee and a person, then they will seek out the resources and training they need.

I don't think there's any one perfect approach, but there are an awful lot of great books and training strategies out there. One that I've adopted – I've used this phrase several times but I recommend it to your leaders – is actually called *The Serving Leader*. When I read that book many years ago, it absolutely blew me away and gave me a new framework to think about how I might lead and serve at the same time. So, I'll mention that as a possible approach.

**Brubaker:** I see that pyramid that we spoke about earlier being flipped upside down, and I see the best leadership coming from the younger members of the organization. Growing leaders from the grassroots level, from the ground up. Millennials crave responsibility, accountability, and coaching. They want to be coached, and they have a desire to improve. I think that when you can reverse-mentor – you're seeing a lot of this in companies with social media, they have what's called reverse-mentoring – you have the Millennials teaching the Baby Boomers, the older generation, "Here's how you drive the results to a greater level with social media." It's the younger members of the community teaching the veterans. I see that as the future because technology is only going to play a greater and greater role in this global marketplace that we're all in.

**Woodfin:** I think more of what you're doing will probably continue to grow. I really think that your creativity is awesome; putting stuff like this together; getting different people's thoughts and opinions on one forum or topic from people that are living it out or trying to live it out. It's fantastic.

Social media will continue to grow, and leaders will continue to put out leadership material or training through social media. I think that technology will continue to grow and grow and that will be a big platform for leadership training.

**Crandall:** I think we've landed in a really good spot as it comes to leader development. More people are getting there where we understand leader development, not as training in specific skills – that training is certainly still valuable and a lot of organizations continue to do that – but this notion of self-awareness, reflection, and understanding. Who you are, what you believe, and how you bring yourself as a leader every day; reflecting on that and making it a self-directed process of making yourself better. I really think that is resonating with a lot of organizations. It's tough to argue with authenticity, and I think people enjoy the freedom to think, "Hey, I can lead. I don't have to be somebody else to lead."

This notion of authenticity has really taken hold, and I think it's got staying power. Leadership development has changed quite a bit in its short history from different theories and ways we should teach it. I don't see us departing any time soon from the notion of developing authentic leaders.

**Lubin:** I think a lot of it is going online. I think most of it is going be through podcast, through audio books. One thing I really like, that I've seen become really effective, is through live WebEx training. I think these are great ways to be much more efficient than taking an entire day to drive to Boston, fly to Dallas, or fly to Florida to sit down and take the time out of the office to go focus on this stuff.

The brain works really well in small snippets versus taking an entire day to go to a leadership training where you're still only going to take 10% of what you learned. If you can do a leadership training once a week or bi-weekly, do it all online, and in the comfort of your own home – a lot like where education is going with online courses – I think that's sort of the direction that leadership is going to be going. I'm a big fan of downloading books or downloading new podcasts onto my iPod or onto my phone. When I go do my endurance training for 2, 3, or 4 hours at a time, I'm learning something. I constantly have the voice of some aspiring leader or some leader pumping into my head. It's amazing how your body and your mind react to this stuff when you're in motion, learning the stuff and how well it retains it.

So, I think that's the direction that most of this is going. Believe me, it's very well needed, doing the face-to-face thing, but I think overall, 90% of your leadership training could be done, doing the things you're doing, by listening to podcasts, listening to audio books, and doing that whole thing.

# FAVORITE QUOTE

## What is one of your favorite quotes?

**Goldsmith:** One of my favorite quotes is: "The leader of the past knew how to tell. The leader of the future will know how to ask."

**Medcalf:** I really love, "Greatness isn't sexy. It's dirty hard work." The same thing with Francis Chan's quote about making sure that we don't succeed at the wrong things. That would be the greatest failure in life is succeeding at the wrong things. Then, C.S. Lewis's quote, "When we put first things first, second things aren't suppressed but they increase."

**Woodfin:** I have this hanging in my office – "You've never lived a perfect day until you've done something for someone who will never be able to repay you." Again, going back to generosity and service, two things I wish I would have done more of a long time ago.

**Clark:** I think the one we've used that I've borrowed is "We want to do it better than it's ever been done before." The reason we say that is not to be arrogant but it's to say: "Okay, this is how they've practiced, this is how they worked, and this is whatever has happened before. Be our own team." We're constantly using that as a motivator to try and do things better than they've been done before, wherever we are.

**Olson:** I guess I've got two. I'm looking at one right now – "God is more interested in what you are becoming than what's happening to you." That's a big one to me. The other piece for me is – "Things that are built to last are not built fast." I mentioned that earlier; that's from Keli McGregor. Clint Hurdle and I talk a lot about being a simple man in a complex world. That means things that are built to last are not built fast. I need to go slow and remember that I'm in process in every day. If I can be humble, that's a huge deal. Just keep learning. Let's learn one new thing a day; it's a win.

**Isom:** When I was an athlete, one of my favorite quotes was "Hard work beats talent when talent doesn't work hard." That was one that I loved when I was a kid and always clung to it. Hard work beats talent when talent doesn't work hard.

Another one of my favorite quotes and one I think most applicable to my life is actually a passage of scripture. It's in Romans 5:3-5, and it calls us to "Rejoice in our adversity because adversity produces perseverance, perseverance produces character, and character produces hope. Hope never fails us." And that just rocked my world, especially after I lost my dad because it was such a radical call to do something so different. Not to mourn, to grieve, to hide, but to rejoice in our adversity because it's only grooming something good in us: character, perseverance, and hope. It's just so true. So, Romans 5:3-5 is my all-time favorite.

**Brubaker:** "It has to be a mentality before it's a reality." That's actually a quote from yours truly. You know I'm a big believer in the mental game: the mental game of sports and the mental game of business. I think that if it's not a mentality first, if you don't have that vision, you're never going to have the victory. Success always happens twice. You go there in your mind first, then it actually happens in the boardroom or on the playing field.

**Janssen:** It comes from George Bernard Shaw. He says, "The people who get ahead in this world are the people who get up and look for the circumstances they want. If they can't find them, make them." That just always resonated with me. If you want to be successful, go and find those situations where people have been successful. Get around them. Learn from them.

That's what I have the awesome privilege to do. If things aren't exactly the way you want them to be, don't complain about them and don't moan about them. If you can't find them, make them. Figure out a way to get that done. That just resonated with me since I was a teenage kid and still is resonating with me decades later. So much so that it's up there so I get to see it every single day walking into my office.

**Anderson:** My favorite quote is kind of an in-your-face quote from Zig Ziglar who said, "Being late is the arrogant choice." I love that quote because I have a real problem with people who are late. So, that one sticks close to my heart.

**Lubin:** One of the things I said earlier: "Formal education will make you a living, but self-education will make you a fortune." If we could get that into minds of the people in the US or the minds of our kids – once they're out of school, to always be learning something – this world would be significantly better. If you took a half an hour of your day and read a book for half an hour every morning before you get up, before you started your day, or before you went to bed, the amount of information and the amount of learning you would have would just be exponential. So, I think that's a key for success in today's time.

**Petrick:** I'm looking at it right here in my office in my house. I have it up on the wall. "The vision of a champion is someone who is bent over, drenched in sweat at the point of exhaustion when nobody else is watching." I think it was the North Carolina Soccer Coach [Anson Dorrance] who said that. I love it because through sports and life – When I was an athlete, I would work out by myself, for the most part. I would envision someone else like me who is trying to improve and work harder than me. I didn't want that to happen. It drove me to work harder by picturing someone else working harder than me; I was competing with that person. Life taught me a lot. Every day, I have to be in charge of my meds, what time I take them, what I eat (so the meds work), and my little girls. It takes a lot of motivation to keep me going because no one is going to hold my hand to get it done. I have to be in charge of that.

**Beebe:** "Where would you rather be than right here, right now?" and "When it's too tough for them, it's just right for us." by Marv Levy. Also, "You never lose until you quit trying." and "Quitting is not an option."

**White:** One of my all-time favorite quotes – I used to have this up when I was a kid is "Don't wait for your ship to come in – swim out and meet it." Nothing is ever going to come to you, you have to go out and get it. I like "There is no shortcut to any place worth going." One of John Wooden's: "If you don't take the time to do it right, when will you have time to do it over?" "The things you do for yourself are gone when you're gone, but the things you do for others remain as your legacy." George Raveling just tweeted that the other day. It was just very profound because I think that's ultimately what it's all about. I think that's ultimately how we make a difference.

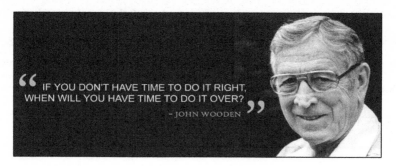

**Crandall:** Yes, the one I mentioned from Warren Bennis, "We begin to become leaders at the moment we decide for ourselves how to be." Anything that Bruce Brown's ever said is one of my favorite quotes. I recommend that anybody who's out there become familiar with Proactive Coaching. I've learned a ton from Bruce Brown and think he brings a lot. I learned from him recently; he said that a lot of times we mistake someone's remark back to us as defiance when it's really a lack of clarity. His practical wisdom like that is just huge.

**McCabe:** "Anything you ardently desire, sincerely believe in, vividly imagine, and enthusiastically act upon must come to pass." – Paul J. Meyer. It was a quote that we used to laugh at when coach used to read it to us. We had it instead of "Win Today" or something like that. That was the quote that we had above our locker room door. After I got out of playing – I was in grad school – I started thinking back on that quote and I thought, "This thing is pretty damn right." Anything that you really, really want; you've got to really, really want it. Anything that you can see yourself doing – you're willing to work your absolute tail off for – has to come to pass. It doesn't get any better than that. Too many people want the easy way. What that quote is saying is: You have to be willing to out-work, out-vision, out-see, out-do and out-believe everybody else. If you're willing to do that, you'll get the success that comes your way.

# FINAL THOUGHTS

## Do you have any final thoughts that you would like to add for the aspiring leaders reading along?

**Gordon:** Yes, if you embrace the principles in my book *The Carpenter* and you love, serve and care, that's the key to leadership. People often ask me, "Jon, how do I become a leader? How do I lead from where I am?" I say, "Love the people that you're with, love what you do, love your organization, love your customers, serve people where you are, and show that you care. You'll stand in a world where most don't care. You do those three things where you are, your influence will grow and you'll grow into the leader that you're meant to be."

**Janssen:** I'm going to challenge people and let them know that your leadership skills have a big impact if you're a coach of a team or a student-athlete as a captain on a team. But, my challenge is to go out and use those leadership skills, not just in the sports world, but in your everyday community, your state, or even around the world. The absolute thing that I am most proud of is, over the last several years, we've had groups of student-athlete leaders go to Kenya, Ecuador, Chicago, New Orleans, and Washington, D.C., and use their leadership skills to help people who are a lot less fortunate. We've built schools there. We've refurbished schools. We've done leadership training for teenagers in Ecuador. That's what I'm going to challenge people with. Don't just limit your leadership skills to your sports team but to see how these same skills of building a team and inspiring people can make a big difference on your campus, in your community, or somewhere on the other side of the world. That's what I would challenge people to do.

**Olson:** Number one: Leadership is important. But, along with that in this day and age, what we are starting to see is everybody is considering themselves a leader. I would say this: Don't be a book with legs. They always say, "Don't say don't." But in this case, what we mean when we say "don't be a book with legs" is don't be a blogger, a social media guy, or author; all you do is write stuff but never experience it. The thing that is going to separate people in the twenty-first century in the next ten to fifteen years is – what's your experience? Are you a virtual blogger-leader-writer? Or are you someone that has truly experienced leadership and been a part of it? I would challenge young leaders to go get involved, get experiences, and don't just write about it. Actually experience it and be a part of some companies, organizations, or teams, where you truly are in it and experience the ebb and flow of leadership. So many people, now, have their own website, have their own deal, and are experts. You are going, "Wow. How are you an expert? What did you do?" "Well, I wrote three books, and I have 100,000 people following me on my blog." You say, "Yeah, but that's not what I want. If I'm going to try and get through a divorce, I'm going to want to talk with someone who has been through it and come out of it. I don't want to talk to someone that writes about it." That would be my biggest challenge. In this day and age, where can all self-market ourselves, we all need to be real careful that we don't start drinking our own Kool-Aid. We really need to get out there, experience life, and be a part of it. Not just write about it.

**Isom:** Probably the biggest would be: You are the only you, and you are the best at being you. So, own your weird. Own your different. Own you.

I'm so sick of looking out into the world and seeing cookie-cutter copies of everybody trying to do and say the same thing. Be you. You are gifted, and you are skilled uniquely. You are placed where you are at right this minute to do something where you are right this minute, to use those skills and those talents.

I would really encourage anyone who's looking to lead – understand the stage's range and size. Good leadership can look like one-on-one interaction with someone as easily as it can look like standing up on a stage in front of 10,000 people. Know that you have a stage. Know that you have a platform to lead. Know that you are gifted, you are skilled, and there is someone out there who is seeking exactly what you have to offer. You're valuable, you're important, and you have the ability to lead. So, lead where you are, lead with the tools you have, and lead well.

**Goldsmith:** I'm going to share one technique. It's going to take two minutes a day. It'll help your listeners get better at almost anything and cost nothing. Are you ready? Now, some people might be a little skeptical right now thinking, "Wait a minute. Two minutes a day? I'll only get better at everything, and it costs nothing? Seems too good to be true." Half the people who have tried this quit within two weeks. They don't quit because it doesn't work; they quit because it does work. This is called the Daily Question Process. Here's how it works: Get out a spreadsheet and write a list of questions that represent what's most important in your life. This could involve friends, family, health, work, or leadership. Whatever is important to you. Every question has to be answered with a yes, no, or number. Seven boxes across; one for every day of the week: Monday, Tuesday, Wednesday, Thursday, Friday, Saturday, and Sunday. Every day fill out that questionnaire. At the end of the week that excel spreadsheet can give you a report card. I'm going to warn you in advance – that report card at the end of the week might not be quite as pretty as that values plaque up on the wall. Because you learn if you do this every day, life is really easy to talk. It is really hard to live. I've been doing this for years. I could tell you it works, and it's hard to do. A lot of people can't do it. If you'd like an article about it, send me an e-mail and put Daily Question. I'll send you the article about how the process works, but it's a fantastic idea.

**White:** There is one thing to remember, and this is one thing I try to remind myself daily. You get better or worse, and you never stay the same. Always have a hunger to improve. Always be humble enough to take constructive criticism. Always be open enough to listen to other suggestions. Never be afraid of a debate. Never be afraid to be challenged. Healthy debate and healthy challenges are critical to our growth.

When you're in a leadership position, your growth then directly impacts the growth of the people that you're leading. You're open to seeing more of their growth as well. When you're in a leadership position, it's a disservice if you don't and we don't prepare future leaders. My job, where I am right now, is to prepare our players to be the best players that they can possibly be. I also want to prepare the next head coach in the WNBA. Let's prepare future leaders to take our job one day.

**Kouzes:** There is one story I can tell you about the secret to success in life, if you think people would be interested in knowing the secret to success. There is only one story that we tell that has survived five editions of *The Leadership Challenge*. It's a story from Major General John Stanford who was the Head of Military Traffic Management Command for the United States Army when we interviewed him. He later, when retired from the army, became the county administrator for Fulton County, which is where Atlanta, Georgia, is located. Then, Superintendent of Schools for the Seattle Unified School District. John led a very distinguished public service career. When we first interviewed him, I asked him the question if he could please tell me, similar to this question, "What advice would you have for aspiring leaders, based on your experience, on how to develop themselves as leaders?" He said to me, "Whenever anyone asks me that question, I tell them I have the secret to success in life. The secret to success is stay in love. Staying in love gives you the fire to really ignite other people, to see inside other people, and to have a greater desire to get things done than other people. A person who is not in love doesn't really feel the kind of excitement that helps them to get ahead, to lead others, and to achieve. I don't know any other fire, any other thing in life, that is more positive or exhilarating of a feeling than love is."

I did not expect to get that answer from a major general, but when I think about all of the people we've interviewed over all these years about leadership – when talking about their personal best leadership experiences – it's very clear to them that leadership is not an affair of the head. Leadership is an affair of the heart.

**Elmore:** I really believe the essence of leadership is – can I solve problems and serve people? If those are my aspirations rather than power, I find that power is often a by-product. If I serve people, they make me more influential; they like me. If I'm solving problems, that's the fastest way to gain leadership in a group of people. I'm solving problems. So, make that the aspiration; something that's in your control. I can serve people, I can solve problems, and then, let the power thing just follow naturally.

**Anderson:** I teach a law in my workshops called the Law of the Mirror. The Law of the Mirror is all about taking responsibility. I think that's essential for leaders. It simply says this, "It is my personal decisions, more than external conditions that ultimately determine my success." Sometimes we blame conditions, but it always goes back to decisions. So, focus on what you can control on a daily basis because it's a lot. Your attitude, your work ethic, your character choices, where you spend your time, with whom you spend it, who joins the team, who has to leave it, whether or not you're going to grow. There is so much that you can control that you don't have to get hung up on the things going on around you. Focus on what you can control and that keeps moving you forward. You focus on external conditions, you turn into a victim. Lord knows we have enough of those out there in society right now.

**Medcalf:** On your deathbed you won't wish you won more tournaments.

You'll wish you developed deeper relationships and loved people more. I learned as a nine-year-old, when I pulled my best friend and little brother out of our pool, that life is fragile and very short. Sometimes people wonder why I do what I do. It somehow ties back to that. We try and love people deeply because we know they can be gone tomorrow. When we put first things first, second things aren't suppressed; they increase. Your value comes from who you are, not from what you do. You are a child of God who happens to lead. Don't let your identity be defined by what you do. It's a recipe for disaster.

Cultivate unconditional gratitude every day. Visualize yourself leading at your best, but also visualize yourself overcoming the inevitable challenges and adversity that come in sports and life. Become your own best friend by practicing constructive and beneficial self-talk. Make sure you're the Rock of Gibraltar for those you lead. Make a commitment to a "no excuses" lifestyle. Take responsibility; never blame anyone, including yourself. Make sure what you do with your 86,400 seconds every day in your willingness to sacrifice; they are in direct proportion to the size of your dreams. Burn your goals. Focus on the mission for your life.

Fall in love with the process and the journey. Let the results take care of themselves. Develop true mental toughness. Use your sport or your company, whatever circumstance you find yourself in, as a vehicle. Please don't be another person who gets used by it. Comparison is the thief of all joy. Do the best you can with what you have, right where you're at. Remember, the person at the top of the mountain didn't fall there. Greatness always looks easy to those who aren't around when all the training is going on. People who are average at what they do are always convinced that there are shortcuts to becoming great but there is only blood, sweat, and years of delayed gratification and deliberate practice. Either pay the price of regret or the price to become great. Dream bigger, think smaller. Be faithful with all the small stuff in your hand. Judge less, love more and become the change you wish to see in the world.

**Petrick:** Have fun whatever you are doing. Life is about being fun. Don't take things so seriously. Slow down and smell the roses; slow down and play with your kids. Try to keep the things that are most important in life in check. Don't let it slip by to where suddenly, you are a big leaguer, but you have lost stuff on the way.

**Eikenberry:** Get on the path. Leadership is a journey. Whether you are aspiring or whether you're in the midst of it, commit to yourself and commit to your team that you're going to learn and get better at it. Reading this book is part of that. But, get on that journey, and if you really are aspiring or just brand-new in the role, I really would encourage you to go to *budtoboss.com* which is all of our products and services around the new supervisor, new manager role. I think you'd find a lot of great value right there.

**Gray:** I think that at one level, life is really short. There are precious moments, and we have to find ways to do that. On another level, we've got time. We've got time to grow, develop, and learn. We don't have to do everything overnight. Within us, we're all champions. We're all champions that were contenders at one point and then found a way to step up, grow up, and become the champion that we want to be.

So, for me, I just want to encourage people to take their time. They don't have to beat themselves up if they're not exactly where they want to be in their career. They've got big dreams, but I really think that one of the things in our culture that people are struggling with is they'll have a dream and that dream won't come fully to fruition. They'll get depressed and frustrated. So often that can lead to a really bad result. I think there's an epidemic of depression going on in America when people don't feel like, "Oh, I haven't lived up to my potential." But, the Lord defines what our potential is. If we're all moving in the right direction and trying to get better, then anything is possible. Change is possible, and we can constantly find a way to get better. I just want to encourage people to stay after it and never give up. Show up. Dress up. Get ready and be ready because chance favors the prepared mind. It's the idea that when that opportunity presents itself, if you're ready, then boom! You can capitalize on it.

I'll leave you with that quote "chance favors the prepared mind" and, hopefully, your listeners will latch on to something that I've said and use it in their own life. I hope that if they do, and they have a good result or even a bad result, I hope they'll pop me an e-mail, send me a note or tweet, and let me know that it's made a little difference in their life. Or, they want to modify a thought that I might've had because I'm not too bold to think that I have it all figured out. I want to have a humble spirit in how I approach things. If people have ideas about how I can improve as a leader after listening to my thoughts, listening to how I think about things, then I'd love to hear their feedback and see what I can do to improve and get better in my own leadership.

**Beebe:** I can humbly say that there were guys that were more talented than I was. I should have never played in the NFL, but I really believe that I played for two reasons.

1) I just out-worked them. I out-trained them. I had passion. I didn't care if anybody was watching me. I would get up at 5:00 am to go work out. I just wanted it.
2) It was my calling in life. At a very young age, when I accepted Christ, I knew that I wanted to do two things: I wanted to play sports, and I wanted to please God. I was just following His lead, not mine.

I was very fortunate and blessed to be able to do what I have been able to do. I really believe that my role, today, is more important than it has ever been in my life.

**Brubaker:** I think the most important thing that we can all remember as leaders is that not everyone is playing at the World Championship, Major League, or Fortune 500 level. Not everyone is at that elite level. People all strive to be there, but I think that focusing on that destination actually derails you. I'll go back to my mentor – 45 years in the business of coaching – and he did it on the back roads of college athletics. I think that the journey, or his lesson, is one that we need to remember. That's where the real work is, and that's where you have an opportunity to make the biggest difference.

It's kind of like another journey from another time that I'm thinking of. There are two other people who rode to Lexington at about the same time Paul Revere made his famous ride, which I'm sure everyone remembers. Those two people's names you never heard of. Never heard of William Dawes or Dr. Samuel Prescott. Think about this. No one remembers those names. They remember Paul Revere, but their mission and their impact was just as important: to let the citizens of Boston know "the British are coming, the British are coming" – right? Their route had them take the roads less traveled, kind of like my mentor. They took the back roads to Lexington, not the main drag. On their mission, they saved lives as well. I think something we need to realize is we can all do big things in small places, and the journey is the reward and really that's where the real work is.

**Woodfin:** I think really trying to do what you say you're going to do is very, very, very important to lead. It's really hard. We all have flaws. We all have issues, but constantly asking yourself, "Would I be doing this if everybody I'm leading was right here with me?"

Good leaders are good leaders when they're with their people, but what are you doing when you're not with your people? The small decisions that you're making are always going to allow you to continue to have leadership over those people. Doing what you say you're going to do and following through with the little things are really important.

**Clark:** All these things that we've talked about are so important. You mentioned positive energy. God is so important to me, as being a leader is being positive and also just the leading by example. It's not just about what I say, it's about what I do.

**Crandall:** Leadership is really hard work. I've heard that from people who read our book, like, "Wow, I read this, and it's inspiring. I agree with a lot of it, but it just seems like really hard work." Absolutely. This is a personal notion and something I've found that's not true of everyone. It's true of me, and I'll just share it. If I've gained any credibility while sharing with you today: The only thing that matters when you lead is caring about the people you lead. To me, it's why I do it. Whatever you're doing – if you can be laser focused on the needs of those you lead and take care of them. I think that's a moral imperative of leadership that will make it that much better. It's not about you. It's not about you. It's about the people you lead.

**McCabe:** Don't try to be somebody you're not. Be you. Too many people try to become something that they're not; try to be a coach like their mentor was. They see another leader of an organization, and they try to embody their leadership styles. Be your leadership styles. You have a different fingerprint for a reason, and your fingerprint must be developed. You have to have an open mindset – a growth mindset – of learning. Challenges are not definers of you; they're developers of you. Find your own leadership style. Find your own vision. Don't just learn from one tree. Reach out of your comfort zones, and go to other coaches that have different philosophies from you. Even if they're completely contradictory of yours, you can learn something. You may learn that yours is actually pretty good, or you may learn that yours maybe isn't as good. Leaders need to get out of their comfort zones. Try to develop your own footprint.

When you're a leader, it's not the last time in your life you'll be a leader. You may change organizations, you may change companies, or you may change other things. You can't be doing it for approval. You do it for what you believe is right. At the end of the day, if it all washes out and you're successful, you're one step closer. If it's not successful, you learn, and you'd be willing to make those changes again.

**Lubin:** I think one of the things is realize what you don't know. A lot of people I know think they know everything. As I get older and as I do more, I realize how little I don't know. So, as an aspiring leader, you have to always be willing to learn new things, be willing to educate yourself, and to just throw it out there. Don't be afraid. Take some risks. If you don't take risks now, you're going to be upset that you didn't in twenty, thirty, or forty years, when you said I wish I had done that.

BEHIND THE SCENES WITH THE
**TOP LEADERSHIP EXPERTS
IN SPORTS**

---

If you have had a positive experience
with the *Leadership VIP* Program and
would like to share a testimonial to be
featured in future editions, please e-mail
Testimonials@LeadershipVIP.com

---

# FOR MORE FROM MATT MORSE, VISIT MATT-MORSE.COM

# FOR MORE FROM BRETT BASHAM, VISIT BRETTBASHAM.COM

# ADDITIONAL VIP RESOURCES

## MentalGameVIP.com

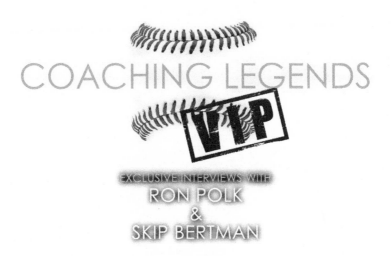

## MentalGameVIP.com/CoachingLegends

Made in the USA
Monee, IL
12 August 2020